Seed Provision & Agricultural Development

T0319582

Seed Provision & Agricultural Development

THE INSTITUTIONS OF RURAL CHANGE

Robert Tripp

Research Fellow
Overseas Development Institute, London

OVERSEAS DEVELOPMENT INSTITUTE · LONDON
in association with
JAMES CURREY · OXFORD
HEINEMANN · PORTSMOUTH(N.H.)

© Overseas Development Institute 2001
First published 2001

All Rights Reserved. Except as permitted under current legislation
no part of this work may be photocopied, stored in a retrieval system,
published, performed in public, adapted, broadcast,
transmitted, recorded or reproduced in any form or by any means,
without the prior permission of the copyright owner

James Currey is an imprint of Boydell & Brewer Ltd
PO Box 9, Woodbridge, Suffolk IP12 3DF, UK
and of Boydell & Brewer Inc.
668 Mount Hope Ave, Rochester, NY 14620-2731, USA
www.jamescurrey.com
www.boydellandbrewer.com

Heinemann
A division of Reed Elsevier Inc.
361 Hanover Street
Portsmouth, NH 03801-3912
USA

Overseas Development Institute
111 Westminster Bridge Road, London SE1 7JD

ISBN 978-0-85255-421-0 (James Currey cloth)
ISBN 978-0-85255-420-3 (James Currey paper)
ISBN 978-0-325-07075-9 (Heinemann cloth)

Transferred to digital printing

Typeset in 10/13 Times by Saxon Graphics Ltd, Derby

This publication is printed on acid-free paper

Contents

Preface & Acknowledgements

Seed is at the forefront of many contemporary debates about development. It features in concerns about globalisation and intellectual property rights, and controversies over the future of biotechnology focus on the impact on seed systems. At a more general level, farmers' access to seed is one of the overriding concerns of many agricultural aid and rehabilitation programmes. This book does not enter directly into specific debates, but rather attempts to provide a comprehensive overview of the nature of seed provision. The aim is to contribute to a more reasoned and informed discussion of the challenges of agricultural development.

The book is based on six years of research at the Overseas Development Institute (ODI) that has examined various aspects of seed system development. My early work examined the management of government seed regulations in developing countries. Regulation addresses problems of information management, and during the research I became aware of the broader issue of how information is exchanged in seed systems. I also began to think more carefully about the incentives for formal seed trade and the emergence of seed enterprises. This led to further research on commercial seed systems in Africa, Asia and Latin America, as well as an examination of many of the small-scale seed production initiatives promoted by donors, governments and NGOs. The challenge of identifying the conditions for seed enterprise growth also motivated a review of historical evidence from industrialised countries. At the same time, the research raised fresh questions about the nature of local seed systems and encouraged me to review anthropological and other studies on farmer seed management and to compare them with results emerging from my own fieldwork.

Because this research on seed systems is closely related to the issues of information and incentives, I was drawn to the literature on institutional analysis, particularly New Institutional Economics and New Economic Sociology. Although these suffer many of the problems of excessive formalisation and jargon experienced by any academic fashion, I found that institutional analysis provided a useful way of organising the multiple threads of my research and for presenting a unified view of seed system development. It also helped me to understand why many developmental aid efforts in the seed sector are unsuccessful. Indeed, the institutional analysis of seed systems has helped me reconsider my own perceptions of the nature of development.

There are many people who have contributed to my understanding of seed provision. My former colleagues in the Economics Program of the International Maize and Wheat Improvement Center (CIMMYT) have done groundbreaking work on various aspects of public and private seed systems, and I am particularly indebted to Michael Morris, Melinda Smale, Paul Heisey and Derek Byerlee for advice and ideas over the years. Since joining ODI, I have enjoyed the support of Elizabeth Cromwell, Kate Longley and John Farrington, whose work on seeds, biodiversity and agricultural development has helped shape my research. Much of my understanding of seed regulation has been the product of collaboration with Niels Louwaars at the Centre for Plant Breeding and Reproduction Research, Wageningen.

Some of the fieldwork in Africa was carried out as part of a project with the International Crops Research Institute for the Semi-Arid Tropics (ICRISAT) that gave me the opportunity to work with David Rohrbach, Richard Jones and Patrick Audi. Research and support for field studies of African seed systems have been provided by many people, but I would particularly like to thank Joseph Rusike, Alex Phiri, Rowland Chirwa, Patrick Kambewa, Lydia Kimenye, Paul Omanga, Ed Zulu, Francisco Miti, Bean Lyoba and John Milimo. Fergus Lyon's research in Ghana provided new insights on seed enterprise development. In India I had the good fortune to collaborate on two research projects with Suresh Pal of the National Centre for Agricultural Economics and Policy Research (NCAP). My knowledge of seed systems in Nepal is largely based on the work of Krishna Joshi. Research for ODI projects in Bolivia and Peru was carefully organised and conducted by Jeffery Bentley.

Most of the research described in the book, as well as the opportunity for writing this synthesis, has been supported by several grants from the UK Department for International Development (DFID). I am most grateful for their support, and it should be clear that they bear no responsibility for my conclusions or interpretations.

The book has been through several drafts that have been organised and managed by Mel Woodland and Patsy de Souza. I am particularly grateful for the admirably efficient editorial support of Margaret Cornell.

1 Agricultural Development

Introduction

Any discussion about agriculture or agricultural change leads inevitably to the subject of seed. Seed is farmers' most precious resource, and concerns about the viability of traditional agricultural systems centre on the diversity and stability of seed supply. Technological change in agriculture, symbolised most forcefully by the Green Revolution, is often described in terms of 'new seed'. More recently, the debate over biotechnology and corporate agriculture is being waged in terms of control over seed resources.

When considering agricultural development, the metaphorical qualities of seed are obvious. Seed production is the outcome of careful planning and selection. A seed's growth follows predictable laws of nature but is also affected by the intervention of human management. The yield is utilised for renewal and advancement. Seed is seen as a resource of farming communities and as a symbol of their integrity and self-sufficiency.

However, this book focuses on practical issues of seed provision and their relation to agricultural development. It examines the origins, growth and performance of seed provision systems and relates these to the principal issues facing agricultural development. For instance, many development debates are based on conflicting views of traditional agriculture. What is the nature of farmer seed systems and how do they evolve and adapt? Until recently, the state has played an important role in seed provision in developing countries. In an era of liberalisation, what is the future of the public seed sector? Commercial seed trade is an essential feature of industrial agriculture. How do seed enterprises emerge, and what conditions foster their growth? Globalisation, rapid changes in technology, and the increasing importance of intellectual property protection are altering the character of agriculture. How do these changes affect the future of seed provision in developing countries? Development assistance to agriculture includes a wide range of seed projects. What has been their impact, and how can such assistance be more effectively organised?

One of the major challenges for development policy is to find a balance among three elements: the rights and resources of individuals, the potential of the market, and the support of the state. Seed provision encompasses all of these elements. Farmers, commercial enterprises, and governments all participate in seed provision. Plant varieties may be developed and improved by farmers in remote villages, by researchers in universities or government institutes, or by scientists working in corporate laboratories. Seed is distributed through exchange and trade among farmers, as an important commodity in agricultural input markets, and as an element of government organisations and programmes. Seed is a source of subsistence, an embodiment of technological change, and a vital input for commercial agricultural production.

This book uses seed provision as a lens through which to examine the broader subject of agricultural development. Agricultural development can be analysed in various ways. It is often described in terms of technology development and diffusion. New crop varieties, and the seeds in which they are embodied, are prime examples of agricultural technology. Agricultural development is also linked to the growth of human capital, including support for farmer training and agricultural research. But our approach to development will use a different focus, one that emphasises the growth of institutions. There is increasing interest in applying an institutional approach to the study of development. This approach emphasises the importance of information, and considers the ways in which individuals and groups exchange information, establish rules to guide their transactions, and structure incentives to achieve specific purposes.

There is a growing body of social science theory that informs this institutional perspective on development, and our analysis will draw upon some of those studies. However, it should be emphasised that the objectives of this book are practical rather than theoretical. First, the book summarises a considerable number of empirical studies that illustrate how seed systems perform. We need access to this type of information in order to break through many of the stereotypes that have emerged about both farm-level and commercial seed provision. Secondly, the adoption of an institutional approach allows an understanding of the conditions and incentives that contribute to the growth and evolution of seed systems. This type of analysis will show how institutional growth is related to agricultural development. Finally, an understanding of the institutions of agricultural development contributes to a critique of development policy and points to alternative strategies that will contribute to the emergence of an equitable and productive agricultural sector.

This first chapter begins with a brief review of the concept of development. This is followed by an examination of the nature of agriculture and some of the major theories explaining the direction of agricultural change. In the second chapter the discussion shifts to introduce the elements of institutional analysis, following the two major currents in the literature, New Institutional Economics and New Economic Sociology. This is followed by an attempt to synthesise these theoretical concerns and to identify a pragmatic approach to institutional analysis that can be used in the rest of the book.

Development

There is no universally acceptable definition of development. The literature on development presents us with a growing list of characteristics and objectives associated with the concept. This book does not attempt to expand or refine that list, but any attempt to discuss development must at least acknowledge the major interpretations and contradictions associated with the concept. Perhaps the principal difficulty in pursuing a definition of development is the fact that the term can signify both an end and a means; development may be a goal or a process. It is best to begin with a brief examination of these two conceptions.

When development is treated as an end, it has traditionally been associated with economic growth. Thus a nation's state of development may be judged by measures of per capita income, gross national product, or employment levels. Dissatisfaction with the use of these economic measures in setting the agenda for development programmes has led to the amplification of development indicators. One of the earliest attempts to complement growth and income measures for development planning was the concept of 'basic human needs' (Streeten and Burki, 1978). This concept focused attention on six areas: nutrition, primary education, health, sanitation, water supply, and housing. More recently, the United Nations Development Programme has begun compiling a 'human development index' in which a country's development status is assessed on a combination of health, educational and income measures (UNDP, 1999). In 1997, the World Bank began to publish a yearly compendium of 'world development indicators' that ranks countries' performance in approximately 80 areas of health, employment, education, environment, economic growth, finance and trade (World Bank, 1999).

Development may also connote the process by which social and economic growth is achieved. In this case we must specify the driving force behind the process. In their comprehensive historical analysis, Cowen and Shenton (1996) distinguish between 'immanent development', an historical process that unfolds without conscious planning, and 'intentional development', a manifestation of state policies. They trace the changes in the meaning of development during the rapid social and economic transformations in Europe in the mid-nineteenth century. The meaning of development shifted away from an organic, immanent process and came instead to signify a formal strategy for addressing economic and social problems, which was applied to the challenges of colonial expansion and administration. Development was the 'means by which the state might serve to actively contain the disorder of unemployment and destitution' (ibid.: 61).

Today, there is a strong tendency towards the 'intentional' interpretation of the development process. Development is often thought of in terms of policies and projects directed at a particular problem. It may appear that virtually every state-sponsored activity in the South is described as development, so that the term loses any meaning. In the North, public agencies and voluntary organisations channel funds to other countries for improving agriculture, industry, education, and health under the name of development, although the donor countries themselves rarely use the term to describe their own domestic plans and policies in these areas.

Despite this undeniable shift in the representation of development towards the intentional side, we must recognise the importance of immanent development. Many of the most significant and enduring changes that occur in the arena of development are the products of individual and collective initiative, independent of the intervention of any development agency. But it is difficult to accept a clear distinction between intentional and immanent development. In addition, it is misleading to see immanent development as the manifestation of some universal human purpose. It is rather the outcome of the pursuit of complex and shifting goals that are mediated and defined by various human institutions. Development must be seen in the context of laws, customs, and other institutions. Change may take place without any attention from the state, or even despite official state policy, but it can not be understood in isolation from the institutional context in which it evolved.

One way to accommodate the contradictions between development as goal and process, and between immanent and intentional development, is to focus on the growth of human capacities and opportunities.[1] Summary statistics of output or wealth may help gauge progress towards a defined goal, and governments or other agencies may enable the development process to proceed, but the emphasis should be on the expansion of human potential. In reviewing the concept of development, Sen (1988, 1999) stresses the importance of enhancing people's freedom to choose. A society's development is assessed by its capacity to offer its members a choice among a range of productive activities.[2] Development leads to the growth and diversification of opportunities for engagement and creativity. If development implies the expansion of choice, it follows that individuals must be able to elect their own goals for development. These goals will certainly change over time. Heterogeneous values and purposes are inevitable parts of the development process, and they make the definition of development particularly problematic.[3] This book examines the course of development in the context of agricultural change. It considers the agricultural development process in both its immanent and intentional manifestations. Although development is a function of individual choice and preference, it is also legitimate to discuss the ways that groups, societies and polities contribute to it. Access to physical resources, the growth of knowledge, and the enhancement of organisational capacity are all important factors. The state and society provide an environment in which such interaction takes place. Thus we must include a consideration of government and donor contributions to the provision of incentives and opportunities for development.

Agricultural change

The character of agriculture[4]
Our examination of development is confined to the example of agricultural change. Most

---

[1]See Cowen and Shenton, 1996: 448—452 for a review of this approach.

[2]The centrality of choice to the concept of development is shared by a wide range of observers. It is a key to Marx's view of development (Cowen and Shenton, 1996: 449), and P.T. Bauer, the conservative critic of development, suggests that '[e]xtension of the range of choice of people as consumers and producers is perhaps the most satisfactory criterion of economic development' (Bauer, 1984: 22).

[3]Although it is relatively easy to chart the progress of an economy in monetary or material terms, assessing individual satisfaction with that growth is much more difficult. An individual's well-being depends partially on income level, but also on the quality of his or her participation in the economy. See Lane (1991) for a thorough examination of the meaning of participation in the market.

[4]For a more complete discussion of the factors that distinguish the agricultural sector, see Timmer (1998).

of the problems associated with defining development are evident in any discussion about the farming sector. There are four issues that require particular acknowledgement. The first is agriculture's unique status as a source of both subsistence and income. A related issue is the fact that agriculture is a variable source of livelihood for rural dwellers; agriculture is often a part-time occupation. Third, agriculture is perhaps more a subject of competing ideologies than any other area in development debates. Finally, agriculture is more characterised by small firms (family farms) than any other economic sector.

In conventional development terms, agriculture may be seen as simply one sector of the economy that contributes to national production and income. But, unlike manufacturing or mining, agriculture is not simply a commodity sector. It is also an important component of rural people's social organisation and culture. Agriculture is a source of production and income, but it is also the core of subsistence and a refuge from the uncertainties of the larger economy. Farmers are both producers and consumers, and farms often utilise a significant amount of family labour. This second viewpoint directs attention away from interpreting agricultural development in purely production terms and encourages an appreciation of agriculture's wider role in rural societies.[5] It is often difficult to separate the household farming enterprise from agriculture's contribution to the social fabric of the community. We must therefore understand that farming populations are subject to a range of incentives and objectives, and differ greatly in the strength of their articulation with the larger economy.[6]

Agricultural development should not be equated with rural development. In many countries, there are large numbers of rural residents who own no agricultural assets and earn most of their income in non-farming activities. In addition, many people described as 'farmers' have complex livelihood strategies in which agriculture may play only a secondary role (Ellis, 1998). Our interest in agricultural development focuses on those rural residents for whom crop cultivation makes a significant contribution either to their subsistence capacity or to their cash income. We shall not attempt to examine the relationships between agricultural change and other aspects of the rural economy.[7] But we must be aware that agriculture is often only one of several sources of household income, and this affects farmers' opportunities and incentives.

An issue of particular relevance to intentional agricultural development is the fact that farming is the subject of quite contradictory policies and images in the North. On the one hand, farming is often treated like any other industry. But at the same time, it is subject to

---

[5]One expression of these conflicting visions is the debate in the literature on peasantry regarding the relative importance of subsistence and market motivations. Wolf (1955) distinguishes peasants, whose aim is subsistence, from farmers, whose focus is the market. Ellis (1988: 12), on the other hand, defines peasants as farm households 'characterised by partial engagement in markets'.

[6]There is not a strict correlation between technology use and commercial orientation in agriculture. For instance, Low (1986) describes how the use of hybrid seed and fertiliser in Swaziland often contributes to a household's subsistence rather than commercial goals.

[7]See Lipton and Longhurst (1989) for a review of the interactions between technology change and the welfare of farm labour. For an introduction to the debate regarding the degree to which agricultural development contributes to the growth of the surrounding rural economy, see Haggblade and Hazell (1989) and Harriss (1987).

an extraordinary amount of protection. This is partly the result of political pressure from its constituents, but is also the result of a more general public sentiment in favour of the idea of the family farm. Although large-scale commercial agriculture predominates in many industrialised countries, the image of an independent and self-sufficient way of life plays an important part in the conduct of agricultural policy.[8] Of particular relevance for our concerns, agricultural development programmes and projects directed at the South are often subject to the same controversies. Agricultural development policy is portrayed either as an (often unrealistic) march towards industrial agriculture or alternatively as an attempt to preserve (often imaginary) communities of self-sufficient cultivators. We must therefore pay particular attention to the influence of such ideologies in the assessment of agricultural development.

Finally, a particularly noteworthy aspect of agricultural development is the fact that the preponderance of small farms provides extraordinary scope, and indeed necessity, for innovation at the level of the individual farm. The provision of technology from external sources is an important element of agricultural development, but in most cases that technology has to be adapted to individual circumstances. Technological change in agriculture is often the result of decisions made independently by large numbers of dispersed farmers. In addition, much development of agricultural technology is done by farmers themselves (Biggs and Clay, 1981). Farmers' capacities and incentives for innovation are important elements in determining the course of agricultural development.

The nature of agricultural change

The potential for agricultural change is determined by both natural and economic conditions. Biophysical resources set limits on the direction of agricultural change. Climate and soils provide the basic parameters within which farmers can work and experiment. These parameters define the length of the growing season and the types of crops that can be grown. They also determine the plant diseases, pests, and weeds that farmers must confront. Farmers' innovations in response to these differences in natural conditions determine the diversity and complexity of farming systems found today (Ruthenberg, 1976).

Within any given farming system, the availability of economic resources, particularly land and labour, provides further parameters for agricultural change. One of the earliest attempts to show how labour availability could account for differences in agricultural practices is found in the work of the Russian economist Chayanov. Writing in the early part of the twentieth century, he tried to explain the behaviour of peasant households by looking at the ratio between dependants and workers (Kerblay, 1971). As the ratio of dependent children to adult producers rises, the intensity of labour use and the amount of land cultivated increase to meet subsistence needs. As children mature and begin to contribute to household labour, or leave to establish their own families, the ratio falls, with consequent changes in land and labour use. These observations were elaborated to develop a theory of a distinct peasant economy.

---

[8]For a discussion of the controversy over policies to protect the small family farm as a production unit and a symbol for a way of life in the US, see Browne et al. (1992).

A more comprehensive treatment of the relationship between population and land is found in Boserup's (1965) theory of agricultural development. In her view, as population expands cultivators turn towards increasingly intensive techniques. Far from being a threat to agricultural stability, population growth stimulates innovation and growth. Boserup traces the ways in which population growth is responsible for the evolution from fallow systems to permanent cultivation to irrigated agriculture. These changes are accompanied by the development and adoption of new technology. Digging sticks are replaced by hoes, which in turn give way to ploughs. As intensification proceeds, farmers develop new techniques of soil fertility management, adopt new crops, and (where feasible) perfect techniques in irrigation management. These changes are generally marked by an increase in output and labour investment and by a decline in labour productivity.

A recent study in eastern Kenya (Tiffen et al., 1994) highlights some of the strengths and weaknesses of Boserup's hypothesis. The study found that substantial growth in rural population density in Machakos District has been accompanied by agricultural intensification and the adoption of a range of new crops and farm management techniques. Despite dire warnings by the colonial authorities regarding the fragility of the environment, the increased population pressure led to innovations in Machakos that have apparently been responsible for a decrease in the extent of soil erosion. Many farmers have constructed terraces; there is an increased use of manuring and composting; and new crops and varieties have been adopted.

But these results also underline lacunae in Boserup's formulation. Although many of the changes in Machakos are the result of local innovation, a significant part of the transformation is dependent on developments in the external environment. The growth of Kenya's market economy was a source of increased demand for agricultural produce. It also provided additional opportunities for diversifying incomes through off-farm labour. In addition, many of the new technologies used by Machakos farmers were developed elsewhere, by public and private agricultural research. The disposition of physical resources and the responses of land management to population pressure are not sufficient to explain the course of agricultural change. We must also look at the availability of externally produced technology and the growth of the wider economy.

Technological change in agriculture includes changes in management (such as new crop rotations), the use of new crops or varieties, the increased utilisation of locally available inputs (such as manure or crop residues), or the application of externally produced inputs (such as chemical fertiliser or machinery). The role of agricultural technology has been a prominent subject in agricultural development theory. One of the most influential contributions in the 1960s was that of Schultz (1964). In contrast to many development economists writing at the time, he argued that traditional agricultural systems represent a rational use of resources. These techniques are the products of a long tradition of experimentation and experience. Attempts to reallocate farmers' resources would not result in any significant improvement, hence Schultz's judgement that traditional farmers are 'efficient but poor'. Change must come from outside, particularly in the form of new technology (and the education that is required to manage and understand it). His writing had considerable influence in directing agricultural development programmes towards technology provision.

If agricultural technology is often developed externally, how does it respond to local needs? One of the most comprehensive answers is found in the theory of induced innovation, elaborated by Hayami and Ruttan (1985). The core of the theory focuses on the way that agricultural technology development reflects changes in the economic environment, particularly in the relative prices of factors of production. Technology helps facilitate the substitution of abundant factors for scarce ones. Examples from the nineteenth century include the development of mechanical (labour-saving) techniques for US farms and fertiliser-responsive ('land-saving') crop varieties in Japan. The theory of induced innovation helps explain how external (private and public) technology development responds to farmers' changing circumstances.

The relationship between the growth of the wider economy and agricultural change is one of the enduring themes in the study of agricultural history. The industrial revolution in Europe was accompanied by an agricultural revolution that included a reduction in the agricultural labour force, an increase in the use of external inputs and machinery, and the production of a wider range of agricultural commodities in response to urban demand. However, these changes were far from a simple, unilinear response by the agricultural sector to industrial growth. Agricultural innovation and adjustment took varying directions in different countries in the face of the industrial revolution.[9]

Despite the fact that European farming's response to the industrial revolution was complex and heterogeneous, the most influential theories of agricultural development of the 1950s and 1960s featured a preoccupation with industrial growth. Perhaps the most prominent example is Lewis's (1955) two-sector model. He saw development characterised by the relations between a modern capitalist sector and a subsistence sector. It was the function of the subsistence sector to transfer labour to the capitalist (industrial) sector. This would in turn lead to the modernisation of the agricultural sector. The expected performance of agriculture in the context of industrialisation is often described as 'structural transformation' (Johnston and Kilby, 1975), the principal features being a declining share in the national labour force and total output and a concomitant expansion of the manufacturing sector. The agricultural sector is seen as a supplier of excess labour and ultimately as a beneficiary of capitalist development that eventually leads to the elimination of subsistence farming.

Structural transformation implies a specific pathway for agricultural development. As more labour moves to the industrial sector there is an increased demand for agricultural products, which should increase farm income. Export markets for agricultural products also become available. The expanding economy offers increased opportunities for off-farm labour that contribute to rural earnings. Structural transformation also includes 'backward linkages', in which agricultural development contributes to growth in the

---

[9]Grigg (1982) reviews the character of this transformation in Europe, as well as pointing to evidence of significant agricultural change before the industrial revolution. Thirsk (1997) presents significant evidence for agricultural innovation during three periods of economic depression in English history.

industrial sector. Farmers demand more inputs, machinery, building materials, and consumer goods. The end of structural transformation is a smaller but more dynamic agricultural sector that contributes to strong economic growth.[10]

It is obvious that theory and reality are far apart in agricultural development. Agricultural change in many countries of the South is still far removed from this vision of structural transformation. Industrial and commercial development have neither absorbed rural labour nor provided sufficient stimulus for increasing farm productivity. For many rural people, agriculture is still a component of subsistence strategies more than an income-generating activity; they have neither the resources nor the incentives for commercial agricultural production.

The picture is not completely bleak, however. There are also many instances where agricultural development has occurred and farm household welfare has increased. Of particular relevance to our interests are important examples where farmers' capacities and options have expanded. Some of these cases are purely the result of local initiative, while others are the outcome of consciously designed development strategies. The following chapters of this book will draw lessons from these examples. It must be acknowledged, however, that judgements regarding progress are hampered by both the complex, heterogeneous nature of the agricultural sector and the widely differing viewpoints and ideologies of commentators.[11]

We shall judge agricultural development on a number of criteria. Farmers must be able to respond to new opportunities while paying adequate attention to resource conservation. This implies increasing organisational capacity and technical knowledge. Farmers require increased access to sources of technology, and they need to be able to exert pressure on their government for the relevant research, extension, and other support. In addition, farmers must be able to deliver their products to the market and to gain access to useful inputs. This requires the organisation of rural enterprise.

A particular feature of agricultural development that will be emphasised throughout the following discussion is the gradual, organic nature of the process. Agricultural development often takes place in response to changes in the wider economy, and it benefits from external technological innovation. But it must depend to a large extent on internal growth and the expansion of the capacities of farmers and entrepreneurs to take advantage of new opportunities.

Seed provision embraces these various aspects of development. When development is treated as a goal, seed is both an essential input for a productive agricultural sector and a key element for household food security. When agricultural development is seen as the

[10]For a concise review of theories of agricultural development see Staatz and Eicher, 1998.

[11]No better example can be provided than the diverse interpretations of the term 'Green Revolution' and the startlingly different images that it arouses. See Tripp (1996) for a discussion of the varying interpretations of the Green Revolution. The literature on it is immense. Lipton and Longhurst (1989) provide a comprehensive, although now somewhat dated, interpretation of the literature. An example of a long-term study of the positive impact of technological change is Hazell and Ramasamy's (1991) study of rice technology in southern India. One of the most moving accounts of the human costs of technical change in agriculture is Scott's (1985) study of the adoption of new rice technology in Malaysia. Technology change in agriculture encompasses much more than the use of purchased inputs. A summary of advances in the field of 'sustainable agriculture' is presented in Pretty (1995).

expansion of choice, the types and sources of seed available to farmers are relevant measures. When development is taken to be the growth of individual capability, we note that seed provision offers opportunities for innovation, organisation and investment, the pursuit of which will depend on the diverse knowledge, objectives and values of the rural population. The way in which people organise themselves to enhance seed provision – on the farm, in commercial enterprises, and in public agencies – is the subject of this book. It is hoped that this focus on seed provision can help to shed light on the broader subject of agricultural change and development.

These features of agricultural development depend heavily on the management of information. Information is essential for innovation within farming communities, for public service provision, and for commercial transactions. Development theory may recognise the importance of information, but does not see it as a particular challenge. Technology is usually assumed to spread through well-understood patterns of diffusion and communication.[12] Similarly, it is assumed that open markets will efficiently translate demands for farm produce or agricultural inputs into responsive supply.

A growing body of evidence now questions these assumptions. We now recognise that information flow is mediated by a range of institutions that play a large role in the direction of development. The following chapter presents a brief review of some of the most prominent efforts at institutional analysis and provides a guide for the examination of agricultural institutions in the rest of the book. Seed and information are both essential elements of all agricultural systems, from the most traditional farming communities to the most advanced commercial agriculture. The book examines how the institutions of seed provision developed in industrial economies and assesses the performance of contemporary seed institutions in the South. The idea is not to present a unilineal scheme of seed system development, but rather to show that the challenges of building viable institutions that enhance the production and availability of seed are similar in all agricultural economies.

[12]See Grigg (1982), Chapter 11; Rogers (1962).

2 Information & Incentives

AN OUTLINE OF INSTITUTIONAL ANALYSIS

An institutional approach is finding increasing applications in the study of development. Although many of these efforts represent no particular political ideology, they generally share a scepticism about much of the intentional development policy that has been in force. The institutional approach emphasises the importance of understanding and drawing upon the capacities and incentives of the people who are the subject of particular policies, rather than attempting to design structures and organisations in a top-down fashion. It also points to the limitations, and the often perverse incentives, of government agencies involved in development.[1]

Two major areas of socio-economic research address the analysis of institutions relevant to our interests in agricultural development. One focuses on the ways in which information and incentives affect the motivations and conduct of participants in economic and political transactions. This area is often called the New Institutional Economics. The second looks at the social context of economic life and the ways in which information flow is mediated by a complex set of social norms and interactions. These latter approaches are quite diverse; we shall describe them as the New Economic Sociology.

New Institutional Economics

Much of the recent thinking on institutions has come to be known as New Institutional Economics (NIE).[2] It includes a number of different interests but all of them are concerned with correcting the assumption of neo-classical economics that markets operate in an environment of perfect information. Instead, NIE focuses on how the quality, complexity and availability of information determine the way markets operate, business transactions are managed, and institutions develop.

Before going further, it will be useful to give a working definition of institutions. Although the term is subject to almost as many interpretations as development, we shall

[1]Some viewpoints can be interpreted as part of a right-wing agenda, and indeed institutional analysis has found favour with those who support a more laissez-faire approach to development (e.g., Dorn et al., 1998). But much of the writing on institutional issues falls within the mainstream of development thinking (e.g., Clague, 1997; Ostrom, 1990).
[2]NIE can be contrasted with the work of several earlier economists who were also interested in institutions. For instance, Veblen (1899) wrote about the way market demand is determined by the social system, and Commons (1934) explored the legal basis of markets (Mulberg, 1995, Chapter 4). These might be referred to as examples of 'old institutional economics' (Nabli and Nugent, 1989).

adopt one widely used definition: 'Institutions are the rules of the game in a society or, more formally, are the humanly devised constraints that shape human interaction. In consequence they structure incentives in human exchange, whether political, social, or economic' (North, 1990: 3). Examples include the laws and customs that determine the conduct of commerce, define land tenure, or provide a system of education. Institutions need to be distinguished from organisations, which are 'groups of individuals bound by some common purpose to achieve objectives' (ibid.: 5); examples of which include political parties, unions, co-operatives, or schools.[3]

Institutions contribute to the efficient management of information. Several types of information are relevant to the concerns of NIE. In any market transaction, information on prices and on the technical characteristics of the goods or services being exchanged is obviously important. Market participants also seek to learn about the quality of the items on offer, information that is often not easily available. People also seek information about the reputation of the other parties in the exchange. The volume and complexity of this information can be overwhelming. The limited human capacity to process this information is often described by Simon's (1959) term, 'bounded rationality'; we inevitably make decisions on the basis of information that is incomplete or difficult to interpret. In addition, the complicated information environment allows scope for opportunism, or 'self-interest seeking with guile' (Williamson, 1985: 30). Institutions may arise to limit these risks of deception.

The themes included under the rubric of NIE range from analyses of business contracts to explanations of the political process. Only a brief summary of the major aspects of NIE is possible here. The discussion will follow a classification suggested by Nabli and Nugent (1989) in their review of the relevance of NIE for development studies. They distinguish two major branches, each with its own subdivisions. The first is generally concerned with economic institutions. The second applies some of the concepts of economic analysis to the understanding of political institutions.

Economic institutions
The acquisition and interpretation of information entail considerable costs. The concept of transaction costs is central to NIE. Transaction costs have been defined as 'resource losses incurred due to imperfect information'; they are found at all stages of an economic interchange and can be divided into 'search and information costs, bargaining and decision costs, and policing and enforcement costs' (Dahlman, 1979: 148). It takes time and effort to learn about a new technology or service; to obtain sufficient information about a potential partner in a commercial relationship; or to monitor the performance of an agreement. 'Transaction costs are the economic equivalent of friction in physical systems' (Williamson, 1985: 19); they are the pervasive resistance that causes exchange and commerce to deviate from the ideal trajectory predicted by neo-

---

[3]Uphoff (1994: 202) emphasises the difference between *rules* (institutions are 'complexes of norms and behaviours that persist over time by serving collectively valued purposes') and roles (organisations are 'structures of recognised and accepted roles'). By this definition, there are instances of overlap; a central bank or a university might be considered as both an organisation and an institution.

classical market theory. NIE is interested in how institutions respond to transaction costs. Two major approaches to transaction costs can be identified, based on a distinction between the *institutional environment* and *institutional arrangements*.[4] The institutional environment includes the broad political and social institutions that determine the ways in which economic exchange can take place. Institutional arrangements, on the other hand, are concerned with the micro-level institutions that determine how specific economic organisations interact.

The most prominent analyst of the institutional environment is the economic historian Douglass North, who sees institutions as a natural response to the complexity of the information environment. 'The major role of institutions in a society is to reduce uncertainty by establishing a stable (but not necessarily efficient) structure to human interaction' (North, 1990: 6). Although their primary function is to provide stability, institutions may adapt or change to take advantage of new economic opportunities. North describes the emergence of institutions in the following way:

> The costs of transacting arise because information is costly and asymmetrically held by parties to exchange and also because any way that the actors develop institutions to structure human interaction results in some degree of imperfection of the markets. In effect, the incentive consequences of institutions provide mixed signals to the participants, so that even in those cases where the institutional framework is conducive to capturing more of the gains from trade as compared to an earlier institutional framework, there will still be incentives to cheat, free ride, and so forth that will contribute to market imperfections. (ibid., 108).

This perspective on the institutional environment has been used to examine the evolution of trade and commerce and the emergence of institutions that allow the transfer of capital, the exchange of information, and the management of risk. Formal commercial laws and regulations, customs governing market behaviour, trade associations and partnerships, and mediums of exchange and measurement are all examples of institutional development in response to the costs of information management.[5]

In contrast, the micro-level view of transaction costs (institutional arrangements) concentrates on the institutions that promote day-to-day commerce. This subject is best represented by the work of Oliver Williamson. Williamson is particularly interested in the relative efficiencies of hierarchies and markets. The best example of a hierarchy is a firm, an organisation that combines several distinct functions that could also be managed independently. The subject traces its origins to a paper by Coase (1937) which asked why firms emerge in market economies. His answer was that firms exist because they are able to lower the costs of negotiating and contracting among individual specialist producers. Williamson looks in considerable detail at the options for contracting and the emergence of governance structures, which are 'the institutional matrix within which transactions are negotiated and executed' (Williamson, 1979: 239). He is particularly interested in how the form of contract and the level of integration between parties in a

---

[4]The distinction is made by Davis and North (1971) and has been used by Dorward et al. (1998) in their review of NIE.

[5]Historical examples include the development of traders' coalitions to co-ordinate negotiations and enforce contracts in eleventh-century Mediterranean trade (Greif, 1993) and the evolution of merchant law in medieval European trade (Milgrom et al., 1990).

transaction are determined by the degree of risk, the frequency of the transaction, and asset specificity (the degree to which facilities, equipment, or personnel are dedicated to the specific activity).

A major aspect of institutional arrangements is the incentive structure. This is explored in the literature on agency. An agency relationship occurs whenever one individual directs the actions of another for the former's benefit. The person directing the action is the principal, while the one taking the action is the agent (Pratt and Zeckhauser, 1985). The principal-agent relationship is problematic because of the asymmetrical distribution of information; the agent usually knows more than the principal about the task in hand. The challenge is to motivate the agent to perform in the principal's interest. Much of the principal-agent literature is concerned with the design of efficient monitoring and incentive systems. Various types of contracts (e.g. salaries, piece rates, shared investments) may be devised in order to provide the most effective incentives for a particular situation (Lazear, 1987; Prendergast, 1999). In broader terms, the literature on agency and incentives describes how one party can formulate a contract that ensures compliance and performance from another.

An important component of the 'incentives' literature focuses on property rights. Demsetz (1967) holds that the institution of property rights emerges in order to guide incentives for 'internalising' the externalities (costs and benefits) of a transaction. These incentives often arise in relation to changes in technology or markets. One of his examples involves the emergence of private land ownership by certain groups of Native Americans who were involved in the fur trade. The development of the trade placed increasing pressure on the animal resources in previously communally managed territory. Private ownership emerged because of the incentives to conserve the resource base and to profit from individual hunting and trapping. Much of the institutional literature on property rights examines issues such as corporate ownership, shareholding, and liability (e.g. Furubotn and Pejovich, 1972). In addition to rights over physical property, an issue of increasing importance for agricultural development is intellectual property protection, which is subject to the same principles and incentives.

The issue of incentives has also proved useful for thinking about the management of public sector enterprises. Employees of government organisations are agents of the public. What type of incentive structure elicits the maximum amount of service for the principals (the citizens)? Because public agencies are fundamentally different from commercial firms, the identification of appropriate incentives is difficult. One solution might be performance-based pay regimes, but such a reform would also require lowering monitoring and enforcement costs in public organisations (Klitgaard, 1997). Attention has also been given to improving the incentive structure of public infrastructure provision (such as roads or water systems) by directly involving the users in planning and monitoring the work (Ostrom et al., 1993). Such innovations have been referred to as 'co-production', which 'implies that citizens can play an active role in producing public goods and services of consequence to them' (Ostrom, 1996: 1073). All of these attempts to improve the incentive systems in public organisations depend on a more efficient flow of information.

Political institutions

The second branch of NIE identified by Nabli and Nugent (1989) is principally concerned with political behaviour. There are two major bodies of literature here. The first relates to collective action and the management of common property. One of the most widely cited examples of this approach is Mancur Olson's *Logic of Collective Action* (1965). Olson discusses the problems faced by groups or coalitions that are formed in relation to collective or public goods. Examples include the management of common grazing land, the lobbying of a union, or the establishment of a co-operative enterprise. The major challenges relate to incentives and information. Because the benefits of group action are spread very widely, an individual's incentive to contribute to the effort is reduced. In addition, group members have inadequate information about others' motives and actions, and this discourages commitment to the effort. Thus deficiencies in the management of information mean that group action may not emerge, even when it is in the clear interest of all the participants.

The other area involves examining the behaviour of the state and explaining the rationality of apparently detrimental policies. This approach is sometimes referred to as public choice theory, rational choice theory, or new political economy (Staniland, 1985). The approach focuses on the rationality of individual actors in the political process. Although the political arena theoretically reflects the outcome of bargaining among all citizens, the uneven distribution of information and incentives leads to domination by particular interest groups. If institutions are created or modified by economic agents pursuing their own welfare, then 'an agent would have to loom large in the market before being willing to incur the costs of organising the new institution... Lying behind the economic theory of institutions, then, is a political story, one in which big interests possess an initial advantage' (Bates, 1989: 90). It is possible to use the political arena to achieve advantages that cannot be obtained in the marketplace. Although NIE's image of institutional change is couched in the language of market interchange, the theory must acknowledge that its 'entrepreneurs' may be 'political, economic, or military' (North, 1990: 84).

Applications of NIE to agricultural change

This rapid sketch of NIE has touched on a wide range of research interests. But they share two important premises. First, they all recognise the crucial importance of information; a significant proportion of economic and political life is concerned with seeking and interpreting information. Second, all of these approaches address the problem of motivation; change will only occur if appropriate incentives are present.

Although NIE has been developed and debated largely in the context of Western market economies, it is also beginning to make contributions to the study of agricultural development.[6] Changes in a society's institutional environment may have a significant effect on the organisation of economic life. For example, a study in northern Kenya

---

[6]For summaries of the application of NIE to a range of development issues, see Harriss et al., (1995); Nabli and Nugent (1989); and Clague (1997).

traces the entry of the pastoralist Orma to the market economy beginning in the 1930s (Ensminger, 1992). Their conversion to Islam facilitated interaction with Arab traders through a shared set of values and laws. The colonial government's introduction of courts, a banking system, and standard weights and measures further facilitated market participation.

There are also examples of the application of the study of micro-level economic arrangements to agricultural institutions. One of the prime examples is the analysis of tenancy institutions, particularly sharecropping (Bardhan, 1989). Sharecropping serves to lower the costs that a landowner would have to pay to monitor farm labourers, while providing a mechanism for risk-sharing between tenant and owner (Otsuka and Hayami, 1988). NIE has also been used to examine the variation in rural labour contracts and the degree to which labour, credit, and access to land may be interrelated (Bardhan and Rudra, 1981).

Hayami and Ruttan (1985) include institutional change in their theory of induced agricultural innovation. They describe an example from a village in the Philippines where technical change was responsible for modifications in tenancy and labour institutions. The principal technological changes were the extension of the national irrigation system to the village and the introduction of modern rice varieties and management techniques. Yields increased from 2.5 to 6.7 tonnes per hectare. The new technology was also responsible for two significant institutional changes. The majority of farmers were leasehold tenants, and there was a significant shift to (illegal) sub-tenancy agreements, which took advantage of the fact that the rent paid to landlords was below the equilibrium rent that would be reflected by the new technology. In addition, farmers changed the way that landless labourers were contracted for harvest. The significant yield increases implied a windfall for harvest labourers, who were accustomed to receive one-sixth of the harvest as payment. The new arrangements obliged them to supply additional (unpaid) weeding labour in order to qualify for their harvest share. These changes are examples of how institutions that regulate tenancy and labour are modified in response to shifts in the resource base and the availability of technology.[7]

NIE has also found application in understanding how institutional arrangements determine farmers' access to markets. Dorward et al. (1998) have examined how information and incentives affect the provision of credit and inputs for smallholder cash cropping. They show how imperfections in these markets are addressed by the evolution of 'interlocking' contracts, in which a trader's access to the farmer's expected output is used as a guarantee for the loan of production inputs.

Principal-agent theory has been used to suggest how to structure a shift towards private provision of veterinary services to African farmers (Leonard, 1993). The farmer is the principal and the veterinarian the agent in this case, but there are significant

---

[7]Hayami and Ruttan respond to the criticism that these changes may have increased efficiency but not equity. They point out that subtenancy allowed more of the landless to become farm operators, and that the alternative to readjusting harvesting shares was the adoption of mechanical harvesting that would have displaced most of the landless labourers.

problems with the efficient monitoring of the agent's performance. One possible solution is the formation of professional veterinary associations that can perform the role of third-party enforcement and help to reduce monitoring costs for farmers.

Public choice theory has also been applied to agricultural development. Bates (1981) describes the process whereby the urban elite in Africa capture the political agenda that determines agricultural policy. The use of marketing boards, price controls and export taxes extracts surplus from farmers and keeps food prices artificially low for urban constituents. The results of this anti-agriculture bias have been demonstrated in a wide range of countries (Schiff and Valdés, 1998). Because much agricultural research and regulation is supplied by the public sector, it is particularly important to understand the incentive system of public agricultural agencies.

A specially interesting example for testing theories of collective action in agriculture is provided by a study of irrigation management in Andhra Pradesh (Wade, 1988). It describes how certain village councils seasonally select and employ village members as 'common irrigators'. Their tasks include guarding the village's access to the main canal, arranging access to irrigation water to avoid excessive loss, and improving supply to those fields furthest from the canal. This institutional innovation only occurs in certain villages, however. The study examines the ecological, social, and economic conditions that facilitate the emergence of this type of collective action.

This review of NIE indicates how institutional analysis is relevant to the study of agricultural development. Farmers react to changing economic conditions and the availability of new technology by modifying local institutions that allocate land, labour, and other resources. The nature of incentives determines farmers' technological innovation and adaptation. The quality and availability of information conditions their interactions with the marketplace. The emergence of rural enterprise is also dependent on the adequacy of information. New economic opportunities may lead to changes in the institutions governing property rights. Finally, the effectiveness of public provision of agricultural technology is a function of the incentives within public institutions and the control of agricultural policy.

New economic sociology

There is another area of research that deals with institutions and information and is relevant to the study of agricultural development. Although it has parallel interests to NIE, and there are significant overlaps, it is based on a quite different set of assumptions about institutional performance.

Despite the fact that NIE challenges some of the basic premises of neo-classical economics, it still focuses on conventional economic parameters. The management of information and the provision of incentives are both seen in terms of the calculative self-interest of individual actors. In addition, although many adherents of NIE acknowledge the conservative aspect of institutions, the emphasis is on their responsive, endogenous nature. Institutions are no longer an external 'given' for economic analysis, but rather an integral part of the equation. In this view, institutions are formed and modified in response to economic interests.

These NIE assumptions are not universally accepted. Information has a social as well as an economic dimension and communication must be seen as part of a much more complex environment than that delimited by market transactions. Similarly, it is difficult to see all market institutions as emerging from the self-interested bargaining of economic agents. If all norms and rules are endogenous, there is a problem of infinite regress. Instead, there must be 'norms established through the process of socialisation [that] provide part of the framework within which individuals pursue their self-interests' (Field, 1984: 705). It is necessary to examine the cultural and social dimensions of institutional performance.

Sociologists have long been interested in economic organisation, and economic sociology is a well-established field of enquiry, in which a number of recent developments of relevance to the study of institutions have captured an important place in current development theory. This work is more heterogeneous than that of NIE, but we shall refer to it collectively as New Economic Sociology (NES) (Smelser and Swedberg, 1994). Three themes are of particular relevance: networks, social capital, and trust.

We saw that NIE is concerned with the way information moves among individual economic actors; institutions arise to facilitate its management, but are defined as rules rather than actual collectivities or organisations. Thus, in this view, economic transactions involve the exchange of goods and information among individuals who have no necessary social or historical relations with each other. Whether economic life can be abstracted from social organisation in this way is a familiar debate. What became known in anthropology as the 'formalist-substantivist debate' revolved around the question of whether developing economies could be understood in the terms used to analyse conventional markets; the formalists held that this was possible, while the substantivists saw much of what was defined as economic life as dominated by patterns of reciprocity and redistribution that defied maximisation theory.[8] A similar debate can be found in political science. James Scott (1976) developed the concept of 'the moral economy' to argue that peasant subsistence, in the face of capitalist or colonial oppression, is often better served by a collective stance whose obligations preclude the operation of calculative self-interest. Others (e.g. Popkin, 1979) argue that peasant behaviour can be interpreted as rational maximisation.[9]

Granovetter (1985) provides a useful compromise by arguing that economic life is not as embedded in society as the substantivists and the moral economy school might believe, but that economic theory, including NIE, is based on an 'undersocialised' view of human action. He criticises the work of Williamson on markets and hierarchies in particular. While Williamson holds that market negotiation is characterised by impersonal and antagonistic behaviour, Granovetter believes that 'the anonymous market of

[8]Polanyi et al. (1957) is one of the original sources of the substantivist school. Various perspectives on the debate can be found in Firth (1967).
[9]For a useful review of the debate, see Peletz, 1983.

neoclassical models is virtually non-existent in economic life and that transactions of all kinds are rife with...social connections' (1985: 495). He argues that the option of the firm cannot be seen as necessarily resolving the problems of trust and control encountered in the market; social relations in a firm may serve to constrain rather than facilitate information flow and may block innovation. It is difficult to abstract economic transactions from networks of social relations that 'penetrate irregularly and in different degrees in different sectors of economic life' (ibid., 491). The concept of networks has found considerable application in understanding phenomena such as the mobilisation of capital and information and the diffusion of innovations in an industry.[10]

There are certainly instances where the operation of networks is an important factor in explaining differences in agricultural development. Long (1968) describes how those farmers in a Zambian community who were Jehovah's Witnesses tended to take better advantage of commercial agricultural opportunities. They 'frequently utilise links with fellow churchmen to gain access to such resources as expertise, farming equipment and labour...' (ibid: 200). The network provided by church membership served to transfer information about techniques and reputations, that helped farmers improve their farming.

More recently, attention has shifted away from networks to the related concept of social capital – a term which has caught the imagination of many development theorists. One of its popularisers defines it as those 'features of social organisation, such as trust, norms, and networks, that can improve the efficiency of society by facilitating coordinated actions' (Putnam, 1993: 167). One of its first uses was by Coleman (1988), who was concerned about the influence of family and community on educational performance. He identified three resources that constitute social capital: an environment of obligations and trustworthiness; the existence of effective information channels; and the presence of norms and effective sanctions. Putnam utilised the concept to explain differences in the economic success of northern and southern Italy, arguing that the relative success of the north could be correlated with the high density of civic associations. According to this interpretation, a region's economic development depends less on its initial economic resources than on the depth of its civic endowments.[11]

A broad definition of social capital would include the adaptation of traditional modes of organisation to new situations. The Kofyar of Nigeria are recognised as being particularly diligent and successful farmers. In some instances farmers migrate, at least temporarily, to areas where they can practise shifting cash cropping. The migrants to one site often come from different communities and so cannot organise themselves through pre-existing kinship or political relations. But the traditional Kofyar voluntary work party has been used by the migrants to help meet the increased labour requirements of the new cropping patterns. Although relatively little used in the home villages, it has

[10]See Powell and Smith-Doerr (1994) for a review of research on networks.
[11]The concept of social capital has also been examined in a study of Tanzania that correlates the breadth and heterogeneity of group membership in a village to average income levels in the village (Narayan and Pritchett, 1997).

taken on new importance in the face of new agricultural opportunities (Netting, 1968).[12]

Another element in the discussions of networks and social capital that has attracted particular attention is trust, although there is little agreement on a precise definition.[13] Trust is also prominent in NIE writings, but its role in an institutional context seems to be mediated by factors more familiar to sociology, such as societal norms, political organisation, regulation, professional standards, networks, and corporate culture (Williamson, 1993). Trust can be seen as an expression of social capital, the growth and development of which contribute to the lowering of transaction costs.

NES insights broaden our scope for examining agricultural development. It is important to recognise that the actors exchanging information may have a significant history of interaction. The structure of current and past social exchange is an important determinant of future institutional innovation. Households in a farming community interact on many different levels, and this will affect their incentives for taking advantage of new economic or technological opportunities. Potential participants in agricultural markets also bring with them memberships in networks that may facilitate, or impede, the development of commercial relations.

Limitations of Institutional Theory

The concepts of NIE and NES are finding increasing application in the study of economic development. The analysis in the remainder of this book will draw on many of these ideas. But before synthesising these concepts it is necessary to discuss a number of weaknesses. In particular, it is useful to draw attention to inadequacies in the treatment of power relationships, problems with objective verification and measurement, and uncertainties in defining causality in institutional change.

Power

Bates comments on the 'bloodless language' of NIE (1995: 47). A world described in terms of information flow is one in which problems can be resolved with better organisation or advice. In the words of a recent World Bank publication, 'developing countries have fewer institutions to ameliorate information problems, and the institutions they do have are weaker than the counterpart institutions in industrialised countries' (World Bank, 1998: 72). In this view, an unequal distribution of power can hide behind fashionable terminology; ruthless control of resources becomes 'information asymmetry', gross corruption 'rent seeking', or dispossession 'institutional innovation'. Although our examination of agricultural development will focus on information and institutions, we should not lose sight of the fact that the inefficient flow of information may be caused by structural inadequacies or the inequitable control of resources.

[12]See Smale and Ruttan (1997) for a description of the adaptation of traditional mutual assistance groups to tasks of soil conservation in Burkina Faso.
[13]A recent popular treatment of the subject assumed a very broad scope (Fukuyama, 1995), while scholarly treatments debate the degree to which the concept is open to quantitative analysis (Humphrey and Schmitz, 1996; Dasgupta, 1988).

There are two areas related to institutional innovation in agriculture where power relationships are particularly relevant. One is market development. Large farmers may be able to dictate the terms and conditions under which other farmers can bring their produce to market. In addition, market structures may be far from equitable. Harriss-White (1996) describes the complexity of grain markets in South India and demonstrates that merchants exhibit a very unequal distribution of assets and ability to control the market. 'Repeated network transactions may lower transaction costs but the costs of switching networks or enforcing contract law are so high that repeated transactions also solidify relations of super- and sub-ordination. Weak trading parties are often deprived of choice with respect to sources of information, trading contacts, credit, access to storage and transport' (ibid., 320). Inadequacy of information is not the only factor that constrains market development.

The second area of relevance is the generation of agricultural technology. The theory of induced innovation presumes that agricultural research has the capacity to respond to the needs of the majority of farmers. Because most agricultural research in the South is conducted by the public sector, the nature of the research product is a function of the political process. In many instances, public science responds to client demands 'through negotiation, persuasion, and coercion' (Busch et al., 1991: 49). Even the architects of induced innovation theory acknowledge that 'the supply of institutional innovations is strongly influenced by the cost of achieving social consensus (or of suppressing opposition). How costly a form of institutional change is to be accepted in a society depends on the power structure among vested interest groups' (Hayami and Ruttan, 1985: 96).[14]

Subjectivity

A second problem with institutional analysis is the subjectivity of many of its concepts. For example, it is usually impossible to quantify transaction costs.[15] Even the identification of what constitutes a transaction cost is sometimes confused, and the term is often loosely applied to any situation where there are uncertainties or delays. 'The suspicion remains that the concept of transaction costs is simply a gloss, or at best a re-specification, of what used to be known simply as market failures' (Mulberg, 1995: 141). Care must be taken in defining precisely what constitutes a transaction cost in a particular situation.

The notion of incentive is even more problematic. Incentives are not observable (Toye, 1995: 56), and there is a temptation to offer ex-post explanations of the success or failure of a particular transaction by reference to the adequacy of the incentives involved.

NES concepts can be similarly difficult to pin down. Social capital seems to have no fixed definition and is often portrayed in very broad terms. Ostrom (1997: 158), for instance, defines it as 'the shared knowledge, understandings, institutions, and patterns of interactions that a group of individuals bring to any activity'.[16] When given such a

[14]See Koppel (1995) for a critique of induced innovation theory.
[15]An interesting exception is provided by analyses of the transaction costs of formal and informal credit. For instance, see Ahmed (1989).
[16]See Harriss and de Renzio (1997) for a useful (and sceptical) review of social capital.

vague definition, it can become a handy rationalisation for explaining various development successes and failures.

Similarly, the role of networks in economic change is also subject to variable interpretation; they are sometimes seen as facilitating interchange (as with ethnic trading communities) and at other times are blamed for impeding progress (as with the obligations of the extended family imposed on entrepreneurs) (Moore, 1997). Networks can promote information flow, but they can also exclude potential participants and control access to information.

Culture and change
Institutional analysis provides a useful idiom for describing change, but its predictive powers are still to be demonstrated. North (1990: 86) explains institutional change in the following way:

> A change in relative prices leads one or both parties to an exchange, whether it is political or economic, to perceive that either or both could do better with an altered agreement or contract. An attempt will be made to renegotiate the contract. However, because contracts are nested in a hierarchy of rules, the re-negotiation may not be possible without restructuring a higher set of rules (or violating some norm of behaviour). In that case, the party that stands to improve his or her bargaining position may very well attempt to devote resources to restructuring the rules at a higher level.

This uncertainty of NIE in explaining change (which type of norm can be violated? under what conditions?) is highlighted by its oblique treatment of the concept of culture. North (1990: 37) defines culture as 'the transmission of knowledge and values from one generation to the next'. Hayami and Ruttan (1985: 111, fn57) also consider 'cultural endowments', which they define as 'those dimensions of culture that have been transmitted from the past'. It is tempting to conclude that, for NIE, norms or values that are susceptible to change are 'institutions', while those that do not respond are 'culture'.

'Cultural barriers' have long been a popular explanation for the failures of development projects. Culture never manages more than a footnote in Hayami and Ruttan's (1985) theory of induced innovation, and in a later article Ruttan (1988) worries about what anthropologists might contribute to the understanding of institutional change. The concept of culture has been subject to various definitions. One of the classic anthropological texts on cultural barriers to change presents examples of fatalistic attitudes, feelings of pride or modesty, and conflicting belief systems (Foster, 1962). But it also includes many down-to-earth examples of incompatibilities in resource management. A smokeless stove is rejected because smoke is needed to control the insects that infest the hut roofs; a new bean is unappreciated because there is insufficient fuel wood to cook it. This presentation of cultural barriers as a mixture of vague attitudes, codified beliefs, and the practicalities of household management makes the reader appreciate the importance of understanding local livelihoods, but does little to advance the case of culture as some separate, identifiable entity.[17]

---

[17]Foster (1962) also describes 'social barriers to change' which include obligations to kin, the local power structure, leadership, and factionalism.

It is instructive to consider how the anthropologist Fredrik Barth (1967) interprets social change. Patterns of behaviour in a society can be seen as aggregates of individual behaviour, which may be thought of as customs. Individual behaviour is an allocation of time and resources, and new allocations are observable and have consequences. Entrepreneurial activity produces

> new information on the interrelations of different categories of valued goods. The information produced by such activity will render false the idea that people have held till then about the relative value of goods, and can reasonably be expected to precipitate re-evaluations and modifications both of categorisations and value orientations. In other words, it changes the cultural bases that determine people's behaviour ... (ibid., 664).[18]

Barth's analysis of change is remarkably similar to that of North cited earlier. Barth's 'cultural bases' are North's 'hierarchy of rules'. We may follow Barth's view of culture as the manifestation of an iterative process where individuals continually renegotiate their allocation of time and resources; or choose the NIE view of culture as an awkward residual bequeathed to an otherwise efficient system of responsive economic institutions.[19] But in either case we have to acknowledge that we are still a long way from being able to explain how and why change takes place. Institutional analysis allows us to appreciate the interplay of interests and values that defines economic change, but our ability to predict the direction or specify the causality of that change is still very limited.

An institutional approach

Despite the limitations discussed in the previous section, a focus on institutions and incentives is a useful way to approach the study of agricultural development. We shall adopt a somewhat eclectic approach, rather than strictly following the formulae of any one school of NIE or NES. The approach is based on the following premises:[20]

i   Information is important and we are often guilty of underestimating the difficulties associated with its transmission and interpretation. The high cost and scarcity of information about technical characteristics and quality impede the diffusion of technology and limit the development of markets for products and inputs. Information inadequacies are as evident at the village level as they are in the commercial sphere.

ii   Information about the trustworthiness of partners is also required for development. Owners of diverse skills, knowledge and resources need to be able to interact and to co-ordinate their efforts. They may do this through collective action, by establishing a long-term business relationship, or by bargaining in the market. In all of these

---

[18]Ensminger (1992) presents an appreciation of Barth's early work and its intuition of the emergence of NIE.
[19]Or we may simply opt for Kenneth Boulding's (1966: 86) 'first revised law of economic behaviour: we will do today what we did yesterday unless there are very good reasons for doing otherwise'.
[20]The idea of trying to identify these key points (as well as some of the points themselves) is borrowed from Hodgson's (1994) discussion of 'institutionalism'.

cases they require information that allows them to establish, monitor, and enforce equitable relationships.

iii Institutions may help to facilitate the flow of information, but people can only be expected to respond when this information elicits appropriate incentives, which may be economic or may take other forms. An understanding of the incentives available to farmers, entrepreneurs, and public officials helps us to interpret the direction of institutional change.

iv Institutions cannot be considered in isolation. Human interaction is structured within societies and cultures. Individuals have a wide assortment of means and motivations for interacting with each other, and it is sensible to consider the way in which an economic transaction or technological change may be embedded in a wider pattern of social interchange. Networks can be used and adapted in innovative ways when opportunities are available.

v Economic systems are not perfectly responsive, nor are cultures and societies rigidly fixed. Both are 'subject to processes of cumulative causation' (Hodgson, 1994: 69) and individual preferences are in a continual state of adaptation and change. Preferences are a function of 'habit and routine…occasionally punctuated by acts of creativity and novelty' (ibid.). Organisations provide stability to economic life, but the innovations of their members lead to new institutions (new rules and modes of conduct).

vi As economies and cultures evolve, there are inevitable disequilibria. There are winners and losers in any process of change. Development should reward the creativity of entrepreneurs but limit their concentration of power. Many of the challenges of agricultural development cannot be separated from the problems of unjust distribution of resources. It is the task of development policy to manage the balance between incentives for innovation and safeguards for equitable access to opportunity.

These principles may appear somewhat crude compared with the elegant theories of NIE and NES. The choice of this broader approach is a pragmatic one. Although we can offer no promise of mechanistic causal explanations nor infallible predictive capacity, this approach will allow us to develop plausible explanations for many of the successes and failures in agricultural development. These explanations will in turn contribute to principles that can guide the formulation of agricultural development policy.

The institutional approach implies that we shall find the same problems of information and incentives in all agricultural economies. However, the institutions that arise to address these problems will vary widely, according to culture, history, and technology. It is our task to understand how a wide range of institutions develops to answer a basic set of challenges for agricultural development.

There is a second reason for eschewing a strict interpretation of institutional theories. NIE holds that ideologies play an important role in helping us to interpret the world around us (North, 1990: 111). Ideologies may provide useful models that allow us to communicate with each other, but they can also stand in the way of understanding complex phenomena. This danger is particularly relevant to the study of development. NIE, the theory that provides us with these insights into ideology, is itself in danger of being used in a rigid and formulaic manner. As such, it joins many other development ideologies and beliefs that posit omniscient (or primitive) farmers, responsive (or predatory) markets, and benign (or oppressive) states. This book seeks to provide an empirical examination of one aspect of agricultural development. It will take advantage of the observations and experience of institutional analysis, but its aim is to provide a background for useful policy advice, rather than to advance particular development fashions or vocabulary.

The organisation of the book

Our primary interest is agricultural development as a process. The strategy is to see how particular incentives are transformed into the organisation of resources and the development of agricultural innovations. One important factor is farmers' ability to develop, acquire and utilise technology that furthers their own interests. Our discussion of agricultural development in the following chapters will focus on one activity: seed provision.

It is difficult to find a better example for examining the agricultural development process. Since the emergence of agriculture, the capacity to select and maintain seed has been in the hands of every cultivator. The diversity of contemporary seed systems is a product of the ingenuity and investment of countless farmers over the ages. Seed has also been a subject of private enterprise for several centuries, although commercial seed activity has developed most rapidly in the past half century. In addition, seed provision has been a focus of specific government intervention and support. Of particular interest to our study is the wide range of government and donor programmes aimed at developing national seed provision capability. Because seed provision can be managed by farmers, commercial firms, or state agencies, it is a particularly appropriate instrument for examining the course of agricultural development.

Chapter 3 provides an overview on the subjects of seed (a physical input) and varieties (a genetic resource). It offers a brief summary of the biological aspects of plant breeding and seed production that will be useful for the analysis that follows. It also discusses the structure of seed production and seed trade and introduces the types of information that are required to foster seed exchange and seed enterprise development.

Chapter 4 examines farmers' variety development and seed provision. It includes an examination of farmers' incentives for the selection of their crop varieties and an analysis of the imperfect information that is available to them. It also examines seed flows among farmers, and shows how these are embedded in wide social and economic networks.

Chapter 5 describes the evolution of the commercial seed sector. It discusses the incentives that are required to elicit commercial seed activity and describes how information is exchanged between seed enterprises and their customers. Particular attention is given to the transaction costs that affect the development of seed enterprises. The chapter also discusses the issue of property rights and the seed trade.

Chapter 6 discusses the public seed system. In many countries, publicly funded agricultural research and extension are responsible for the development and delivery of new crop varieties. The chapter pays particular attention to the organisation and incentives for these public activities. It also describes the flow of information about public sector technology. In addition, there are still a number of public seed companies in the South, and their performance is discussed. Another element of public participation in the seed sector is the provision of regulations with the rationale to facilitate the flow of information between seed producers and consumers; the adequacy of these regulatory frameworks is reviewed.

Chapter 7 examines several types of donor and government interventions to improve local seed provision. Some of these projects are in response to emergency situations caused by drought or civil disorder. But many of them are attempts to encourage village-level seed provision capacity or to stimulate small-scale commercial activity. All of these activities will be examined with regard to the adequacy of incentives and the mechanisms for addressing the significant transaction costs involved in seed system development.

Chapter 8 reviews the factors that have contributed to the evolution of farm-level, commercial and public seed activities. It discusses the strengths and weaknesses of different donor approaches to seed system development. It emphasises the fact that institutional growth is a slow process. Institutions cannot be imposed from the outside, but must emerge from the experience, negotiation, and compromise of the actors themselves. External aid can make a difference, but the primary responsibility for seed system development rests with farmers, entrepreneurs, and responsible governments.

3 Seeds & Varieties

Introduction

Before examining the institutions of seed provision, we shall use this chapter to establish some basic information about seed. The subject often causes confusion because seed is actually two different things. First, it is an embodiment of genetic information that is selected, improved upon, and utilised in succeeding seasons. Different varieties carry different sets of genetic information. Secondly, seed is a physical input and a traded commodity. We shall begin by looking at its biological and genetic components, including a review of seed biology and an examination of the nature of variety selection and plant breeding. We shall then shift to an analysis of seed as a physical input, including the rationale for seed demand, the development of the seed trade, and a review of the individual components in the seed provision process.

Seed biology[1]

The cereals and pulses (or grain legumes) that constitute the majority of our food supply are grown from seed. The seed is the product of the fertilisation of the female reproductive organ of the flower (pistil) by pollen from the male organ (stamen). The pistils and stamens may be in the same flower (as in wheat) or in separate flowers on the same plant (the silks and tassels of the maize plant).[2] The type of fertilisation has important implications for seed production. If fertilisation normally occurs within the flower of a single plant, the crop is called self-pollinated; wheat, rice and beans are important examples. If pollen from one plant normally fertilises the pistil of a different plant, the crop is called cross-pollinated. The pollen may be carried between plants by the wind (as in maize) or by insects (as in pigeonpea). Some crops, such as sorghum and cotton, reproduce both by self- and cross-pollination.

Cereal crops are all members of the grass family and are called monocotyledons. Their seed consists of an embryo and an endosperm that provides a starchy food reserve when the first leaf of the embryo, or cotyledon, emerges from the soil. Legumes, on the other hand, are dicotyledons, which means that their seed comprises two seed leaves that

[1]Much of this discussion is based on Stoskopf (1981).
[2]In some crops, such as hemp and hops, the male and female organs are in separate flowers of different plants.

begin photosynthesis after germination. In both cases, the energy and nutrients stored for the young plant in the seed are exploited by humans as food grain. Thus, farmers traditionally have had to decide which part of their grain harvest is to be saved for seed use.

In many fruits and vegetables the seeds are surrounded by an edible fleshy fruit. Farmers growing these crops must extract the seeds for next season's planting. In some cases the fruit may be consumed and the seed saved, but in other cases the fruit must be destroyed or allowed to decompose in order to obtain the seed. Some vegetables are grown for their leaves, stems or roots, and their seeds do not develop until after the harvest of the edible portion. Some plants have to be reserved for seed production, which may also require special management and growing conditions.

Seed is a living organism. Provided with the proper conditions, it will germinate and reproduce. Several biological mechanisms help control these functions. The possibility that seed might germinate while still on the plant or in the fruit is limited by the mechanism of seed dormancy. The seeds of many crops will not germinate immediately after maturity; they exhibit a dormancy period of several weeks or months, depending on the crop or variety. Once a seed germinates, the plant's reproductive cycle may be regulated by other factors that help it mature at the proper time. After germination, many crops will flower only during the time of year when days are a specific length. The day-length sensitivity of a particular variety may limit its ability to be cultivated in another environment. Crops planted in the autumn that come to maturity in the spring (such as winter wheat) often require vernalisation by low winter temperatures before their reproductive cycle is initiated.

There are also some important food crops that normally reproduce asexually, rather than through seed production. Potatoes are usually grown from small tubers or parts of tubers, referred to as seed potatoes. Yams are also reproduced in this way. Because farmers must select tubers for seed from their harvest, or acquire them in the market, seed of these crops is subject to many of the information management characteristics that we shall discuss for conventional seed.

Some other crops (such as cassava or sugar cane) are normally reproduced from stem cuttings or from suckers obtained from the base of the plant (such as banana). Because these reproduction systems are very different from the seed systems we shall be examining, these crops will not feature in the discussion in the rest of this book.

This brief outline indicates that seed has two separate functions. First, it is a physical entity that allows the plant to reproduce the following season; it is an input that can be produced and saved on the farm or acquired from outside. Second, seed is a repository of genetic information. The type of genetic information passed from one plant generation to the next depends on the reproductive mechanisms (e.g. cross- versus self-pollination) and on farmers' management of their seed selection. We shall begin by outlining some of the major issues that affect the genetic side of seed management.

Plant domestication and diffusion

Our ancestors began to domesticate wild plants more than 10,000 years ago. Although the exact origins of the domestication process may never be known, a certain amount of archaeological evidence is available. The domestication of wheat and barley in the Fertile Crescent of Mesopotamia is one of the better-documented instances.[3] The survival of early human groups depended on mobility, as people moved seasonally from one environment to another, collecting plants and hunting wild animals. Trade also became an important way to take advantage of the varied environments, and commodities such as obsidian and various foodstuffs were exchanged between areas.

Cultivation began to emerge as a complement to exchange and migration. Early cultivators required as wide a range of plant types as possible, because they had to begin searching for those characteristics that met their particular needs. For instance, the wild grasses from which they were making their selections 'shattered' (dropped and dispersed seed from the plant when it was mature), and plants had to be found that retained their seed until after harvest. The wild grasses often matured over an extended period, which required repeated harvests, so early farmers began to select for uniform ripening (Harlan, 1995). In addition, the tough glumes covering the seeds of early wheat and barley made grinding difficult, and so effort was devoted to finding variants that were more suitable for food preparation. The growth of trade undoubtedly contributed to plant domestication, because it moved the seed of a species from its own niche to those where a wider range of mutants might survive. As new plant types were developed, their grain and seed entered into regional trade, and further cycles of improvement and adaptation were possible.

The process of plant domestication was almost certainly part of a very gradual transition from hunting and gathering to sedentary agriculture, rather than a sudden revolution.[4] The Soviet botanist Vavilov argued that a crop's centre of origin is coterminous with its centre of diversity. It is now known that the situation is somewhat more complicated than this, but it is possible roughly to delineate the areas in which our major crops were first domesticated. The Fertile Crescent was apparently the centre of origin not only for wheat and barley, but also for several pulses such as peas and lentils. Evidence for the domestication of Asian rice can be found in a belt extending from the Ganges Plain to North Vietnam and South China. South-East Asia is the home of crops such as taro, banana and sugarcane. Specific areas in Africa have been proposed as the centres of domestication for sorghum, pearl millet and cowpeas. Mesoamerica is the home of maize and squash, while potatoes, sweet potatoes, cassava, groundnuts, and beans were all first domesticated in South America.

The exceptional story of crop domestication is rivalled by the history of the diffusion of crops from their centres of origin. An analysis of evidence for the diffusion of wheat and barley north-west across Europe shows a fairly steady rate of approximately one kilometre per year, over the course of 3,000 years. There is reason to believe that this expansion represents the actual movement of Neolithic cultivators rather than the transfer of technology from one group to another (Ammerman and Cavalli-Sforza, 1971). Crops of Near Eastern and African origin were being grown in India as early as 4,000 years ago (Evans, 1993). Taro, as well as certain types of yams and bananas, were

---

[3]The following discussion is based on Flannery (1965).
[4]This discussion is based on Evans, 1993: Chapter 3.

apparently brought by settlers from South-East Asia to Madagascar several centuries BC. From there the crops moved to the east coast of Africa and then westward, allowing the expansion of cultivation into forest areas (Murdock, 1959). Maize apparently spread rapidly from its centre of origin in Mesoamerica into South America, but the South American potato moved northwards much more slowly (Evans, 1993).

The age of exploration and empire greatly accelerated the movement of crops around the world. New World crops such as maize and potatoes rapidly found their way to Europe, Africa and Asia. Groundnuts and cassava established themselves as important crops in parts of Africa and Asia. Sweet potatoes were carried by Spanish and Portuguese sailors to the Philippines and Indonesia and subsequently became the major staple in the New Guinea highlands (Biggs and Clay, 1981). Europeans also introduced crops to the New World. Sugarcane, which had been domesticated in South-East Asia and brought by Arab traders to Egypt and Syria, was one of the crops Columbus took on his second voyage to Hispaniola, in 1494 (Brockway, 1988). When European settlers went to the New World, they took with them many of their traditional crops, such as wheat and barley.

This exchange of crops initiated in the sixteenth century contributed to profound changes in agriculture all over the world. On the one hand, many farmers were provided with new species that they could begin to adapt to local conditions and environments, the result being a significant increase in opportunities and productivity. On the other hand, the availability of new species was an important element in the expansion of colonial empires. The organisation of plantation and slave economies to produce foodstuffs, dyes, condiments and other products, based on newly discovered or transplanted species, became a major element in the strategies of colonial states and trading companies (Brockway, 1988).

Many lessons may be drawn from the history of crop diffusion. The fact that this rapid and widespread movement of crops was accompanied by, and contributed to, oppression and colonisation is undeniable. Commentators often use the fact that the major crops of the North have their origins in the South to protest against the uncompensated access to crop germplasm by commercial interests (Mooney, 1979). (The issues of plant variety protection and intellectual property rights will be addressed in Chapter 5.) It is worth noting that the South has also benefited greatly from crop diffusion; indeed, the greater part of crop movement has been not from South to North but rather across zones of equivalent latitude (Harlan, 1988). If North and South are used with political rather than geographical connotations, we must also bear in mind that conquest and expansion were features of crop movement in pre-Columbian times as well. But no matter what political conclusions are drawn from contemplating the diffusion of crops around the world, the overwhelming interdependence of world agriculture is inescapable (Kloppenburg and Kleinman, 1988).

The remarkable distribution of the world's crops also gives us pause when using the term 'traditional' crop or variety. A significant proportion of the crops that farmers currently grow have been introduced from elsewhere. Equal admiration should therefore be reserved for the accomplishments of farmers in centres of crop origin and for the ingenuity of those in other environments who have carefully selected and adapted the species introduced. The work of adaptation has been so successful that for most major food crops the average yields in their new homes are higher than those in their centres of origin (Jennings and Cock, 1977).

Varieties and plant breeding

Early cultivators beginning to select plants for particular characteristics soon found that it was impossible to identify plant types that met all their criteria. One plant type might have yielded well but its seed was difficult to grind, while another produced grain that was exceptionally palatable but did not yield if the rains came late. Different types performed better in different environments. Compromises had to be made, and the result was an increasing number of different plant types. These we shall refer to as varieties, a term simply meaning a population of plants that can be distinguished from others. (Other terms commonly used include 'cultivar', which is a shortened version of 'cultivated variety,' and 'landrace', which often signifies a local variety with considerable genetic heterogeneity.)

The number of crop varieties utilised and maintained by a group of farmers will vary widely, depending on a range of circumstances. Farmers select varieties for their maturity, plant type, grain qualities, and many other factors. In some cases the number of local varieties may be exceptionally large; when Conklin (1957) studied the Hanunoo shifting cultivators of Mindoro in the Philippines fifty years ago, he found they could describe 92 different rice varieties. In most cases, however, farmers manage a more limited portfolio of varieties. (The methods and rationale of farm-level variety management are discussed in Chapter 4.)

Although farmers have been selecting and developing varieties since the beginnings of agriculture, the techniques that characterise formal plant breeding emerged only at the end of the eighteenth century. The scientific basis of plant genetics was not established until the rediscovery, in the early twentieth century, of the work that Mendel had carried out in the 1860s. By the early nineteenth century many farmers in Europe and North America were using the crops in their own fields to select and develop named varieties (Simmonds, 1979). Farmers in Japan developed fertiliser-responsive rice varieties that they exchanged through farmer associations (Francks, 1984). By the late nineteenth century in the United States private seed companies were competing with the Department of Agriculture in distributing new varieties, and in 1903 the American Breeders Association was formed, with academic and commercial membership (Kloppenburg, 1988).

One of the most significant advances was the discovery of hybridisation in the early twentieth century. A plant of a cross-pollinated crop such as maize normally depends on fertilisation from another plant. If it mates with itself the result is called an inbred, and it usually performs much less well than its parent. But if two inbreds (of different parentage) are crossed with each other, the progeny may be much more productive than

31

either of the original parents. This phenomenon is called hybrid vigour, and is the basis for hybrid seed production. The technique was first developed for maize, and by the 1930s hybrid maize was beginning to replace the open-pollinated varieties of the US Corn Belt. The principal drawback of hybrids is that the second generation of seed is less productive than the original hybrid. Thus farmers who grow hybrid seed usually find it unprofitable to save their seed.

The discovery of hybridisation had a profound impact on the seed industry. Because farmers would need to buy fresh seed each year, there was a significant incentive for seed companies to favour hybrids. Hybrid seed production also required increased technical and administrative skills to manage the inbreds and the hybrid seed. With regard to the major food crops, hybridisation is most prevalent in maize, but is also important for pearl millet, sorghum, and a number of vegetables. Varieties of these cross-pollinated crops that are not hybrids are called open-pollinated varieties, or OPVs. It is also possible, but more difficult, to produce hybrids of some self-pollinated species. A considerable investment has been made in wheat hybrids, but with no commercial success to date. Rice hybrids have been developed and are widely grown in China, but have not yet been successful elsewhere (Pingali, 1994).

The advent of formal plant breeding has led to the development and diffusion of many new varieties. For the sake of simplicity, we shall refer to any variety or hybrid that is the product of formal plant breeding as a modern variety (MV). The term is far from perfect; it may give an unwarranted sense of superiority, and many of the 'modern' varieties in farmers' fields were developed several decades ago. Varieties that are the product of farmer selections and exchanges will be called local varieties. The distinction may be blurred at times, however, because farmers sometimes adapt and select MVs to meet their own priorities, and it may be unclear at what point, genetically or historically, an MV becomes a local variety.[5] (The development of private and public plant breeding is discussed in Chapters 5 and 6, respectively.)

In recent decades, scientific plant breeding has moved forward with increasing speed (Tudge, 1988). The science of cytogenetics has allowed breeders to cross plants of distantly related species, so that a wild grass may provide disease-resistant genes to a new wheat variety, for instance. Various laboratory techniques have provided opportunities for inducing mutations, from which new varieties can be sought. Advances in tissue culture allow scientists to reproduce varieties of many crops from a single cell.

The techniques of biotechnology, based on an understanding of molecular genetics, are the area of plant science that currently captures most attention. These techniques allow plant breeders much more accuracy and efficiency in assessing the results of conventional breeding and, most notably, permit the transfer of genes between species, resulting in genetically modified (GM) or transgenic crops, the use of which has risen sharply in North America and a few other countries in recent years (James, 1999), with consequent impact on the seed industry. They are currently the subject of considerable controversy in Europe and elsewhere. They are not yet widely grown in the South (apart

---

[5]For further discussion of this issue see Tripp (1996).

from China) where their potential promotion is the subject of debate about commercial control and environmental impact (Cohen, 1999).

GM crops include a wide range of characteristics. Currently the most widely grown are those that feature resistance to some of the herbicides commonly used in industrialised agriculture. Others have been developed with resistance to particular insects, viruses or bacteria, while others feature enhanced consumer characteristics such as longer shelf-life or higher nutrient content. There is also hope that biotechnology can be used to develop plant varieties tolerant to abiotic stresses such as drought or salinity. Much of the controversy surrounding GM crops is based on the fact that these techniques allow for genetic transfer between unrelated species and the uncertainty about the possible environmental effects of such novel varieties.[6]

Seed as input

The previous discussion has focused on the domestication and diffusion of food plants and the ways in which farmers and plant breeders attempt to manipulate the genetic characteristics of the seed they use. Besides being a repository of genetic information, seed is also a physical input. This section examines the ways in which that input is managed.

Farmers can save seed for the following season. In some cases no distinction is made between stored grain and seed, but farmers often select their seed carefully and store it separately. Because seed is a living organism, care must be taken to guard against extremes of humidity or temperature, as well as to protect it from insects and pests.

There are a number of reasons why farmers may not be able to provide their own seed. In these cases they must look outside the farm for an alternative source of seed. The characteristics of seed provision within farming communities are discussed in Chapter 4, while the nature of private and public sector seed provision is presented in Chapters 5 and 6 respectively. Our purpose here is to gain some appreciation of the reasons why farmers may seek seed off-farm and to introduce the way seed is managed as a commodity.

Seed demand

Among the most important factors governing the incentives for seed acquisition are seed requirements and multiplication ratios. These are a function of the biology of the crop and they determine the amount of seed a farmer needs and the expectations for its yield. Table 3.1 presents some typical data for a number of important crops. These figures should be seen as only rough estimates, because planting practices and expected yields vary greatly depending on the environment and crop management practices. Nevertheless, certain patterns emerge from the table. The cereals exhibit a wide range of

---

[6]Among the most spectacular examples are the transfer of a gene for herbicide resistance from a bacterium to various field crops. But many examples of genetic engineering involve genetic transfer between more closely related species, and the techniques are also useful for transferring genes within a species (Ronald, 1997).

seed requirements; the amount of wheat seed that a farmer must save or acquire to plant one hectare is nearly 20 times the amount of pearl millet seed needed for the same area. The multiplication ratios for the cereals also vary, but are quite high and may be well over 100: 1. The ratios shown in the table can easily be exceeded when growing conditions are good, but they can also be lower in marginal environments. For the legumes, higher seeding rates are generally required, and the multiplication rates are significantly less favourable. Because legume prices are generally higher than those for cereals, the investment required for legume seed for a given area is usually higher than that for a cereal. Similarly, a very large quantity of seed potato is required, which makes the investment in seed a significant part of the costs of potato production. For crops that have high seeding rates, the storage of seed for a large farm may require special facilities.

Although the image of self-provisioning farm households, each saving its own seed, is a popular one, there are many instances (some of which have been relevant since the very beginning of plant domestication) where farmers need to seek seed outside the farm. These conditions are the basis for the movement of seed within and between farming communities and the development of informal and formal seed trade. Table 3.2 presents a summary of the major factors that determine the demand for seed from off-farm. It is roughly divided into three types of demand, based on seed availability, seed management, and genetic factors.

One of the most common reasons for seeking seed is the inadequacy of the previous harvest or the necessity for farmers to sell or consume what they would otherwise save as seed. In addition to seed shortage due to chronic poverty, natural disasters (such as droughts or floods) and civil disorder also contribute to seed insecurity.

Other types of seed demand related to supply are more often associated with commercial agriculture. In some cases farmers grow a crop that they do not consume on-farm. Many farmers in Thailand grow maize as a cash crop but prefer to eat rice. They sell their entire harvest and buy fresh maize seed each year (Morris, 1998). In some cases it is impossible to save seed from a crop because it is harvested before the seed is mature. This is the case for many fodder crops and for vegetables.

Table 3.1 Seed requirements, yields and multiplication rates for field crops

Crop	Kg of seed required to plant one ha	Typical yield (kg per ha)	Typical multiplication ratio (grain: seed)
Rice (transplanted)	40	2,000–3,000	50–75
Wheat	90	1,500–3,000	17–33
Maize	20	1,500–3,000	75–150
Sorghum	10	800–1,500	80–150
Pearl millet	5	800–1,200	160–240
Soybean	50	800–1,200	16–24
Chickpea	40	1,000–1,200	25–30
Groundnut	80	800–1,600	10–20
Potato (tonnes)	1.5–2.0	15–30	10–20

Source: Modified from Louwaars with Marrewijk (n.d.)

Table 3.2 Types of seed demand

Source of demand	Examples
Supply	
1. Unplanned seed shortage.	Previous harvest inadequate; farmer sold or consumed all seed.
2. Crop usually not stored for seed.	Cash crop; entire harvest is marketed.
3. Crop not harvested for seed.	Crop harvested as a green fodder crop: vegetables sold before seed can be extracted.
4. Hybrid seed.	Yield decline in second generation.
Seed management and quality	
5. Seed management problems.	Seed-borne diseases in farm-saved seed.
6. Seed conditioning problems.	Difficulty in removing weed seeds.
7. Seed storage.	Seed is too bulky to store: humidity problems in storage.
Genetic factors	
8. Varietal purity.	Purity difficult to maintain in cross-pollinated crops.
9. Access to a new variety.	Farmer obtains seed of a new variety.
10. Seed exchange.	Customs that move seed between neighbours' fields.

Farmers who use hybrid seed usually do not save the second-generation seed. In theory, hybrid use requires repeated seed purchase, although there are significant exceptions. A study of seed use in Malawi showed that up to 9% of 'hybrid' seed was recycled seed (Smale et al., 1991). This is not uncommon among smallholder farmers who may find that although the yield in the second generation is lower, it is still an acceptable alternative to investing in fresh hybrid seed or planting a local variety. These trade-offs are familiar to commercial farmers as well; in some years up to 20% of Argentine maize farmers may recycle hybrid seed in response to high seed prices and low grain prices (Jaffé and van Wijk, 1995).[7]

There are also cases where farmers prefer to get their seed from areas that are more suited for seed multiplication. Farmers producing commercial potato varieties in Peru, for instance, must replenish their planting material every three or four years to reduce aphid-transmitted viral infection. They purchase seed or barter for seed tubers with farmers from higher elevations (Zimmerer, 1996). Seed-borne diseases may be transmitted and multiplied on-farm, causing farmers to seek chemically treated commercial seed or seed from an area with less disease pressure. Farmers may not have adequate seed cleaning methods, leading to significant contamination by weed seed or other impurities, and causing them to look for commercial seed. Seed may be too bulky to store, or it may require special care. Soybean seed is fairly sensitive to temperature in storage; in Indonesia, many farmers prefer to buy soybean seed from traders who are

---

[7]The degree to which hybrids can be usefully saved by farmers depends very much on the type of crop, the type of hybrid, and the farming system. The situation for maize is reviewed in Morris et al.(1999).

able to move fresh seed from one production zone to another (van Santen and Heriyanto, 1996).

On-farm seed maintenance may also be difficult because of problems in maintaining varietal purity, particularly for open-pollinated crops. In southern Mexico, farmers plant several different local maize varieties and MVs. One of the most common is a short-statured, open-pollinated MV for which farmers purchase fresh seed every 3 or 4 years, when they find it is losing its desired characteristics (Bellon and Brush, 1994). In some areas, farmers believe that seed needs to be moved or exchanged frequently to maintain the potential of the variety.

Finally, a major reason for farmers to acquire seed off-farm is to acquire a new variety. In some cases the farmer may see the variety in a neighbour's field and ask to buy or borrow some seed for the next season. In other cases, the farmer will buy commercial seed to gain access to the new variety. In our discussion of the genetic and commodity aspects of seed we have now come full circle, as the farmer goes off-farm to acquire seed with new genetic characteristics.

Seed trade

We have seen that the origins of plant domestication are associated with the movement of seed from one environment to another. Trade in seed is literally as old as agriculture. There are numerous ways in which seed moves within farming communities, including through gifts, loans and cash purchases.

Formal commercial seed trade is hundreds of years old. One of the first recorded instances of seed trade in England was the case of two merchants at Huntingdon who began supplying leek seed to Scotland by packhorse in 1296. By the middle of the sixteenth century markets and shops in London were supplied with a range of vegetable and pulse seeds by growers who specialised in seed production. Seed was also imported from abroad. A pamphlet from a seedsman in 1732 describes seed imported from Italy, Turkey, Egypt, France, Portugal, Holland and Brazil (Thick, 1990a).

In the US, the use of farm-saved seed declined throughout the nineteenth century, due largely to the increasing commercialisation and specialisation of US agriculture. Farmers no longer had the time or interest to process and store seed that was readily available in the market. By 1918 it was estimated that the majority of seed sown for crops such as alfalfa, millets, forage sorghums, and many vegetables came from commercial sources (Fowler, 1994). The American Seed Trade Association was formed by 34 companies in 1883 (Kloppenburg, 1988); it currently has over 500 members.

A significant stimulus to seed trade beginning in the late nineteenth century was the development of modern plant breeding. In the case of European wheat breeding, private breeders took the lead in France and established commercial seed operations, while in the Netherlands government institutions developed the early wheat varieties (Lupton, 1988). In the US, the majority of plant breeding was done by the Department of Agriculture and by the land grant agricultural universities that were established in the late nineteenth century. State experimental stations helped establish crop improvement associations that multiplied and disseminated new varieties. The significant role of government seed provision in the early twentieth century drew increasing complaints from the private seed trade, but commercial plant breeding did not come to the fore until the 1930s, with the advent of hybrid maize (Kloppenburg, 1988).

In most of Europe and North America commercial seed enterprises replaced government seed operations. Until recently, the seed industry has been characterised by small, independent and often family-owned firms, but this pattern changed drastically in the 1970s with mergers and take-overs often involving companies with other interests, such as chemicals or food processing. This trend is particularly marked with regard to biotechnology, where five multinational corporations control most of the market. Ten seed companies control about one-third of the commercial seed trade (RAFI, 1999). However, there are still many small family seed businesses in operation; for instance, there are more than 300 companies producing maize seed in the US (Duvick, 1998).

The transition to private seed production has been less evident in the South, where public plant breeding has usually been accompanied by the establishment of state seed enterprises. In India, the National Seeds Corporation was established in 1963, and this was followed by the establishment of state-level seed enterprises. The public sector dominated the seed trade until significant changes in policy in the 1980s allowed more scope for private companies. Currently, public and private sector seed enterprises compete in India, with the private ones dominating the market for hybrids (Table 3.3).

In Africa, parastatal seed companies were established in many countries, but many of these have been dismantled or sold off as part of structural adjustment or in response to inadequate performance. In most countries where parastatal activity continues, private seed companies are beginning to make inroads. In Latin America, most formal seed trade is dominated by commercial firms.

It is estimated that total world-wide annual seed use represents a value of over US$50 billion. Approximately US$30 billion of this is part of commercial transactions (Le Buanec, 1996). Table 3.4 shows the size of the internal commercial seed market for the eight most important countries.

Table 3.3 Public and private seed trade in India[a]

Crop	Total area (m ha)	% of market volume in hybrids	% private varieties	% private seed
Wheat	24.1	0	0	10
Rice	42.4	0	0	20
Maize	5.9	90	33	80
Sorghum	14.4	90	20	80
Pearl millet	10.5	90	15	80
Rape/Mustard	5.8	0	5	30
Sunflower	1.4	35	35	90
Soybean	2.5	0	0	10
Castor	0.7	75	0	70
Cotton	7.5	35	10	60

[a] Based on figures for 1990/91
Source: Turner, 1994

37

Table 3.4 Estimated value of internal commercial seed markets for the top eight counties

Country	Internal commercial market US$m
USA	4,500
Russia	3,000
Japan	2,500
China	2,000
France	1,800
Germany	1,500
Brazil	1,200
India	800

Source: Le Buanec (1996)

Seed provision

The term seed provision has been chosen carefully to describe the subject of this book. The term encompasses the collection of activities required to develop crop varieties, produce and process their seed, and ensure that the seed reaches farmers' hands. These activities demand a wide range of skills and experience. At the farm level, all of these responsibilities may be managed by the members of individual households. But even in the most isolated and subsistence-oriented farming system interactions among households and between communities are usually important for seed provision. As seed provision systems develop, a growing number of actors provide their services. Both private and public sector entities begin to engage in seed provision. This book is concerned with how the management of information affects the course of agricultural development. In order to understand the performance of seed systems, we need to see how the various components of seed provision are co-ordinated, to understand the incentives that motivate the participants in each of them, and to analyse the ways in which farmers, commercial firms, and public organisations make their contributions.

Figure 3.1 gives an outline of the principal components of seed provision. These are the activities that will occupy our attention in the remainder of the book. The figure describes the components in language most appropriate to formal seed provision, but we can also discuss farm-level provision in the same terms. The figure illustrates the principle types of information flow that determine the efficiency of the seed provision process. The remainder of this section introduces each of these components.

1. *Plant breeding.* Seed provision begins with the identification of appropriate varieties. Until recently, all crop varieties were the product of farmer selection. Farmers gradually improve and refine the varieties that they grow, as well as keeping an eye out for new material that appears in their fields or on neighbouring farms. Their seed selection techniques contribute to the maintenance and improvement of local varieties.

The growth of public and private plant breeding activities in the past century has contributed a large number of new varieties from which farmers may choose. The public sector has played a strong role in plant breeding in most countries. Even though seed multiplication and marketing in industrialised countries are managed almost exclusively by the private sector, public plant breeding is still very important. Even in the case of

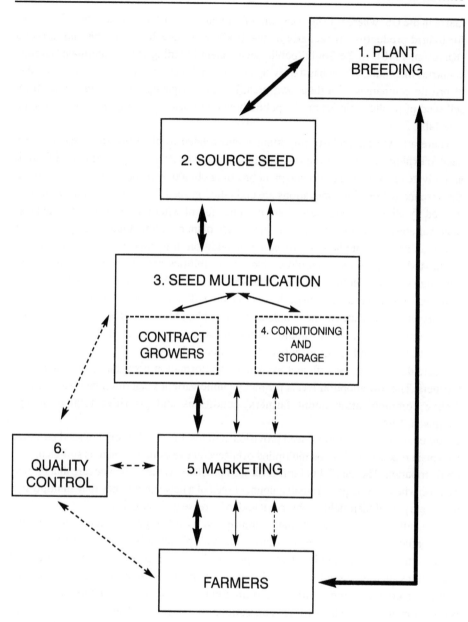

Types of information flow

Characteristics of variety ━━━━━

Price of seed ─────

Quality of seed ─ ─ ─ ─ ─ ─

Figure 3.1 The components of seed provision

maize in the US, where private companies dominate, 50% of the maize inbred lines used for hybrid production as recently as the 1980s were developed by the public sector (Knudson, 1990). In the South, public sector plant breeding is still dominant. Even in countries like India, which has a thriving commercial seed sector and a growing number of private companies with their own plant breeding capacity, many commercial firms sell seed of public varieties or use public breeding lines to develop their own varieties (see Table 3.3).

There are two particularly important issues related to plant breeding that we shall need to explore. The first is the way in which incentives affect the performance of public and private plant breeding. Private plant breeding obviously responds to a profit motive. Because many breeding innovations are embodied in seed that can be saved by farmers, or used by other plant breeders, there is a question of what level of property rights for plant varieties is appropriate to stimulate private plant breeding. Plant variety protection is also an issue for public plant breeding. In addition, it is important to define how the public and private sectors should divide responsibilities and define their relationship. Although there is a feeling that the public sector should take particular responsibility for basic research, the exact nature of the partnership will depend on a number of factors.

A second issue relates to the mandate of public plant breeding. It is widely agreed that public agricultural research should address those issues, and serve those farmers, for which there are insufficient incentives for commercial research. The completion of this mandate depends on the efficient exchange of information between farmers and plant breeders. The low adoption levels for many public varieties can often be traced to ineffective communication about farmers' conditions and priorities (Haugerud and Collinson, 1990).

2. Source seed. In most formal seed provision systems, the small amount of seed produced by a plant breeder needs to be multiplied over several cycles before there is sufficient seed for distribution. The parallel in farm-level seed provision is the particular care that farmers exercise when they acquire a small amount of seed of a new variety; they may multiply it in a separate part of their field to observe it and to increase their supplies.

We shall refer to the seed that is multiplied as a bridge between breeders' and commercial seed as source seed. Source seed multiplication is usually subject to fairly strict controls, with particular attention paid to the earlier generations. The number of generations of source seed required depends in part on the multiplication ratio for the particular crop and the technical requirements (e.g. disease control) of the seed production process. The various generations of source seed are described in two different terminologies. In OECD terminology seed generations proceed from breeders' seed to pre-basic, basic, and certified seed.[8]

Source seed production requires particular skills and experience and it may be undertaken by specialists. The organisation responsible for commercial seed multiplication may or may not produce its own source seed. In general, large seed companies usually

---

[8]The other major terminology is that of AOSCA (Association of Official Seed Certifying Agencies), and features breeders', foundation, registered, and certified seed. We do not need to be concerned here with the precise definition of these stages nor with the equivalence of the two terminologies.

manage and maintain their own source seed, while small companies may rely on other suppliers. In India, private seed companies may produce their own source seed of public varieties, or purchase source seed from other companies or state seed enterprises.

A viable source seed production mechanism is essential for seed enterprise development. Information is a key factor. Because it usually takes several seasons to produce sufficient source seed of a particular variety that can be used for commercial multiplication, very clear signals of demand regarding quantities and varieties are required. In addition, small enterprises need to know where they can acquire source seed for multiplication.

3. Seed multiplication. The production of a seed crop for the next season is the core of seed provision. But it is important to realise that it is not the only operation and hence should not receive exclusive attention in analysis, or in the design of seed provision. In a typical commercial seed operation, the costs associated with the multiplication of seed account for one-third or less of the final retail price of the seed.

Although seed multiplication is at the core of any seed enterprise, it is a function that is almost always contracted out. This is because it is uneconomical for an enterprise to own the major resource, land, required for seed multiplication. Thus most public and private seed enterprises contract growers to multiply seed in their own fields.[9] There is usually a contract between the company and the grower specifying the type and quality of seed to be produced. Seed growers usually engage in extra practices they would not normally follow in the production of a grain crop, and are compensated by being paid a premium above the grain price.[10]

The management of seed multiplication contracts shares many of the problems typical of contract farming (Little and Watts, 1994; Porter and Phillips-Howard, 1997). Contract growers may be disappointed by the prices paid by the seed company, the timing of the payment, or the application of poorly understood quality provisions. Companies, on the other hand, face the risks that growers will not comply with their contracts, will be tempted to sell their seed to other buyers, or will attempt to adulterate or otherwise misrepresent their harvest. Contracts can address some, but not all, contingencies, and the successful evolution of contract seed growing requires the development of trust between the company and the growers.

4. Conditioning and storage. The processing of harvested seed is usually called 'conditioning'. This includes drying, cleaning, grading, treating and bagging the seed. At the farm level, household members are usually responsible for selecting the seed for the next season, cleaning it, and storing it safely, often in special bins, pots, or other receptacles. On a commercial scale, these operations often require considerable organisation in order to accommodate large quantities of seed. In some cases all of the conditioning

[9]Some parastatal seed companies use their own land or government farms for seed multiplication. The available evidence indicates that this is less efficient than contracting private growers (Abeygunawardena et al., (1990).

[10]The economics of land use dictates that seed companies must establish contracts with individual growers. In other industries, changes in technology have affected the economics of contract production. The development of central sources of power helped convert 'putting out' in the weaving industry to a centralised factory system (Alchian and Demsetz, 1972).

operations may be carried out manually, but usually special equipment and facilities are required. Seed storage may require large buildings, and storage facilities have to be designed to regulate temperature and humidity and to discourage insects and rodents. Logistical challenges include siting the conditioning facilities as close as possible to the seed production area, and learning how to manage facilities and labour that are often subject to seasonal peaks and troughs in demand.

Large seed companies usually own their own conditioning and storage facilities, but it is also possible for a company to rent these facilities from another company, an entrepreneur, or the government. Such contracting adds to the transaction costs of the enterprise, but saves investing in equipment and storage space that might not be fully utilised.

5. *Marketing.* Seed must reach farmers in time for the next season. At the household or village level this is usually no problem, but distribution and marketing are among the principal challenges for a large seed enterprise. There is widespread agreement that the state has shown a poor record in seed marketing and that this is an operation that should be left in private hands (Jaffee and Srivastava, 1994). Even in countries where parastatal seed companies still operate, they are being weaned away from inefficient government input distribution networks.

Seed merchants have to manage two sets of relationships: with the seed company and with the farmers who are their customers. Merchants often have to order seed from the company well in advance (often before the company does its seed multiplication). Merchants are often unable to return unsold seed, which may have either to be sold as grain or be destroyed, so careful planning is required.[11] Retailers must be provided with good information about the varieties and seed that the company has on offer. A well-developed seed enterprise usually devotes considerable resources to maintaining a network of retailers.

A relationship of trust between the seed merchant and the farmer is also essential. It is instructive that in many parts of the United States large seed companies still market their products through a network of local 'farmer-dealers' who sell inputs to their neighbours (Zulauf and King, 1985). It can be assumed that this system is effective because farmers are more likely to rely on the experience and reputation of one of their neighbours than on a large retail outlet.

6. *Quality control.* Seed embodies genetic qualities (as a variety) and physical properties (as an input) that farmers may not be able to assess until after the crop is planted or even until it is harvested. Seed quality control addresses these two concerns. Genetic quality is controlled by monitoring the source seed used for multiplication and by visiting seed multiplication plots to ensure proper isolation distances and to remove off-type or diseased plants. If these operations are carried out by a designated third party they constitute the core of seed certification. In addition, seed testing is undertaken after harvest to monitor characteristics such as moisture content, germination capacity and cleanliness.

There are two types of approach to seed quality control. The first places primary responsibility on seed sellers' and consumer vigilance. Well-established enterprises with

---

[11]These problems are not restricted to the South. For instance, uncertain seed demand has a serious effect on the size and range of retailers' stocks in the US (Houston et al., 1988).

reputations to protect may sell seed that has no official certification. Such seed is often described as 'truthfully labelled', as it bears a label describing its minimum standards, any divergence from which can be challenged by the consumer in court, and the company punished by the customers switching to competitors. When seed is sold in this way, the company itself may manage all of its own quality control operations, or it may contract an independent laboratory to do so.

A second approach is independent certification, which may be undertaken by a public or private agency, and be voluntary or mandatory. In the European Union, seed certification for field crops is mandatory. The certification may be done by government organisations, although the seed companies themselves may be licensed to carry it out. In the US, certification is voluntary and managed by private agencies. In the South, many countries have mandatory government seed certification regulations.

Seed provision is a complex process comprising a number of components, each of which requires particular skills and resources. As seed provision systems develop and expand, choices need to be made about the management and integration of these elements. Large seed firms usually manage the majority of these components, often including plant breeding. At the opposite end of the scale, the traditional farmer also represents an integrated seed provision operation, managing everything from variety selection to seed utilisation. In between these two extremes, and presenting the major challenge for seed enterprise development, are the myriad possibilities for combining, collaborating and contracting among different organisations to achieve improved seed provision. Contributions may be made by the public sector and by a range of commercial operations, co-operatives, and individuals. The success of these endeavours depends crucially on the information and incentives that are available to each of the actors.

Summary

Seed carries two types of information. First, it bears the genetic information of a particular crop variety. This information determines the agronomic performance of the variety and the characteristics of the harvested grain, fodder, or other products. Secondly, seed is a commodity whose physical qualities are often not immediately obvious at the time of a transaction. A purchaser seeks information not only about the variety, but also about the purity and viability of the seed. The development of the seed trade requires mechanisms for transmitting information about seed quality.

The genetic information embodied in crop varieties has been modified and manipulated by humans for more than 10,000 years. Farmers identify plants that look promising, save the seed, and manage subsequent cycles of selection and adaptation. This process responds to farmers' requirements for production in particular environments, meeting subsistence needs, and participating in markets. The ability to utilise plant genetic information has been enhanced by the exchange of seed between farmers within communities, and by the movement of plant varieties as part of trade, migration and conquest. The science of plant breeding has developed within the past century, and specialists have emerged who breed varieties for public research institutes or universities, or for private seed companies. The productivity of the plant breeding enterprise requires an efficient exchange of information between breeders, farmers, and consumers.

Seed is a commodity that can be produced and saved by farmers, or can be acquired off-farm. Although farmers have traditionally saved the bulk of their seed from season to season, seed has also been a traded commodity since the emergence of plant domestication. In commercial agricultural systems there is a growing tendency for farmers to purchase seed, and even in so-called subsistence agriculture a considerable volume of seed is regularly obtained off-farm. The motivations for seeking seed range from inadequacies in crop production to problems in maintaining physical seed quality, to the search for different varieties. All of these seed transactions, whether between neighbours or in commercial markets, require institutions that channel information about variety characteristics and seed quality.

As plant breeding and the seed trade have developed, they have stimulated the emergence of commercial systems that include everything from family-run businesses to multinational corporations. Formal seed provision involves a number of distinct functions. Although there is a tendency to think of seed provision as essentially the undertaking of seed multiplication, this is only one part of the process. Formal seed provision usually involves access to plant breeding capacity, and requires a system to produce source seed for commercial multiplication. Seed provision also encompasses the processing and storage of the seed, the management of quality control, and the organisation of distribution and marketing. In some cases of seed provision, a single firm performs all of these functions, while in other cases they may be divided among several distinct organisations. In addition, some of the functions may be performed by public sector entities, while others are in private hands. An understanding of the organisation and performance of formal seed provision thus requires analysis of the institutions mediating the transfer of information among the various actors in the system.

The next chapter examines how information about seed and varieties is managed at the farm level. This will form the basis for an analysis of the evolution of formal commercial and public seed provision systems, and will also provide an understanding of how farmers interact with these formal systems.

4 Farmers' Seed Management

Introduction

This chapter examines the practices of farm-level seed provision. It reviews farmers' motives and methods of variety selection, briefly discusses the process of farm-level seed production, and presents evidence on the ways in which seed moves from farmer to farmer.

The purpose of the chapter is to establish a baseline regarding the performance of the seed provision that takes place without the intervention of any formal (public sector or commercial) seed system. The examples used are mostly contemporary ones, drawn from a range of developing countries. A few historical examples from industrialised countries are also discussed. It is often difficult to make an absolute distinction between local and formal seed systems, but many of the examples are drawn from situations where formal seed provision plays a minor role. It should be emphasised, however, that the purpose is not to reconstruct some original pristine state of farmer seed management. Most of the examples are drawn from situations that have experienced considerable agricultural change. In particular, many of these examples of local seed provision are found in the context of extensive agricultural markets, and as seed becomes a traded commodity it is difficult to separate the 'local' from the 'formal'. Nevertheless, the discussion attempts to draw a line and reserves the examination of the emergence of commercial seed provision for the following chapter.

The emphasis in the discussion is on the way information is managed by farmers for identifying crop varieties and distributing seed, and on the incentives for the development of local seed provision. It examines the type of information needed for variety selection, the ways in which that information is embedded in the social life of rural communities, and the imperfections and compromises that characterise its management. It also examines the ways in which seed moves between farmers, and discusses the types of information that accompany these local transactions.

Technology development: New varieties

The motives for diversity
Despite the advances of modern plant breeding, most of the crop varieties planted in developing countries are the products of farmer selection and innovation. They exhibit a

45

remarkable range and diversity. What have been farmers' incentives for developing so many different varieties? Part of the answer is found in the diversity of environments in which farmers operate, which occasions a search for varieties adapted to specific growing conditions. Another part of the answer can be found in the various uses that farmers have for their crops, leading to selection for specific qualities for food preparation or other end uses. As trade develops, farmers also plant varieties that are in demand in the market. In addition, the selection and use of different types of variety often reflect social factors or aesthetic preferences.

The spectrum of crop varieties developed by farmers allows them to exploit a remarkable range of environments. There are many examples of varieties adapted to particular climatic and soil conditions. Some of the maize varieties grown by Native Americans occupying arid parts of the US south-west are able to produce a harvest with a minimum of rainfall. One of their characteristics is their ability to be planted at extreme soil depths (above 30 cm), where they are more likely to encounter moisture. Most maize varieties cannot emerge after germination at this depth, but the adapted varieties are able to extend the stem shoot to reach the soil surface. In addition, although most varieties produce a large number of branching roots, these drought-tolerant varieties produce a single seminal root that is able to force itself deep into the soil in search of moisture. These varietal characteristics, combined with careful crop management, have allowed farmers to produce acceptable harvests in even very dry years (Collins, 1914).

Selection based on climatic conditions may lead to a range of varieties. Sorghum is an important crop throughout the drier areas of West Africa. In the driest (northern) parts of this region, the local sorghum is not photoperiodic; it matures in a fixed number of days after planting. Farmers can thus vary their planting times depending on the arrival of the rains and, in the driest areas or years, can choose the earliest maturing varieties. Further south, where rainfall is more abundant, many of the sorghum varieties are photoperiod-sensitive. Regardless of the time they are planted, they will not flower until the day length begins to shorten. This allows them to mature at the normal end of the rainy season (and helps the developing ears escape the fungi and insects that are prevalent at the height of the rains). If the rains begin early, these varieties can be planted and will accumulate additional biomass and nutrients before they begin their reproductive phase (Bunting and Pickersgill, 1996).

Farmers also select varieties to adapt to micro-environmental differences. It is not uncommon for them to have access to several different field types that require different varieties. A study in a rice-growing village in the coastal plain of Orissa, India shows how variety choice is influenced by land type (Kshirsagar and Pandey, 1996). Farmers planted a total of 33 local rice varieties (as well as 11 MVs). They distinguish three major field types. Upper terraces are well drained and prone to drought, requiring early maturing varieties. Middle terraces are suitable for varieties of medium maturity. The lower terraces require flood-tolerant varieties. The study shows how farmers' access to field types determines the number of different varieties grown (Table 4.1).

There are many other environmental factors in addition to climate and soils that motivate farmers to develop different crop varieties. Diseases and pests evolve along with

Table 4.1 Rice variety and field types (Orissa, India)

Number of field types	Proportion of farmers	Average number of varieties grown
1	24%	3.4
2	52%	4.4
3	24%	6.3

Source: Kshirsagar and Pandey (1996)

crops, and farmers need to select varieties that can accommodate changing disease and pest pressure. In some cases a particular variety may be resistant, while in other cases farmers may plant a mixture of varieties to make it more difficult for pests and pathogens to adapt (e.g., Martin and Adams, 1987). They must also select varieties that are compatible with the rest of their farming practices. Varieties may be selected that compete well with local weed populations, that are easy to harvest, or that are adapted to intercropping.[1]

Farmers also select varieties in accordance with their end uses. The range of food-preparation techniques in the world rivals the diversity of crop-growing environments. Culinary techniques and preferences co-evolve with crop varieties. Farmers select varieties that are suited to the local diet, but food-preparation techniques must also accommodate to environmental parameters. The mature kernels of most maize varieties are quite hard and usually have to be ground into flour to prepare a range of flat breads, porridges, and other maize foods. However, certain varieties have large, soft kernels that allow them to be quickly toasted on a griddle, as well as being ground for flour. But these types will grow only at very high altitudes, because they are highly susceptible to insects and diseases. So it is mostly Andean farmers who have the luxury of toasted maize in their diet. Potatoes are also well adapted to the cooler temperatures of the highlands, but at very high altitudes most varieties are susceptible to frost. Andean farmers plant certain potato varieties that tolerate frost; their disadvantage is that they have an unpleasant, bitter taste when boiled. So farmers have developed techniques for freeze drying these varieties that make them more palatable when cooked (Zimmerer, 1996).

Farmers select varieties not only for their acceptability as food but also for their contribution to other farming requirements. Those who keep livestock often devote significant attention to the fodder qualities of their varieties.[2] Crop residues are often used for construction or fuel. In parts of northern Ghana, where fuel wood is exceptionally scarce, one of the major selection criteria for sorghum varieties is the suitability of the stalks for firewood.

Crop varieties are also chosen using non-utilitarian criteria. Particular varieties may have ceremonial uses, or some may be selected partly on aesthetic criteria. In the late

[1]In the drier areas of Central America, farmers intercrop sorghum and maize, planting both crops at the same time. The maize varieties are earlier maturing than the sorghum, which is photoperiod-sensitive. In a year of good rainfall the maize will mature before the sorghum begins to flower, and the maize plants can be cut or doubled to allow more light to reach the sorghum. If the rains have been poor, the drought-tolerant sorghum may provide the major part of the harvest (Hawkins, 1984).
[2]See Byerlee et al. (1989) and Kelley et al. (1991) for evidence of the exceptional importance of fodder quality to some Asian farmers.

nineteenth century, many US farmers devoted considerable time to selecting and perfecting their maize varieties. One of the most successful was James Reid, who

> liked ten-inch ears that were almost cylindrical, with eighteen to twenty-four straight rows of kernels. He himself wanted ears that were somewhat smooth, for he thought they were easier on his hands when it came to husking...He treasured the cylindrical, ten-inch ear which was well covered over the butt and tip (Wallace and Brown, 1988: 72)

In the early 1900s, the popularity of 'corn shows' spread throughout the Midwest (ibid.). Entries were judged on the size and uniformity of the maize ears presented. Champion farmers could sell their prize-winning cobs for considerable sums, and they were accorded great prestige in their communities. The popularity of these contests waned only after it was demonstrated that the winning selections were not necessarily the highest-yielding varieties.

A study in Sierra Leone (Richards, 1986) describes the care and energy that farmers invest in selecting and developing rice varieties. Granted that they have a number of different field types, it is still noteworthy that in a small village farmers recognised a total of 70 rice varieties, 49 of which were grown at the time of the study. The maintenance of this diversity of varieties has obvious practical importance, but it also 'is invested with rich cultural significance. If rice is a "currency" in which many social relations – relations of patronage and clientship – are computed, then rice varieties have assumed something of the significance of gambling chips in a game of social mobility' (ibid: 145).

Despite profound economic and political changes in the highlands of Peru, the cultivation and use of diverse native crop varieties have been preserved. Zimmerer's (1996) meticulous study of farming in southern Peru reveals that it is the wealthy (who have the extra resources required to manage both traditional and modern varieties) and the poor (who have few alternatives) who are most likely to grow the widest range of these varieties. 'On the one hand, for the well-to-do, the diverse crops harnessed prestige and reinforced status, frequently helping the leaders host a community or religious feast... For the poorest farmers who could not afford anything else, on the other hand, the diverse crop plants were more an unchosen item in their hardscrabble diets' (ibid: 93).

In this Peruvian example, as in many other cases, farmers have the additional option of growing MVs, mostly the products of public sector research. We shall postpone examination of these varieties, their promotion and utilisation, until Chapter 6. But the criteria outlined above (including environmental adaptation, farming system compatibility, consumption preferences, and social strategies) that define the incentives for local crop variety development are the same as those used in the decisions to grow MVs.

These criteria help explain the remarkable diversity of varieties found today, but it would be incorrect to accept an over-idealised notion of farmers carefully and consciously moulding plant genetic resources to their specific requirements. The process is certainly more complicated, involving a co-evolution of crop types, management practices, and consumption preferences. 'A more realistic view is that farmers have created and managed environments where crop varieties could evolve under a range of changing and contrasting selective pressures' (Wood and Lenné, 1997: 117). A study in three areas of southern Peru (within approximately 30 km of each other) showed that only a very small amount of the total genetic variability found in the potato varieties examined was due to differences among the areas. This is perhaps explained by the considerable gene flow occasioned by trade and exchange (Zimmerer and Douches, 1991). In Malawi, on the other hand, an examination of differences among bean populations throughout the country shows greater variability between than within regions, probably reflecting differences in environments and in consumer preferences between different parts of the country (Martin and Adams, 1987).

Incentives for innovation

We have highlighted some of the major factors responsible for the development of a vast array of crop varieties. The entire history of agriculture is one of adaptation, experimentation and innovation. To a considerable degree, each farm is an enterprise that faces individual circumstances; farmers must be ready to assess and to respond to particular conditions. But it is worth examining further the nature of innovation in agriculture. Is it pursued collectively or individually, and what are the incentives for innovation?

A useful review of farmer experimentation by Sumberg and Okali (1997) distinguishes between 'proactive' experiments that require conscious planning to create conditions for observation and assessment, and 'reactive' experiments that are the result of chance circumstances. Richards' (1986) description of the development of rice varieties by farmers in Sierra Leone includes both types. Farmers may notice an unusual type of rice in their field. If it is undesirable the farmer will make sure that it is not part of the harvest that will be used for seed, but if it has interesting traits it may be set aside. In the early stages of experimentation, a new variety may be planted in a carefully managed plot near the house, where it can be protected and observed. Subsequently it will be tested in field types that are judged to be most appropriate. In many cases these new varieties are found growing spontaneously in the field (the result of a mutation or seed dropped by an animal or another farmer). In other cases, farmers actively seek new varieties in neighbouring villages or further afield when they travel.

It is also important to remember that farmer observation and selection are not always aimed primarily at crop improvement. Farmers in Mexico carefully select their maize seed, but they rarely articulate a strategy for modifying or improving varietal characteristics. The selection process is seen primarily as a way of maintaining the integrity of particular varieties (Louette and Smale, 1998).

The Sumberg and Okali study examined instances of farmer experimentation in several locations in Africa. The authors found that the propensity to experiment was not distributed evenly among locations or between farmers in a community, and they identified a number of factors relevant to understanding the incentives for local variety development. Farmer experimentation was found to be more widespread in areas facing particular challenges, such as declining soil fertility or frequent droughts. A clearly defined problem was a stimulus for innovation. They also found that experimentation was more likely among individuals with a full-time commitment to farming. A diversity of livelihood sources reduces the likelihood that an individual will have the time or the interest to devote to agricultural innovation. Although all types of farmers may experiment, an additional stimulus for innovation is the existence of a robust commercial market for the output.

Although the majority of farmers experiment, at least in the 'reactive' sense, there are relatively few with the skills and incentives to devote significant resources to this activity. In many cases these farmers are well known by others as good sources of seed. Wallace and Brown (1988) describe the Illinois farmer George Krug who in the early 1900s was responsible for developing the highest yielding non-hybrid yellow maize variety ever found in the Corn Belt. Krug is described as a polite, relatively uneducated, unassuming man who devoted great attention to the selection of his seed. He chose ears from strong stalks and carefully checked the kernels for their appearance. These ears were kept in baskets that were then individually examined during the winter months to make the final selection for the next season's seed. Krug was a charter member of the local farm bureau but he did not attempt to make any commercial gain from his innovation. Indeed, he worried that his growing reputation would cause him to lose some of his friends through jealousy.

Although formal education is not required for successful variety selection, persistence and devotion to the task are essential. An agricultural diary from early nineteenth-century Japan shows how the careful testing, rejecting and adapting of rice varieties over a period of 58 years were accompanied by an increase in the varieties' maturity (and hence an increase in yield potential) by 17 days (Smith, 1959).

If it is a mixture of curiosity, prestige, and economic self-interest that motivates particular farmers to experiment and to select promising varieties, how are their results shared with other farmers? There is hardly any evidence of organised systems of experimentation or diffusion among groups of farmers. Varieties, and knowledge about them, vary across communities, but concepts of community development or ownership of plant varieties are not empirically valid.

Information about innovations travels among farmers. In some cases, physical features may help determine the speed of flow. If farming is done in open plains where fields are contiguous, the appearance of a new variety or technique is relatively easy to spot. If farmers cultivate isolated forest plots, there is less opportunity for widespread observation. Sumberg and Okali (1997) refer to this factor as the 'transparency of the landscape'. The nature of social networks also plays an important role in determining the flow of information about innovations. The Sierra Leone rice farmers described by Richards (1986) may have isolated fields, but the subject of rice varieties is a 'social currency' and an item of frequent conversation. In the more open derived savannah of Ghana, on the other hand, Sumberg and Okali (1997) found that fields were often accessible, but fears of accusations of witchcraft prevented farmers from showing excessive interest in their neighbours' activities.[3]

We have seen that the wide range of local crop varieties is mostly the product of

---

[3]A similar contrast can be made between the maize farmers of Jalisco, Mexico, who actively seek varieties from other communities to test (Louette and Smale, 1996), and the farmers of Alta Verapaz, Guatemala where the closed, corporate nature of communities means that most seed is obtained from relatives (Johannessen, 1982).

selection by individual farmers, in the context of natural circumstances that are often beyond farmer control. The variety selection is often 'reactive', as farmers notice a novel characteristic in the field or in the grain store, but it is sometimes the product of consciously planned selection and experimentation. Individual farmers are motivated to look for new varieties because of the yield advantages that may result, the prestige that may be accorded the discovery of a useful variety, or the exigencies of pressing production problems. A few individuals may devote considerable time to variety selection, but for most farmers innovation is the product of chance observations. The result of the judgements and selections of individual farmers is often a very wide range of varieties grown in a community or area, but there is little evidence to show that farmers are motivated by the abstract concept of diversity.[4]

Although there are incentives for individual experimentation and selection, the emergence of more organised variety development is limited by high transaction costs and low incentives. It would take considerable time and planning to organise collaborative experimentation among a group of farmers. In addition, the rewards for their extra efforts would be widely shared. Information about a new variety is difficult to 'protect' or control at the community level, and variety innovations usually spread fairly rapidly. The following section examines the ways in which information about crop varieties is distributed in farming communities.

Managing information

Although the primary evidence we have for the range of varieties grown by farmers is variety names, these are an imperfect guide to the actual numbers and distribution of varieties. Brush et al. (1981) found the average farmer in highland Peru could name about 35 types of potato. In a single locality, 50 to 70 names might be found, although 10 to 20% of these are likely to be synonyms. Farmers vary in their knowledge; some are meticulous when considering the identity of a variety while others are more perfunctory.[5] In the tropical forest of Peru, Boster (1986) found that kinship was an important factor for Aguaruna cultivators in preserving and spreading information about cassava varieties. Most knowledge of cassava varieties is spread among women, and different kin groups may apply alternative names to the same variety. For an open-pollinated crop like maize, the correspondence between local variety names and genetically distinct entities is particularly problematic (Louette and Smale, 1998).

The management and development of local varieties are thus constrained to some degree by imperfections in variety nomenclature and the limitations in the spread of information. Further challenges to the management of information include the rapid turnover of varieties, the multiple characteristics that are used in selection, and farmers' limited capacities for managing a diverse portfolio of varieties.

[4]More research is required in order to understand if there are instances where farmers try to maintain certain varieties primarily for conservation, rather than for short-term utilitarian considerations (Smale et al., 1999).
[5]Clawson (1985) describes an interesting shorthand for distinguishing among varieties. Certain characteristics (such as cooking quality) may be correlated with the colour of a variety, but for several crops there is also an apparent (and not well understood) correlation between colour and maturity. In some areas of Mexico, four maize grain colours are found (yellow, white, blue-purple and red), and variety maturity is closely correlated with this ordering, with the yellow varieties having the longest maturation period.

There is a common misconception that 'traditional' varieties are unchanging components of the agricultural landscape. On the contrary, many examinations of local variety development emphasise the exceptionally fluid nature of farmers' variety portfolios. Part of this is due to the dynamic nature of agriculture and the constant need to search for better-adapted varieties, but part of it is a product of the insecurity of farming. In the Sierra Leone village studied by Richards (1986), most farm households reported considerable change in varieties. Poorly performing varieties were discarded, but in many instances seed of acceptable varieties was also lost, due to farming misfortune or to unplanned consumption by household members or relatives. The continual movement of seed in and out of a traditional maize-growing community in Mexico means that it is 'unlikely that any farmer in Cuzalapa sows seed derived from a stock bequeathed directly from his parents' (Louette and Smale, 1996: 13).[6]

It is also important to recognise that there is no such thing as a perfect variety. So many potential agronomic and consumption criteria can be used to assess varieties that it is virtually impossible for a single variety to be judged best across the board. This explains why many farmers plant several varieties, but it also explains why variety choice is often an imperfect process. Different members of the household will often have very different priorities in choosing varieties (Ashby et al., 1987). Women may be more concerned about consumption or food-preparation characteristics, while men may focus on agronomic or market characteristics.[7] Farmers are continually making compromises in selecting the varieties they wish to plant. This is an example of the 'bounded rationality' that affects farmer decision-making; it is only possible to consider a relatively limited number of characteristics, and to formulate a limited number of trade-offs, in making decisions about what variety to plant.[8]

The multiple criteria that may influence variety preference, the limited time and resources available for making decisions, and the uncertainties of farming all work against the possibility of a precise decision-making process. Zimmerer's (1996) study of Andean agriculture describes in great detail the resources and criteria that farmers use to maintain an admirably diverse agriculture. But at the same time, he warns persuasively against 'the uncritical and often unstated assumption of environmentally fine-tuned adaptation in the diverse crops' (ibid.: 17).

---

[6]Sperling and Loevinsohn (1992) discuss the factors related to the survival of bean varieties in Rwanda. Varieties that are grown by only a few farmers may easily disappear because of various risks of crop loss, and because farmers tend not to provide seed of new varieties to others until they have multiplied a sufficient quantity for themselves.

[7]Barnett (1969) describes some of the compromises affecting rice variety choice in the Philippines. Varieties are selected on the basis of cooking quality, yield, ease of harvesting and maturity, and trade-offs must be made. For instance, glutinous varieties are favoured for consumption, but their use is limited by the fact that they are particularly susceptible to pest attack. Choice of maturity is partially determined by neighbours' practices; because animals graze the fields after harvest, a farmer tries to plant varieties of similar maturity to those planted in neighbouring fields.

[8]The situation is not confined to traditional agriculture. A study of wheat varieties planted by Kansas farmers showed a number of factors that influence variety choice, including milling qualities, agronomic characteristics, yield, and yield stability. But even econometric analysis was able to throw only limited light on the way decisions were actually made (Barkley and Porter, 1996).

The great diversity of local varieties is often a temptation for inferring a selection process that is more consciously motivated than is actually the case. Several accounts in the literature describe sorghum varieties in Ethiopia that have particularly high protein quality (Mooney, 1992; Berg et al., 1991). The commentators point to the fact that such varieties are given local names such as 'milk in my mouth', which would seem to indicate that farmers recognise their nutritional qualities. But in fact their value for farmers is their early maturity and higher sugar content (Gebrekidan and Kebede, 1979). The varieties are sown in small quantities and used for roasting, when the grain is still immature, and could not contribute significantly to protein consumption. The local names reflect the sugar rather than the protein content. This is an example of the dangers of idealising local variety development.

One of the best ways of illustrating the compromise between farmers' sophisticated knowledge of their environment, on the one hand, and their limited information and resources, on the other, is an examination of the number of varieties sown. Discussions of traditional agriculture are often based on the assumption that farmers plant many different varieties, each adapted to a specific niche or selected for a special purpose.[9] There are certainly instances where farmers plant a significant number of varieties of their most important crop(s).[10] But we should not get the impression that this is the typical situation. Discussions of crop diversity draw heavily on the literature of anthropology, ethnobotany and human geography. Many of these studies are carried out in locations that are chosen specifically because of their (often atypical) diversity. A few examples are cited and repeated, and it soon becomes accepted fact that all traditional farmers are managing a multitude of crop varieties. The situation is in fact much more complex; the number of varieties grown by farmers is related to the diversity of environments available to them and to the diversity of end uses for the particular crop.

A second source of misunderstanding is the confusion between the number of varieties known in an area and the number of varieties grown by an individual farmer. We have already discussed the selection skills of rice farmers in a Sierra Leone village. Although a total of 49 different varieties was grown by these farmers in one year, the average number per household was about three. Similarly, a nationwide survey showed an average of 2.2 rice varieties per household (Richards, pers. comm.). This should not be surprising, since most farmers have limited land and resources and are simply not able to manage a large number of varieties. However, the small figure for individual households should not diminish the significance of the much larger range of varieties at least potentially available to farmers in the village.[11]

---

[9]For instance, a guide for seed system analysis states that 'small farmers usually maintain a very broad portfolio of varieties, to cope with production variability and to fill end use and agro-ecological niches, and will often assimilate an improved variety into this on a limited scale to avoid sacrificing overall variability' (Cromwell et al., 1992).

[10]See Dove (1985) and Freeman (1955) for descriptions of complex traditional rice systems that incorporate a large number of varieties.

[11]In a traditional maize-growing community in central Mexico, farmers plant a total of 26 different varieties, but the average number per household in one season is no more than 2.6. The most popular variety accounts for 51% of the area sown (Louette and Smale, 1998).

One of the methods farmers have for managing a large number of varieties is the use of crop categories and mixtures. The many potato varieties planted by the farmers in southern Peru are managed as three major categories (classified by end use). Within each category, a number of varieties are included. Zimmerer (1996) describes a farmer selecting seed potatoes:

> Working quickly, she did not exert a precise control over the specific landraces that were skimmed toward the mound of new seed tubers...She was...choosing her landraces in mixtures rather than selecting them specifically as single variants. She selected only a few landraces individually, or in some cases, none at all (ibid: 198—9).

The fields of the most important category of potatoes contain an average of about 21 different landraces, and Zimmerer points out that this average is remarkably consistent among farmers. Thus they are able to assemble a mixture of varieties that provides them with what they feel is an adequate range of diversity without investing excessive time in individual selection. Maize varieties are also planted as mixtures, but the average field contains just 2.9 varieties, and farmers devote more time to the selection of the particular varieties to be planted.[12]

The exceptional range of local crop varieties developed by farmers must be seen against the backdrop of a markedly imperfect information system. Farmers' choice of varieties is determined by a large number of potential criteria, but the limited time and scope for making their choice results in inevitable compromises. Variety choice is certainly an example of the operation of bounded rationality. The potential number of varieties is at times very great, but the knowledge of this range, the availability of seed, and the access to production resources are all usually quite limited. Thus even in situations where there are many choices available, it is unusual to find an individual household planting more than a few varieties of one crop. In cases where many varieties are planted, the exigencies of information management often result in their being planted as mixtures. The uncertainties of farming also contribute to the difficulties farmers have in maintaining a stable and well-defined portfolio of varieties, and even highly favoured varieties may be lost. Access to new planting material, or even to information about the alternatives available, is mediated by social networks. The transaction costs involved in searching for information or seed outside of these limited networks may be considerable. The varietal diversity found in farming communities is the product of individual decisions and compromises regarding household preferences and goals, made under severe time and resource constraints; an imperfectly shared body of information about the options available; and the randomising effects of an unpredictable farming environment.

---

[12]Another frequently cited example of variety diversity is beans in Central Africa. Rwandan farmers often plant many different varieties, but these are managed as mixtures. Each mixture is destined for a particular field type. On examination, a mixture may be found to contain a dozen or more different varieties, although the farmer may be able to name only a few of them (Sperling, pers. comm.).

Seed production

Chapter 3 outlined the principal elements of seed provision. Although that framework is most useful for the analysis of formal seed systems, it can also be applied to farm-level seed provision. The previous section has discussed the organisation of farm-level variety selection. This section will examine source-seed management, seed multiplication, conditioning, storage, and quality control as applied to farm-level seed provision. The following section will then examine the distribution mechanisms in farmer seed systems.

First, however, it should be emphasised that, although this discussion focuses on farmers in developing countries, the practice of saving seed is common among farmers in industrialised countries as well. The figures in Table 4.2 try to estimate seed saving in the European Union and the United States. These figures are only approximations, and are based on comparisons of statistics on commercial seed sale with estimates of total seed use. In some cases they will include both farm-saved seed as well as seed provided by another farmer. Nevertheless, the figures give an indication of the importance of informal seed systems in industrialised countries.

Seed production at the farm level begins with the selection of 'source' seed for the following season. Although farmers sometimes dedicate a separate field, or part of a field, for seed multiplication, it is much more common to select seed from the general harvest.[13] The seed may be selected in the field, particularly if farmers value characteristics such as early maturity. Richards (1986) describes how farmers harvest rice by individual panicle and set aside any material of unusual maturity for further observation. Seed may also be selected based on plant characteristics (e.g., by avoiding the use of seed from diseased or insect-damaged plants), but this is relatively unusual.[14]

Although farmers sometimes select seed in the field, in most cases it is selected after the harvest is completed. Farmers in indigenous communities in Veracruz, Mexico select maize seed at several stages. Some may be identified in the field. When the harvested maize is brought to the house, there are further opportunities for selection. Some ears may be identified before storage, while others are identified as the woman removes them from storage for food preparation; these are hung separately in the house. The final selection is made just before planting, when damaged ears from those initially identified for seed are discarded (Rice et al., 1998).

Farmers usually select seed of grains, legumes and tubers on the basis of healthy, above-average appearance, thus contributing to the continuation of these characteristics. This is not necessarily the case with vegetables, however, especially if they are destined for the market. In some cases, farmers select seed from those fruits that are rotten or unacceptable (Louwaars, 1994). This utilises fruits that would otherwise not be sold, but may at times contribute to perpetuating undesirable genetic characteristics.

---

[13]Fields may be planted specifically for seed when the crop is normally harvested before the seed is mature (e.g., a forage crop) or when off-season seed cultivation offers advantages (Almekinders et al., 1994).

[14]An Ohio maize farmer, writing in 1843, describes seed selection: 'During the gathering of the crop, I have attached to the tail end of my wagon a large basket into which is deposited the choice of all ears. My method is to save for seed all the ears where there is more than one to a stock, as it does add to the yield.' (cited in Wallace and Brown, 1988: 55).

Table 4.2 Estimates of proportion of non-commercial seed use in industrial countries (%)

EU (all crops)[a]	
Denmark	5
The Netherlands	25
United Kingdom	30
France	50
Italy	70
Spain	90
US[b]	
Wheat	70
Barley	50
Rice	30
Groundnuts	30

Sources: a) Ghijsen (1996); b) Figures for the US are based on estimates of commercial seed use in the mid-1970s. Adapted from Butler and Marion (1985), cited in Pray and Ramaswami (1991).

When seed is stored separately it is often afforded special care. There is a wide range of traditional seed storage technology (Wright et al., 1994). Limited information is available on the effects of farmer seed management. Sattar and Hossain (1986) found that farm-stored rice seed in Bangladesh compared favourably with commercial seed. Studies in Ghana and Zambia showed that farm-stored seed had acceptable germination (Tripp et al., 1998 a and b).

A few studies have tried to assess the yield differences between farm-managed and commercial seed. Some have shown that farm-stored bean seed (Janssen et al., 1992) or potatoes (Crissman and Uquillas, 1989) is of equal quality to commercial seed. Other studies, however, have shown deficiencies in farm-level seed management (Trutmann and Kayitare, 1991; Scheidegger et al., 1989). Heisey and Brennan (1991) review studies on farmers' ability to maintain wheat varieties that show an annual yield loss ranging from nil to 1.6%.

Farmers also have methods for evaluating the quality of their seed. Asian rice farmers separate empty or rotten kernels of rice from their seed lots by flotation tests with water or brine (Bray, 1986). Farmers all over the world are accustomed to conducting germination tests if they have suspicions about seed quality; a sample of seed is mixed with moist soil and observed over several days.

In summary, farm-level seed production is often difficult to separate from other crop production activities. Seed is sometimes selected in the field but more frequently it is selected before storage (in which case it may be accorded special treatment) or at times just before planting. There may be a single decision taken on seed selection, but often it is an iterative process, influenced by household consumption needs and other exigencies. Farmers usually take sufficient care of their seed to ensure an acceptable harvest, but there are limits to their capacities to guard against all the factors that may affect seed quality.

Seed distribution

Despite the logic and the importance of seed saving, farmers have always had occasion to search for seed off-farm. As outlined in Chapter 3, farmers may look for seed for a number of reasons. They may wish to acquire a different variety, or they may feel that their own seed management does not provide satisfactory quality. In addition, farmers often run short of seed, through bad luck or bad planning, and must look for fresh supplies. This section examines the avenues through which farmers acquire seed. It looks only at seed obtained from other farmers or from local markets, and does not touch on the subjects of formal sector commercial or public seed, which are covered in subsequent chapters.

Certainly the most common source of seed is another farmer. In many cases the links of seed supply are embedded in the social fabric of farming communities. In the words of an English gardening manual from the sixteenth century,

> One seede for another, to make an exchange,
> With fellowie neighbourhood seemeth not strange

(McLean cited in Thick, 1990a: 59)

The search for seed among neighbouring farmers is not necessarily an easy one, however. Most households aim for self-sufficiency and do not always have surplus seed that can be spared. In addition, farmers take pride in seed self-sufficiency, even though it is often not achieved in practice. Asking another farmer for seed may be difficult or embarrassing. It is thus not surprising that a large proportion of seed distribution is mediated by links of kinship or friendship. Table 4.3 summarises the results of a number of studies on farmer seed sources in Africa. In the majority of instances kinship or friendship is overwhelmingly important in determining the provider. Kinship is particularly important in these cases, although the range of people that a farmer considers kin admittedly may be quite broad.[15]

The threads of local seed distribution are well illustrated in a description of a Zambian farming community.

> Cultivators who have run out of seeds beg, borrow, barter or buy what they need from friends and relatives. Kabanda Nyuni has planted groundnuts that he got from Tiku Banda, Kwezekani's widow, and in return he will weed Tiku's maize field; he has planted beans he received from his mother Sonile. Simon Sakala got eight cobs of maize as a free gift from Fatness Manda to use for seeds, (Skjønsberg, 1989: 54).

As this passage illustrates, seed may be provided on various terms. The term 'seed exchange' is often used to describe local-level seed distribution, but in its strict sense this type of transaction is relatively unusual. Farmers may exchange seed of different types,

---

[15]In Kalimantan, Indonesia rice seed is more likely to be given as a gift (or exchanged) within kinship-based longhouses than between longhouses (Dove, 1985).

Table 4.3 Seed acquisition from farmers

Location	Crop	Farmer who is seed source (%)		
		Kin	Acquaintance	No relation
Southern Province, Zambia	Sorghum	62	23	15
Southern Province, Zambia	Cowpea	70	10	20
Western Province, Zambia	Groundnut	56	18	26
Western Province, Zambia	Sorghum	72	12	16
Mzuzu, Malawi	Groundnut	79	*	*
Blantyre, Malawi	Groundnut	64	*	*
Eastern Province, Kenya	Pigeonpea (MV)	8	*	*
Eastern Province, Kenya	Pigeonpea (local)	32	*	*

* No data
Source: Tripp, (2000)

each gaining a new variety in a mutually advantageous interchange. In some instances, farmers may exchange seed of the same variety, often in the belief that seed performs better if it is moved from field to field.[16] Seed exchange should be distinguished from barter (in which one of the partners receives seed in exchange for a quantity of the crop destined for consumption). In Peru, farmers in many areas need periodically to seek fresh seed potato because of disease and pest problems. The best seed potatoes are grown in areas of higher altitude, and other farmers develop relationships with farmers from these areas. 'Often familiar as family relatives, friends, and social kin, many upland farmers tilled five or more parcels of floury potatoes each year' (Zimmerer, 1996: 113).

Although seed may be provided as a gift, or be part of a barter agreement, farmers often have to pay cash for the seed they acquire from their neighbours. Table 4.4 summarises data on seed transactions among farmers from four locations in Africa. The importance of seed purchase varies by locality and by crop, but in most cases it is significant. Several parameters help determine the likelihood of a cash transaction. The quantity of seed is obviously important, and a small amount of seed may be offered as a gift. The relationship between the farmers is also important. Table 4.5 shows the nature of farmers' transactions for pigeonpea seed in a location in eastern Kenya. It is clear that seed acquired from a relative is much less likely to be in exchange for cash. Farmers just beginning to plant pigeonpea are also more likely to obtain seed as a gift than are those who have been growing the crop but require fresh seed. In addition, the type of variety influences the nature of the transaction. Seed of the MV, which is an important cash crop, is more likely to be purchased from other farmers than is seed of the local variety.

---

[16]We found a number of instances of this practice among rice farmers on the north coast of Andhra Pradesh (Pal et al., forthcoming). Diaz et al. (1994) describe how rice farmers in the Philippines sometimes exchange seed with their neighbours for good luck.

Table 4.4 Seed acquisition from other farmers, Ghana and Zambia (%)

Type of transaction	Wenchi, Ghana		Akatsi, Ghana		Senanga, Zambia			Kalomo, Zambia		
	Cowpea	Maize	Cowpea	Maize	Cowpea	Sorghum	Groundnut	Cowpea	Sorghum	Groundnut
Purchase	83	30	33	50	30	19	81	78	73	76
Gift	17	51	22	47	67	77	19	17	19	22
Loan	–	15	–	–	–	–	–	–	2	–
Exchange	–	–	44	3	3	3	–	5	6	2
(N)	(18)	(33)	(9)	(32)	(33)	(43)	(32)	(59)	(52)	(51)

Source: Tripp et al. 1998a and b.

Table 4.5 Probability that a farmer will have to pay cash for pigeonpea seed obtained from another farmer (by type of variety, relation, and occasion), Eastern Kenya (%)

Relation to seed provider	*Local variety*		*MV*	
	First time	*Second time*	*First time*	*Second time*
Relative	5	11	24	33
Not a relative	25	49	77	79

Source: Audi et al., 1999.

In general, seed of higher value crops, and especially cash crops, is less likely to be given as a gift.[17]

Seed loans are also common. In most instances the repayment may be called 'seed' but will often be used for consumption. In some cases, seed loans are provided without interest (as reported by Henderson and Singh (1990) for Ethiopia). In many other cases, however, an additional quantity of seed is expected in repayment. In parts of Andhra Pradesh, rice seed is loaned in the expectation of a return of 50% interest (Pal et al., forthcoming). In an area in southern Mexico, maize farmers are expected to repay double the quantity of seed borrowed (Louette and Smale, 1996). In Sierra Leone, it is common for farmers to loan seed at planting time in expectation of receiving twice the quantity at harvest (Richards, 1986). As borrowers are in no position to demand or enforce seed quality, seed loaned to others may not necessarily be equivalent to that reserved for own-use. Farmers in Sierra Leone carefully rogue their rice that is destined for seed to eliminate weeds and off-types. They report that a particularly persistent weed is more likely to show up in the fields of strangers and those heavily in debt (i.e., those most likely to have borrowed seed) (Richards, 1986).

Seed may also be provided in exchange for work or service, or may form the basis of a sharecropping arrangement. In Lesotho, 'the provision of seed alone is sufficient to qualify a person as a share-crop partner' (Robertson, 1987: 157), and the custom of 'stranger farmers' producing groundnut in Senegal and The Gambia is governed by the host farmer being able to provide sufficient seed (ibid.). Seed plays a variable role in sharecropping arrangements; in southern Mexico the landowner provides the seed (Louette and Smale, 1996), while in Uttar Pradesh, the tenant is responsible for obtaining the seed (Bliss and Stern, 1982).

Although much of the flow of seed (through gifts, loans, or purchases) takes place within individual farming communities, it is misleading to speak of 'community seed systems' if this implies an organised set of obligations based on an ethic of community-level seed security. Farmers who are short of seed must rely on ties of kinship, friendship, or clientship with other individuals. The transactions characterising these ties may be motivated by welfare considerations, but they may also represent quite unequal distribution of power and control of resources within the community.

---

[17]In northern Nigeria, a son who is part of a joint farming household (*gandu*) can expect seed of grain crops, but not of groundnut (a cash crop), from his father (Hill, 1972).

An additional source of seed at the local level is the market. Grain or tubers normally sold in markets or shops for consumption may also be used as seed. If farmers have access to markets or shops, they can use these as additional sources of seed. Tables 4.6 and 4.7 summarise data from a number of studies of seed sources carried out in Africa and Asia, respectively. The use of the market as a source of seed varies widely. If markets are not conveniently located, their use as a seed source will be minimal. The Zambia data in Table 4.6 come from communities in low-population density areas where markets are not well developed. Grain markets are more likely to be important sources of seed when seed type and quality are easy to recognise. Different varieties of grain legumes are often fairly easy to distinguish visually, hence their seed may be particularly likely to be purchased in the market. Markets are also important as sources of seed when few individual farmers are likely to have a surplus of seed to exchange or sell. The importance of markets for wheat seed in Bangladesh and bean seed in Rwanda illustrates this relationship.

There are several possible disadvantages to grain markets as seed sources. Seed provision by traders may be part of inequitable debt relations maintained with farmers.[18] Some merchants are knowledgeable about seed (and may even maintain separate stocks of grain suitable for seed), but they often place little emphasis on the possible use of their grain as seed. Farmers in Sudan often obtain seed from grain merchants, but they express concern about the quality and price of seed obtained in this way (Coughenour and Nazhat, 1985). Similarly, farmers in Rwanda purchase much of their bean seed in local produce markets, but they often do not trust the market sellers (Sperling, Scheidegger and Buruchara, 1996). There are few incentives for traders to invest in maintaining separate seed stocks. The grain destined for seed often represents a small proportion of a trader's business and the trader buys the grain from a number of farmers, making any type of (seed) quality control extremely difficult.

Tables 4.6 and 4.7 also indicate the overall frequency of off-farm seed acquisition. These data, combined with other sources, lead to the conclusion that in developing countries it is very common for one-quarter to one-third of seed to be acquired off-farm, from non-formal (farmer or commodity market) sources.[19] This implies a significant quantity of seed being given, loaned, bartered or sold at the community level.

The appreciable quantity of seed that enters into community-level transactions should be an impetus for specialisation. In many communities certain farmers are known as particularly reliable sources of seed.[20] In some cases these farmers may provide the seed as part of social obligations or as a source of prestige or patronage.

[18]A report written in 1927 in Andhra Pradesh describes merchant lenders' control over poorer farmers. '[T]he loans take the form of advances of grain against the coming crop. Such advances are made for seed as well as subsistence…When it takes the form of advance of seed one and half times the quantity borrowed is repayable at the next harvest…and, if the borrower is…unable to repay the loan…a further interest of half the total quantity due…is repayable at the succeeding harvest.' (cited in Satyanarayana, 1990: 90).

[19]A study conducted in a traditional maize-growing community in Mexico over six seasons found that 47% of the seed lots planted were obtained from other farmers; about one-quarter of these were transactions with farmers from outside the region (Louette and Smale 1998).

[20]Thiele (1999) describes certain farmers in Peru who conserve up to 48 potato varieties and are key contacts for variety diffusion.

Table 4.6 Seed sources, Africa, beans, cowpeas, maize (OPV), sorghum (%)

Crop and location	Farm-saved	Other farmer	Grain market	Formal source	Other
Cowpea, Ghana[a]					
Wenchi	76	8	14	2	–
Akatsi	48	4	39	9	–
Cowpea, Zambia[b]	71	27	3	–	–
Beans, Zaire[c]	59*	1*	59*	–	–
Beans, Rwanda[c]	63*	10*	32*	1*	4*
Beans, Zambia[b]	57	34	9	–	–
Maize (OPV), Ghana[a]					
Wenchi	78	12	–	3	6
Akatsi	76	15	5	4	–
Sorghum, Zambia[b]	73	22	5		

Sources: a) Tripp et al. (1998b); b) Andren et al. (1991); c) Sperling et al. (1996)
*Sums to more than 100% because of multiple sources

Table 4.7 Seed sources, Asia. Wheat and rice (%)

Crop and location	Farm-saved	Other farmer	Grain market	Formal source	Other
Wheat. Pakistan[a]					
(Rice zone, Punjab)	55	21	3†	10	11
(Cotton zone, Punjab)	62	22	2†	8	6
Wheat, Bangladesh[b]					
Small farmers	40	3	30	24	4
Large farmers	65	0	10	24	2
Rice, Sri Lanka[c]	68	24	0	6	2
Rice, Philippines[d]	63	22	0	10	5
Rice, Srikakulum[e], India	40	36	0	19	5

Sources: a) Tetlay et al. (1990); b) O'Donoghue (1995); c) Pattie and Madawanaarchchi (1993); d) Diaz et al. (1994); e) Pal et al. (forthcoming)
† Shopkeepers

If the seed is sold, the price charged is often the same as for grain; a recent review of several studies in Africa showed this to be the case (Tripp, 2000).[21] But in more market-oriented agriculture, seed-producing farmers may be able to charge a premium; a study of rice farmers in Andhra Pradesh showed local seed-producing farmers charging their neighbours approximately 30% above the grain price (Pal et al., forthcoming). Similarly, potato farmers in Bolivia who specialise as seed producers can earn a 20–30% premium if the seed is sold locally, where their reputations are known (Thiele, 1999). In these examples, information about the seller's reputation is a vital part of the transaction. In some cases, other means may be used to convey information about the seed offered for

[21]However, because grain prices may be very volatile, the 'seed' price paid just before planting may be 2 or 3 times the grain price at harvest. See Richards (1986: 127) for an example regarding rice prices.

sale. In Rajasthan, one village is considered to be the best source for a local variety of pearl millet, renowned for producing very long heads. Its farmer seed sellers keep particularly spectacular examples to show potential clients who arrive from elsewhere to purchase seed (Tripp and Pal, 2000).

Although seed saving is part of the almost universal ideal of the self-provisioning farm household, there are many instances where the ideal is compromised. Farmers may look for seed in order to replace a variety or to improve the quality of their seed, but in many instances a poor harvest or other problems mean that seed stocks have been depleted. The most common source of seed is another farmer, often linked through kinship or friendship. The social embeddedness of the transaction is explained by the likely pathways of information flow and the need to identify a trustworthy source. Seed is also often part of wider relationships within farming communities, including those that generate prestige, govern patron-client links, or determine the practicalities of sharecropping and tenancy. In all cases, the farmer seeking seed requires information about the types of varieties available and the quality. In some situations, where farmers (or market traders) have the resources and knowledge and can develop a sufficient reputation, they can specialise in selling seed.

Summary

This chapter has tried to characterise farm-level seed provision. It has concentrated on the performance of variety choice and seed distribution separate from the operation of formal commercial or government seed systems. It has emphasised the importance of information management in the context of the mixture of incentives and limitations that defines small-scale agriculture.

Variable environments and a range of economic and social parameters present a large number of criteria on which farmers may select and develop crop varieties. The result is an impressive diversity of varieties, partly because no single variety is likely to be superior in all characteristics, partly because the changing circumstances of farming require flexibility and adaptation, and partly because of incomplete information. Farmers have imperfect access to information about varieties. Systems of nomenclature are not standardised, and when there are many varieties available few farmers are aware of the complete range. Information about varieties often moves through pathways of kinship and friendship. Imperfect information, lack of resources, and the risks of agricultural production contribute to the fact that an individual farmer is likely to grow at most only a few varieties of any crop.

Most farmers are interested in new varieties when they appear in their fields or in those of their neighbours. But relatively few have the time or resources for a concerted strategy of testing and observation to identify new varieties. Those who do consciously develop or improve varieties are motivated by an interest in improving their farm production, by curiosity, and by the prestige associated with such expertise. These farmers have no way of deriving unusual economic gains from their experimentation, nor is there any evidence of collaboration or formal organisation in the search for useful crop varieties.

The seed production process is usually managed as a part of crop production, but particular care is invested in the selection and storage of seed for the next season. A significant quantity of seed is acquired off-farm, even in situations where no formal seed system exists. Much of this seed is obtained from other farmers, and these transactions are often part of social networks that help disperse information about varieties, seed availability, and seed quality. Seed also flows through relations of patronage and tenancy. Much seed is acquired at the community level, under a range of local customs, but it is the relations and negotiations between individuals, rather than an ethic of community seed provision, that govern access to seed. We may recall that one measure of development is the capacity to choose. In community-level seed provision, that capacity is characterised by considerable contrast. On the one hand, seed choice may take place in a context of impressive variety diversity. But inadequate information, limited resources, and restricted networks for seed access often severely constrain the capacity to choose the most appropriate seed.

Finally, we have seen that there are opportunities for some farmers to establish themselves as seed specialists. As markets develop, this specialisation accompanies the emergence of commercial seed provision, which is the subject of the next chapter.

5 The Emergence of Commercial Seed Trade

Introduction

It is difficult to know where to begin to describe the development of commercial seed markets. As we saw in the previous chapter, seed has been an item of trade since the beginning of agriculture. Farmers often acquire seed in local grain markets, and they provide seed to their neighbours under a wide range of conditions, some of which certainly qualify as commercial transactions. Perhaps the most sensible approach is to recognise that the role of markets in any society can be located on a continuum. Lane (1991: 12) puts forward a number of criteria that signal the degree of 'marketisation', several of which are useful landmarks to help identify the origins of commercial seed markets in agricultural societies. The principal criteria include: the frequency of exchange of goods and services for money; the existence of a network of information on prices; and the achievement of social control and co-ordination within the economy through transactions.[1]

These criteria for a market economy suggest three issues that need to be addressed about the emergence of a formal, commercial seed sector. The first concerns the incentives for commercial seed production. Under what conditions do farmers find it worthwhile to turn to markets for their seed supply? What are the characteristics of agricultural production and the farming economy that stimulate the demand for commercial seed?

The second issue relates to the role of information in seed market development. A seed enterprise endeavours to market a commodity that farmers have been able to provide for themselves. The enterprise therefore needs to present sufficient information to its clients about the advantages of its product, and farmers need to be able to transmit their demands to the enterprise. What does this imply about the type and quality of information transfer required to maintain a seed market?

The final issue concerns the organisation of seed provision. We have seen that seed provision is a complex process, involving several distinct activities (Chapter 3). A commercial seed system may be based on a large number of individual operations co-

---

[1]Lane's other criteria include: maximisation of the principle of substitutability, where values (tastes, people, goods or services) are easily substituted for each other (e.g. capital for labour); co-ordination through the price mechanism; income and profits as criteria for success; the power of wealth to command resources; the importance of 'rational calculation'; the existence of competition (e.g. alternatives); the absence of a single centre of control; and the separation of political and economic authorities (Lane, 1991: 12).

ordinated by market mechanisms or, if the transaction costs are too high, may involve integrated seed firms. What is the role of information and networks in determining the scope and direction of commercial seed activity?

This chapter will attempt to address these issues with a range of data. The following section examines the issues from a historical perspective, concentrating on examples from the development of commercial seed markets in England, beginning in the seventeenth century, and the emergence of the commercial seed system in the US in the early twentieth century. The next section turns to examine contemporary evidence from the South, and features examples of commercial seed enterprise development in India and Peru. The following section focuses on commercial plant breeding – perhaps the most contentious issue in the current debate about the future of seed provision. The discussion pays particular attention to the arguments about intellectual property protection and their relation to the incentives for plant breeding.

Historical examples

Vegetable seed in England[2]

There are records of trade in vegetable seeds in England as early as the thirteenth century. However, this trade experienced a significant expansion beginning in the seventeenth century as market gardening assumed increasing importance in provisioning growing urban populations. Commercial garden acreage around London expanded elevenfold in the 60 years from 1660. At the same time, the English diet was becoming more diversified, following examples from the Continent, and there was an increased demand for a wider variety of fruits and vegetables (Thirsk, 1997). Because vegetable seed production usually involves a process of extraction or extra crop management that requires time, labour and experience, it is not surprising that the seed trade first centred on vegetables. Seed production specialists could provide a useful service to commercial growers and to home gardeners. In addition, many new species and varieties were being introduced to consumers and farmers at this time, and the formal seed trade was often the best way of gaining access to these innovations.

Much of the vegetable seed growing was concentrated in a few areas of eastern England, particularly in Kent and Essex, where the combination of soil and climatic conditions made them particularly appropriate for seed production. These areas receive higher amounts of sunlight and lower rainfall and experience less risk of frost than locations further inland. In addition, they are relatively close to London, which became a centre for seed marketing.

The growth of the seed industry in Kent and Essex also owes much to the farming traditions that had developed there. These areas had become centres for market gardening, and hence the local demand for seed was high. In addition, they had a reputation for developing new varieties of vegetables, and this seed found a ready market in London and elsewhere. Perhaps the most notable characteristic of many of these seed

[2]The material in this section is drawn largely from Thick, 1990a and b and Roper, 1989.

growers was their immigrant origins. Many Dutch, Flemish and French Protestant refugees came to England from the mid-seventeenth century to escape religious persecution. Some of them were farmers and vegetable gardeners, and they brought with them new crops and new techniques. Many settled on lands that were available in eastern England where they helped stimulate a diversifying agricultural economy.

It is no surprise that the majority of commercial seed enterprise was concentrated among these immigrants. 'The mystery of commercial seed growing could pass easily amongst the Dutch gardeners for they were in a close community, bound by nationality as well as by the hostility of many English neighbours' (Thick, 1990a: 63). The Dutch households that arrived to take up farming and gardening were often large enough to be able to manage all the tasks of seed production. The network of social ties with neighbouring households allowed them to organise seed multiplication (e.g. to ensure that nearby seed production plots could not cross-fertilise) and to share technical knowledge.

These market gardeners sold some of their own seed, but seed sale depended to a large extent on merchants in London and elsewhere. In the early years of the seed trade there were no specialists, and seed was merely one item offered for sale by grocers, druggists and others, or by itinerant pedlars. However, there was soon a noticeable growth in specialist seed merchants. One estimate, based on the number of surviving seed catalogues, indicates that there were only three large seed firms in London in 1688, but that the number had grown to 35 a hundred years later.

As the seed trade developed, some seed growers continued to market at least part of their own production, but growers increasingly provided all of their seed on contract to merchants. Seed houses provided a much more reliable vehicle than farmgate sales. Some of the growers developed into seed firms that contracted local growers, while other firms developed from the activities of urban merchants. Merchants and growers developed close relations, as the following passage describing seed production in Essex illustrates:

> [T]he merchant will choose someone in whom he has confidence or who has been recommended to him by a reliable agent (for example a smaller local firm or a grower who has been commissioned to place contracts). In the early days, word would be sent to the prospective grower that the merchant's senior representative, or even the merchant himself...wished to visit the farm. On the day, the grower and his wife, clad in their Sunday best, anxiously awaited the arrival of a personage in top hat, tail coat and gloves... These early contracts and those of many years later were seldom, if ever, signed. It was considered an agreement between gentlemen and, as such, each side had complete confidence that the other would honour the bargain to the best of his ability. (Roper, 1989: 152).

Just as relations of trust developed between seed growers and merchants, there was also an evolution in relations between seed buyers and sellers. In the early years of the seed trade, pedlars played a large role, and they were often found to be selling low quality seed. A report of 1596 vents a gentleman's anger at the many pedlars who were found to 'deliver the seeds which they sell mingled with such as are old and withered, or else without any mingling at all to sell such as are stark naught' (Plat, cited in Thick, 1990b: 106). With no fixed place of business, it was difficult to monitor or punish such fraudulent sale, while more honourable pedlars had a difficult time establishing reputations. We must assume that under these circumstances a farmer would prefer to buy seed from the grower himself. The emergence of large commercial seed houses, with established reputations to protect, contributed to an improvement in the quality of marketed seed. By the early eighteenth century the leading seed merchants were producing gardening manuals and seed catalogues that helped to establish their reputations and to advertise their products. However, the seed houses depended on the integrity and experience of their suppliers, and they could be guilty of unknowingly selling defective seed. This was particularly a problem with imported seed, as a report from the early eighteenth century indicates:

> The greatest Difficulty that attends this Affair in the getting Seeds from abroad, is, the great Cheat that those People, who gather it on the Sea-side, put upon the merchant, and consequently upon us here…so little Faith is to be found amongst those Collectors of Seeds, who no doubt think it no Sin to cheat Hereticks. (Switzer, cited in Thick, 1990b: 114).

As the international seed trade expanded, and as firms developed established trading partnerships, these problems became less prevalent. For instance, a number of seed firms in Essex established trading relations with firms in continental Europe. In one case, an Essex firm established export relations with a Dutch seed firm and members of the Dutch family spent extended periods of residence in Essex, learning the language and the customs of the local trade (Roper, 1989: 153). By the end of the nineteenth century the efforts of established seed firms in England to sell seed under their own brand names had extended to the major firms marketing cereal seed (Walton, 1999).

In summary, the vegetable seed trade in England developed in response to growing demand and the diversification of the economy. Much of the initial demand was met not spontaneously by the average farmer but rather by a group of immigrant entrepreneurs whose social networks and experience allowed them to organise their seed production operations. Their techniques and examples gradually spread to a wider population of seed growers. A weak link in the early years of the trade was the absence of trust in seed merchants. This was resolved by the emergence of specialist seed dealers who invested in maintaining and enhancing their reputations. The growth in the trade brought further diversification at the farm level, as some of the larger growers developed their marketing capacity, while smaller growers established contracts with the emerging seed enterprises.

Hybrid maize seed in the US

Chapter 3 discussed how the development of hybrids was a particular stimulus to the private seed industry because it provided a type of seed that farmers would buy every season. This is particularly clear in the development of the seed industry in the United States. Although private seed companies had been in existence since the mid-nineteenth century, significant growth began in the 1920s with the advent of hybrid maize.

Seed enterprise development in the US Corn Belt followed a number of distinct paths. We shall begin by describing briefly the three leading seed companies in Illinois in the mid-1930s: Funk Brothers, the DeKalb Agricultural Association, and Pfister Hybrid Corn Company.[3]

---

[3]The following discussion is based on Fitzgerald, 1990.

The Funk family was prominent in business, banking and politics in Illinois, and owned 22,000 acres of farmland. In 1890, Eugene Duncan Funk abandoned his university studies and travelled in Europe, where he was impressed by the private plant breeding he saw in France. In 1901 he and 14 other family members pooled their land and began growing and selling seed of maize and other crops. The firm established contacts with the Illinois state experimental station and learned techniques in crossing and selection. By 1914 the enterprise was well established and produced an annual catalogue of its seeds. In 1915 it took the unusual step of hiring a recently graduated plant breeder (who turned down an offer to work for the university). The first maize hybrid offered by Funk Brothers appeared in their 1928 catalogue.

The DeKalb Soil Improvement Association was formed in 1912 by 12 affluent farmers in DeKalb County. The association's initial interest was in soil improvement; it formed a buying co-operative for fertilisers and received advice from university agronomists. The members' broader interests led to the formation of the DeKalb Agricultural Association in 1917, which included seed purchase, and eventually the production and sale of seed, among its activities. By the early 1920s the association was consulting with university plant breeders and testing new maize hybrids. Because they farmed in the northern part of the Corn Belt the DeKalb farmers required earlier maturing varieties. The association's relationship with the university breeding programme was advantageous to both sides, and by the early 1930s DeKalb had developed early maturing maize hybrids that gained widespread popularity.

The third example of seed enterprise development in Illinois, the Pfister Hybrid Seed Company, illustrates a very different pathway. Lester Pfister was born in modest circumstances in rural Illinois in 1897, and left school at the age of 14 to begin farming. Although he had little education and no financial resources, he had the natural ability and determination required to select and breed maize varieties. He devoted long hours to learning maize breeding techniques and experimenting with different varieties, and his skills were soon recognised by the county farm adviser, who began to work with him on yield trials. By 1922 Pfister had begun to produce and sell seed of the highest yielding variety from the trials ('Krug corn', see p.50). He soon became interested in hybrid maize and developed some of his own inbred lines. By 1933 he was selling hybrid maize seed to local farmers and his business expanded rapidly.

Although these three cases illustrate quite different types of seed enterprise development, they share a number of characteristics. In each case, the enterprise began by producing and selling seed of open-pollinated maize varieties. Although the majority of Illinois farmers saved their seed at that time, there was considerable demand for seed of new varieties, and the enterprises established their reputations for their own varieties. Commercial farming was well established by the late nineteenth century and farmers were eager to find ways to expand their production. As the techniques of hybrid seed production were developed, the enterprises took advantage of this new technology. In many cases the hybrids significantly outyielded the best open-pollinated varieties, and they also had characteristics such as stalk strength or disease resistance that attracted farmers' attention and stimulated the growth of the hybrid seed market.

Another common characteristic of these histories is the complex relationship between the private seed growers and public sector research and extension. In each of these cases there was close collaboration between public plant breeding and the emerging private seed enterprises. The university supplied its varieties, and later its inbred lines, for the enterprises to test and, where successful, to market. This collaboration was furthered by the close personal relations that often developed between university personnel and the farmer entrepreneurs.[4]

The seed enterprises also had to establish their reputations among the farmers. The seed business was not new, of course, and companies had been publishing and distributing catalogues in the US since the middle of the nineteenth century. By the 1890s, some mail-order seed firms were receiving 6,000 letters a day (Fowler, 1994: 37). One of the early leaders in hybrid maize seed, Henry Field, had developed a business by selling his vegetable and flower seeds door-to-door. By 1899 he was publishing a four-page catalogue, which evolved into a monthly magazine, *Seed Sense*, that 'combined the elements of a family letter, a round robin, an almanac, and a catalogue (Norskog, 1995: 61). By the mid-1930s, Field's 'Mule Hybrid Seed Corn' was one of the most popular brands in the Midwest.

The establishment of brands was an important part of marketing strategy for the seed companies. The DeKalb County Agricultural Association illustrated its advertisements with a flying ear of maize that became one of the most widely recognised logos in the seed business. Another large company, Northrup King, established several different brands, each aimed at a particular segment of the farming population (Norskog, 1995: 130). The advice in a farming journal of 1938 supports these attempts to promote strong reputations.

> There are shysters in the hybrid seed corn business, just as there are in any other kind of business, and one has to be careful about where one buys seed. The thing to do in this respect, it would seem, is to buy seed from the big reliable companies whose investment in plants, advertising, and research work indicates that they expect to be permanent institutions. (Klinefelter, cited in Fitzgerald, 1990: 194).

The companies also invested heavily in various marketing strategies. Funk Brothers promoted its hybrids through techniques such as providing free hybrid seed to farmers who bought its open-pollinated varieties and giving its hybrid seed to farm boys who wanted to enter state yield contests, in exchange for the names and addresses of other farmers (Fitzgerald, 1990: 218). In the early years of the hybrid maize seed industry, there were many cases in which excessively aggressive marketing led to farmers planting poorly adapted hybrids. But the success of the industry ultimately depended on the performance of the hybrids, and this required the companies to pay attention to adequate targeting and adaptation of their hybrids. As one breeder observed, 'the reputation of a hybrid was influenced by the poorest producer of that hybrid' (ibid: 191).

[4]However, there were also conflicts of interest. For instance, relations between the DeKalb County Agricultural Association and the University of Illinois were often strained because of shared personnel and problems in separating the association's public extension functions from its commercial activities (Fitzgerald, 1990: 184).

The contemporary seed industry in the US is a remarkable mixture of small businesses and enormous corporate finance. The latter element captures most of the headlines, and there is no doubt that the seed market has undergone a significant transformation with the mergers and buyouts that have marked the combination of pharmaceutical, chemical and seed companies positioning themselves for global markets and preparing to take advantage of biotechnology.[5] But small enterprises also remain an important part of the seed sector. In the 1930s, nearly 200 maize seed companies were formed in the US. Many of these have since gone out of business, but others have emerged to take their place. In 1995, more than 300 companies were selling maize seed in the US; 25 new companies were established between 1990 and 1995. However, there is a marked concentration in the industry; in 1995, seven companies accounted for about 70% of the market, a level of concentration which had been constant for more than 20 years (Duvick, 1998).

The small companies occupy a significant niche due in large part to the importance of factors such as local knowledge, networks and trust that determine the course of seed system development. They often serve local markets and are able to target very specific growing environments. In addition, the seed from the smaller companies may have a lower price; they do not have the advertising or technical service budgets of their larger competitors, but can establish their reputations through local networks. Indeed, local reputation is so important that even the larger seed companies market the majority of their hybrid maize seed through local farmers who act as their agents. These tend to be larger farmers who are well known to their neighbours and who sell seed (and at times other inputs) at their farms (Zulauf and King, 1985).[6]

The contribution of small companies is also aided by the existence of a number of so-called foundation seed companies – companies that specialise in plant breeding and sell or license their inbreds to smaller companies which then market the hybrids under their own brand names. In addition, many farming areas have a large number of other small businesses such as seed processors and distributors that contribute to seed provision (Houston, et al., 1988). Although the largest seed companies tend to be integrated operations that perform all the functions from breeding to marketing, the quality of information flow and the concentration of seed enterprises in particular areas in the US lower transaction costs and allow for a wide variety of contracting opportunities.

Examples from the South

Commodity traders and seed

Chapter 3 pointed out that most formal seed provision in the South has, until recently, been in the hands of the public sector. One of the principal exceptions has been the seed

---

[5]The three seed companies described earlier in this chapter have followed different paths. DeKalb was recently purchased by Monsanto. In 1974 Funk Brothers was purchased by Ciba-Geigy, which subsequently merged with Sandoz to become Novartis. Pfister continues as an independent company, marketing maize hybrids, including some that are genetically modified.

[6]The importance of marketing cannot be overemphasised. One seed analyst observes that 'the seed business is more a marketing game today than in the past...Seed corn and cottonseed companies, in our opinion, have reached germplasm equality, which places greater emphasis on service and marketing functions to improve business' (Shimoda, 1996: 8).

provision functions performed by commodity traders. This is particularly true of crops that farmers are not able to maintain through local seed multiplication. For instance, seed potato production is affected by diseases and pests in many farming areas, and farmers must at least occasionally purchase fresh seed from higher altitude production zones. In Nepal and Peru, seed potato from the higher altitudes is often moved to producers at lower altitudes through a network of local markets (Chhetri, 1992; Scheidegger et al., 1989). In Bolivia, certain periodic markets are recognised as centres of informal trade in seed potato. The trade involves many small traders and merchants, and the provision of information is imperfect. Farmers try to purchase from merchants they know who come from areas with reputations for producing high quality seed (Bentley and Vasques, 1998).

One of the most remarkable examples of indigenous seed trade is that of soybean in Indonesia. Soybean production takes place in three different seasons, depending on the ecology of the zone, with stringent requirements for planting time and hence for seed availability. Soybean seed is difficult to store for long periods in tropical conditions, and many farmers prefer to purchase fresh seed. Much of it is purchased from other farmers, but a considerable amount is also sold by soybean traders. Each season grain traders are able to identify recently harvested soybean suitable for seed and offer it to farmers in time for planting. In the December-January period, for instance, traders buy soybean from farmers who have planted in unirrigated rainy season plots. They select seed for sale to farmers who will plant in rainfed wetland plots in February. The traders charge a premium over the grain price (usually about 50%) and are able to perform much more effectively than the parastatal seed company (Van Santen and Heriyanto, 1996).

Seed sector liberalisation in Peru[7]

Until recently, formal seed supply for many of Peru's most important crops was managed by the state. The state agrarian bank contracted private growers in the highlands to produce seed potato that was then provided to potato-producing co-operatives. Rice seed was produced and sold by the government rice monopoly. Maize seed was managed by the national maize research programme. In the early 1990s a number of policy changes took place in the seed sector. The government ended its support of agricultural co-operatives and closed the state rice monopoly. Private seed enterprise was encouraged, and a donor project helped establish departmental seed committees (CODESEs) that were to provide a voluntary seed certification service and, in some instances, access to seed conditioning facilities. The effects of these changes in government policy on seed production varied, depending on the specific crop.

The stimulation of a private seed industry was most effective for rice. The demand for rice seed from commercial farmers is fairly high because the price they receive is determined in part by the type and quality of rice they bring to market. Rice production is concentrated in a few major areas, and several small seed firms have emerged, the majority of them formed by people who had been in government agricultural research

[7]This section is based on Bentley et al. (2000).

institutes or universities and who saw an opportunity in the new policy trend towards privatisation. Many were also affected by the decline in public funding for research, and brought their expertise in rice breeding and agronomy to the seed business. Some of these companies have purchased seed conditioning equipment, while others rent equipment provided by the CODESEs. Some are also able to rent land and other facilities that were previously part of government research stations. Another major player in the rice seed market is a large rice mill. It already had the facilities and storage infrastructure necessary for seed processing. In addition, it has the financial resources to organise contract seed growers and to establish seed marketing.

Some of the companies maintain their own source seed and a few have initiated breeding programmes. Many companies use the rice varieties developed by public research in Peru, while others are exploring the possibility of marketing foreign (European) varieties. In one controversial case, a rice seed company claimed that its breeders had made sufficient changes to a public variety to qualify it for certification as a new, private variety. Their claim was ultimately rejected, but this is an example of how private companies producing public varieties attempt to differentiate, and claim ownership of, their products.

Some private companies are also producing maize seed, especially for yellow maize production in lowland areas that is mostly destined for sale as animal feed. There is one particularly popular public open-pollinated variety that is produced by a number of companies. But, despite liberalisation, there is still significant government participation in maize seed production, particularly through a producers' union associated with the national maize programme. Hybrid maize seed is also available, much of it imported from Argentina and Brazil. The government's liberalisation policies have had little effect on the seed trade for highland maize varieties grown mostly by smaller, less commercial farmers. Much of the seed for this crop is farm-saved and the seed trade is mostly in the hands of grain merchants who sell seed produced by local farmers.

When the government seed potato provision system was abolished, there was an initial flush of activity among highland potato growers to supply the market for certified seed. The CODESEs provided certification services and many small growers entered the market. However, certified seed potato is much more expensive than informal seed potato. Seed represents a significant proportion of the total production costs for potatoes and farmers attempt to save their own seed or to purchase cheap (but adequate quality) informal seed. The few certified producers that remain sell much of their production to NGOs, who distribute it to their clients. Another limitation on the potential demand for seed potato is the fact that most potatoes are currently destined for consumer markets that require certain types of potato but do not pay a premium for high quality potatoes of particular varieties. The fast food industry has grown rapidly in Peru's urban centres, but most of the potatoes it uses for French fries are imported; the preferred variety is not adapted to Peruvian growing conditions. Even if a suitable substitute were found, considerable reorganisation of the current marketing system would be required to ensure that appropriate seed could be delivered to farmers and that the buyers could easily distinguish the preferred variety.

The response of the Peruvian seed system to opportunities for private investment illustrates several of the principles that are central to this book. The opportunities for formal seed provision are determined by demand; crops that are marketed under widely accepted quality standards (such as rice) or that are not consumed on-farm (such as yellow maize) are more likely to involve seed demand. The relative cost of seed is also an issue, and a farmer will carefully consider the large investment needed for seed potato. Developing a seed enterprise requires considerable knowledge and experience. The majority of the new seed enterprises were formed by ex-government employees who had technical knowledge and strong links with the farming sector, and who could use their contacts to facilitate access to government facilities and equipment now available to the private sector. Finally, the development of consumer confidence in commercial seed is facilitated by local seed production and marketing facilities that farmers can trust or (particularly in the absence of private varieties) by a strong brand image that farmers can identify. The seed potato market in particular has none of these qualities and hence is slow to develop.[8]

Pearl millet hybrids in Rajasthan

Although a few private seed companies had existed in India for many years, mostly selling vegetable and flower seed, it was only in the 1980s that policy changes provided the incentives for significant commercial seed activity. One of the major changes was a ruling that allowed private companies to produce and sell seed of public varieties. This was followed by other changes, including liberalised access to foreign germplasm and changes in variety registration requirements (Selvarajan et al., 1999). One of the first entry points for the private seed industry was in hybrid sorghum and pearl millet (Pray et al., 1991). Companies began to produce and market public hybrids, in competition with the state seed corporations. In addition, a number of private companies initiated their own breeding programmes, and proprietary sorghum and pearl millet hybrids were soon available.

The Indian private seed industry has grown very rapidly, and current estimates indicate that approximately 60% of the seed market in India is in the hands of the private sector (Selvarajan et al.1999). Private enterprise now covers a very wide range of crops, but hybrid pearl millet and sorghum continue to be important. These are particularly interesting crops, because they tend to be grown in more marginal areas, by farmers who are often less commercially orientated. It is thus worthwhile to examine how an expanding and quite sophisticated private seed industry interacts with resource-poor farmers. The example that will be discussed is pearl millet in Rajasthan.[9]

The farmers of eastern Rajasthan have access to hybrid pearl millet produced by approximately 15 private companies, as well as by the Rajasthan State Seeds

[8]Such trust and demand can develop, however. In Scotland, companies holding plant breeders' rights for certain potato varieties have attempted to control seed potato production, which has led to a number of former seed growers turning to the production of 'small ware' potatoes, supposedly destined for food use. These are sold (illegally) as seed to potato producers in England (Clunies-Ross, 1996) This clandestine trade in non-certified seed requires exceptional trust between buyer and seller.

[9]This section is based on Tripp and Pal, 1998 and 2000.

Corporation (RSSC). The larger companies market only their own hybrids; other companies may market both proprietary and public hybrids, and some smaller companies, without research capacity, sell only public hybrids (as well as public OPVs). The seed is sold through a large number of private input dealers (some of whom are also agents for the RSSC). Most of these are small shops selling a range of seeds and agricultural chemicals. There is a sufficiently high demand for the hybrids for even some other shops (e.g. electrical goods or stationery) occasionally to sell pearl millet seed. Many companies provide banners, posters, calendars and other items promoting their seed. The seed is packaged in 1.5 and 3 kg packs.[10]

A study was carried out in two contrasting areas of Rajasthan. In one area, traditionally known as Shekhawati, farmers had been introduced to commercial pearl millet seed a few years earlier. In the second area, around the town of Behror, farmers had longer experience with commercial seed markets. The focus of the study was the quality and type of information that flowed between farmers and seed providers (merchants and companies). Farmers made a clear distinction between local pearl millet varieties (*desi*) and MVs (hybrids and OPVs) which, regardless of origin or type, are called *sankar* (a Hindi term meaning 'hybrid'). About two-thirds of the farmers in Shekhawati, and all the Behror farmers, planted at least some pearl millet hybrids.

The farmers plant both public and private hybrids, although the proportion of public hybrids is much lower in Behror. An exact comparison is impossible because of farmers' incomplete knowledge of the varieties they are planting. As Table 5.1 shows, only a small proportion of the farmers knew the names of both the hybrid and the company that produced the seed. Most varieties carry code names (e.g. BK-560, PG-5822) and farmers have difficulty remembering these. Several of the public varieties have nicknames (e.g. 'whiskered', for a variety with bristles) and a popular private variety is called 'plastic bag' to describe its distinctive packaging. Some farmers remember part of the code number, and many of those who plant commercial varieties know the name of the company, but not of the specific hybrid. Even though farmers may know the company name, the concept of different private companies, or the distinction between public and private seed companies, is often not recognised.

How does this imperfect access to information affect farmers' practices? Although they may not know the precise name of the variety they are planting, they can describe its characteristics and list its good and bad points. As Table 5.2 shows, farmers rely heavily on their neighbours and on merchants for advice and information. Merchants have an incentive to sell the seed that provides the highest return, but they also want to keep their customers. Even in Shekhawati, where the use of commercial seed is relatively recent, 61% of the farmers using hybrids in 1997 had purchased seed or inputs from the same dealer previously. In a few cases, farmers who had been unhappy with the hybrid sold to them the previous year had received a refund from the dealer. In Behror, with longer experience in the commercial seed market, farmers were more familiar with company names, and utilised a wider range of commercial seed.

The general performance of most of the pearl millet hybrids is sufficiently good for

[10]Pearl millet has one of the lowest seeding rates of any cereal; 4 kg is sufficient to plant one hectare.

Table 5.1 Knowledge of hybrid planted in 1997, Rajasthan (%)

Farmer knowledge	Shekhawati (N = 100)	Behror (N = 80)
Company and hybrid	23	10
Company only	35	76
Hybrid only	18	1
No knowledge	24	13

Source: Tripp and Pal (2000)

Table 5.2 Source of information for 1997 pearl millet hybrids, Rajasthan (%)

Source	Shekhawati (N = 100)	Behror (N = 80)
Another farmer	48	39
Shopkeeper	36	46
Extension	12	15
Other	4	0

Source: Tripp and Pal (2000)

farmers rarely to plant a completely inappropriate variety. But in many cases they do not have enough information to help them distinguish between the different private and public hybrids that exhibit a range of grain qualities, maturities, and growth habits. Information about the varieties provided by the companies tends to be of a very general nature, and companies invest more in promoting their brand image. Despite the considerable investment in advertising, seed company reputations are established slowly. On the other hand, fears about wide-scale deception in commercial markets seem unfounded, although instances of fraud do occur. Perhaps the most common examples are occasional attempts by merchants to sell outdated seed, or to sell grain in illegally acquired seed bags. The gradual strengthening of company reputations and the emergence of stable and reputable merchants, combined with adequate consumer protection, should further increase the efficiency of commercial seed markets.

Rice seed in Andhra Pradesh
The case of pearl millet illustrates how Indian seed companies responded to the opportunity to market hybrids. This is similar to examples from many other countries, where hybrids are the entry point for private seed development. But the private seed industry is not limited to hybrids, and when appropriate conditions are present private seed production is possible for crops traditionally considered to be largely farm-saved. This section describes one example, the case of rice seed in Andhra Pradesh.[11]

Rice is the most important crop in Andhra Pradesh; the state's farmers grow about 9.6 million tonnes of rice on 3.5 million hectares. About 70% of it is grown during the *kharif* season of monsoon rains and the vast majority benefits from some type of irrigation

---

[11]This section is based largely on Tripp and Pal (2001).

(borewells, tanks, or canals). The state has benefited from a highly productive public agricultural research system, and most of the rice varieties farmers plant are MVs. Although rice seed can be saved from season to season, there is a growing trend among Andhra Pradesh farmers to purchase fresh seed quite frequently. Surveys done in three districts of Andhra Pradesh in 1998 showed that only 20 to 40% of rice seed (depending on the district and season) is farm-saved. There are several reasons for this remarkably high turnover. First, rice is a commercial crop and an important source of income for many farmers. Each season they purchase fertilisers and pesticides, and the additional investment in seed represents a small proportion of their total cash outlay. In addition, many farmers express the view that saved seed results in lower yields. In some rice-growing areas high temperatures and humidity can cause a loss in seed quality, and farmers who do not practise careful roguing or who do not have access to a clean threshing floor may have to plant very impure seed. Finally, the increasing demand further stimulates the competitive provision of reasonably priced rice seed.[12]

The rice seed that farmers buy comes from a number of sources. Between one-third and two-thirds (depending on the district) is purchased from other farmers. Larger farmers in particular often reserve a part of their production for sale as seed to neighbours. They are able to charge a premium of about 30% over the grain price (or provide the seed on loan with the expectation of repayment in kind, plus 50% interest). Most of the rest of the seed is purchased from government seed companies (principally the Andhra Pradesh State Seed Development Corporation), private companies, or co-operative producers. Precise statistics are difficult to obtain, but APSSDC sold approximately 32,000 tonnes of rice seed in 1998, private companies sold at least 20,000 tonnes, and co-operatives sold (approximately) 8000 tonnes. The relative contribution of the private sector has been increasing rapidly in the past few years.

What are the factors that allow such a significant participation of the private sector? One answer lies with the unusual status of Andhra Pradesh in commercial seed production. The northern part of the state presents excellent climatic and infrastructure conditions for seed multiplication of many crops. It was one of the principal areas where the private production of hybrid sorghum and pearl millet began, and many private seed companies have their headquarters in Andhra Pradesh.[13] Although seed production offers only modest economies of scale, it has significant economies of scope, and once a company is producing and selling a range of (usually hybrid) seeds, adding rice seed to the portfolio is straightforward. This is the way several large companies have begun producing rice seed. In addition, some of the larger companies are interested in the potential for hybrid rice and are establishing their position with ordinary rice seed in anticipation of the development of acceptable hybrids.[14]

Besides the larger companies, there is a wide range of other enterprises in the rice seed business. The ability of small enterprises to participate, and the variety of enterprise

[12]Rice seed price in Andhra Pradesh is approximately twice the grain price at harvest.

[13]The Andhra Pradesh Seedsmen Association has 147 member companies.

[14]There has also been considerable public and private investment in the development of hybrid rice in India in the past few years. Significant progress has been achieved in breeding programmes, but the hybrid varieties developed so far have not proved acceptable to farmers. Grain quality is one of the principal issues.

combinations that emerge, owes much to a number of factors that serve to reduce transaction costs for these enterprises. The major factors are illustrated in Table 5.3. They are related to several of the elements of seed provision: source seed, seed multiplication, conditioning, and marketing.

Because private seed companies in India have easy access to public varieties, source seed production is quite manageable. Breeder seed of the varieties developed by the state university network is available through a system in which companies (public, private and co-operative) submit requests ('indents') and a prepayment by an annual deadline. The university stations multiply the requisite breeder seed and companies arrange for its delivery. The companies use this breeder seed to produce foundation seed, which is then multiplied for commercial seed. Although many companies obtain breeder seed through this system, companies can also buy foundation seed from each other.

Table 5.3 Major types of rice seed enterprise, Andhra Pradesh

Function				
Produce foundation seed	Organise seed growers	Process and store seed	Market seed	Examples
	✓			Local organisers are contracted by seed companies to identify and supervise seed growers.
		✓		Individuals who own seed cleaning and storage facilities rent them to seed companies.
			✓	An established seed company that wishes to begin marketing rice seed can buy foundation seed, hire organisers, and rent processing facilities.
	✓	✓		Some organisers own seed cleaning and storage facilities. They may be contracted to deliver processed seed to a company.
	✓		✓	Small operators can buy foundation seed and rent processing and storage facilities
		✓	✓	Owners of processing equipment may buy foundation seed and hire an organiser.
✓		✓	✓	Some large companies may contract organisers, although company staff also supervise seed multiplication.
	✓	✓	✓	Some small operations find it more convenient to purchase foundation seed from other companies.
✓	✓	✓	✓	Companies that have facilities and staff in the area where seed is multiplied perform all functions.

Seed multiplication is carried out by contracted farmers. Because of a ceiling on land-holdings in India, most seed production requires the contracting of large numbers of smallholders. Much of the rice seed multiplication takes place in northern Andhra Pradesh, even though the majority of the cultivation takes place in other parts of the state. The climate is excellent for producing a good seed crop, and many seed companies have offices and facilities in the area. In some cases company staff arrange contracts with farmers, but they often contract someone called an organiser who has strong local political connections and who agrees to deliver a certain quantity of seed and then identifies and supervises the individual growers. Because there is considerable seed production in a concentrated area, there are many experienced seed growers (and organisers) available.

Rice seed conditioning does not require specialised equipment; a seed cleaner and adequate storage facilities are the main requirements. Again, because of the concentration of production activities, many conditioning facilities are available for rent. Some organisers have acquired their own cleaners and storage facilities that they offer as part of their service.

Seed marketing is facilitated by an extensive network of input dealers; there are more than 8000 registered seed dealers in Andhra Pradesh. Major companies designate certain dealers as their distributors and these in turn recruit other dealers. If dealers (or companies) run short of seed, they may come to the major production area in search of seed from some of the smaller enterprises.[15]

Many of the factors that facilitate the emergence of small rice seed enterprises in northern Andhra Pradesh are similar to those discussed in relation to industrial clustering or enterprise zones, where many enterprises of the same industry operate in close proximity (Schmitz and Nadvi, 1999). Such clustering reduces transaction costs by establishing networks that share information and technology and reallocate spare resources. They also act as a magnet for attracting potential clients.

The opportunities for producing rice seed are exploited not only by established seed companies, but also by small enterprises that enter the market through rice seed. There appear to be three principal origins for these small enterprises. Some are begun by individual farmers who are relatively wealthy and have had experience as contract seed growers with public companies or experimental stations. Others have been started by seed merchants, who use their contacts and experience to expand into seed production. Finally, some organisers expand by acquiring processing equipment and begin to market their own seed.

As with pearl millet, we can ask about the quality of information transmitted from the commercial seed system to rice farmers. In contrast to pearl millet, most farmers have a very clear idea of which (public) rice varieties they wish to grow and do not require further information from seed dealers. On the other hand, they have even less information about seed companies than the pearl millet farmers; in the Andhra Pradesh study,

---

[15]Singh et al. (1995) discuss a similar situation for small producers of OPV maize seed in India. In years when there is a shortage of hybrid maize seed, small producers of public OPVs can bring their seed to the market. In years when they are unable to sell their crop as seed, they can sell it on the grain market.

in only 29% of the cases when rice seed was purchased from a dealer could the farmer identify the name of the (public or private) company that had produced the seed.

There is an additional weakness in the interface between public plant breeding and private seed production. Because all of the rice varieties are in the public domain, and many companies produce seed of the same variety, there is no incentive to promote particular varieties. Any investment in promoting a particular variety may simply result in increased sales for a competitor. (Seed quality is also a potential selling point, but until farmers are better able to distinguish among seed companies, this will not be effective.) Thus private companies are not effective sources of information about new public rice varieties, and the state seed companies do not invest much effort on this front either. But farmers eagerly seek out new rice varieties, and there is one particular sector of the seed provision system that exploits this niche. A number of small seed producers have good relations with university experimental stations. They are able to get source seed of new varieties and multiply it for sale. They are often more willing to market these new varieties than the larger companies, who wait until demand is established. However, as we shall see in the following chapter, a significant diffusion of new rice varieties is the result of farmer-to-farmer seed trade.

The incentives for private plant breeding

Since the beginning of scientific plant breeding in the late nineteenth century there have been examples of both private and public initiative. The development of wheat breeding in France and the United States illustrates the contrasting pathways. Wheat breeding in France was initiated by private breeders, most notably Henri de Vilmorin, whose privately marketed varieties dominated French wheat farming up to the mid-twentieth century. It was not until 1921 that the French government began to fund a wheat breeding programme (Lupton, 1988). In the US, on the other hand, most wheat breeding has been the responsibility of state experimental stations, universities, or the Department of Agriculture. Even today, there are approximately equal numbers of private and public wheat breeders in the US (Bohn and Byerlee, 1993), and there is healthy competition between public and private varieties (Barkley and Porter, 1996).[16] To cite another contrast, all potato breeding in Canada is carried out by government research agencies, while most potato breeding in the Netherlands is in private hands (Young, 1990). Nevertheless, the importance of hybrid seed and the high seed demand of commercial agriculture mean that the majority of plant breeding investment in industrialised countries is in the private sector.

The development of private plant breeding in the South has followed a different trajectory. Most plant breeding has been done by government research institutes or universities. Hybrid maize has provided the major opportunity for the emergence of a private seed industry. This is now common throughout Latin America (Morris and

---

[16]An analysis of the 128 principal wheat varieties grown in the US in 1934 shows that 100 had been developed by the public sector, 23 by private individuals and only 5 by seed companies (Kloppenburg, 1988).

López-Pereira, 1999) and hybrid maize was also the entry point for private plant breeding in South Africa and Zimbabwe (Rusike, 1995). A few other cases are evident, including the private vegetable seed industry in several Asian countries and private wheat breeding in Argentina. The previous section reviewed some of the results of the recent liberalisation of the seed industry in India, where there is growing investment in private plant breeding, particularly for hybrid crops.

The increasing reliance on the private sector in agriculture, the uncertain budgets for many public agricultural research institutes, and the growth of international trade all signal a trend towards the increasing importance of private plant breeding. However, a major issue that remains to be resolved is the appropriate level of incentives for private breeding. The question of intellectual rights protection dominates current debates about the future of the seed industry and is one of the most important institutional issues for seed system development.

Because possession of seed or planting material allows the production of exact copies of a particular variety or species, there has always been a problem of establishing property rights for new plant discoveries or breeding innovations. The Dutch monopolised the trade in cloves from the Spice Islands of South-East Asia in the early seventeenth century by destroying the clove trees growing on all islands except one and then carefully controlling production and export (Landes, 1998). Europe depended on imports of indigo dye from India until the French were able to establish plantations and process the dye in the French Antilles during the eighteenth century. British interests in North America were eventually able to acquire seed and knowledge of the dye-making techniques, despite a French edict making the export of indigo seed a capital crime (Brockway, 1988). When the Dutch were able to acquire superior varieties of cinchona (the bark of which is a source of quinine), the Bolivian who had helped smuggle this seed out of the country was imprisoned for treason (ibid.).

Despite the problem of protecting a new species or variety, plant breeding by private individuals flourished from the mid-nineteenth century. We can only speculate about the precise incentives for this activity. Much early plant breeding was done by 'gentleman farmers' with the time and resources to engage in research, and who were not necessarily interested in making an immediate profit. Most of the farmers, wealthy or otherwise, who dedicated their efforts to variety selection and plant breeding were certainly motivated by the opportunity to participate in a rapidly expanding scientific endeavour and by a desire to improve the agriculture of their regions. The opportunity to establish a reputation was also important; a catalogue of cereal varieties from Scotland in 1852 shows that about 9% of the names are those of the introducer or promoter of the variety (Walton, 1999). The early development of maize varieties in the US was characterised by the open exchange of germplasm among farmer breeders, either through personal friendships or through organised fairs and agricultural shows.[17]

---

[17] A paper written by a farmer in *The American Agriculturalist* of 1843 responds to an earlier favourable mention of his variety, and he devotes considerable space to explaining his breeding methods. 'As you did me the honor to mention my corn crop in your paper, contrary to anticipation, your notice has brought me a liberal amount of orders for seed, and I feel under obligation to give some explanation of the process by which I obtained it' (Hendrikson, cited in Wallace and Brown, 1988: 55).

However, commercial incentives were not absent from early private plant breeding. For crops that farmers bought regularly as seed (such as fodder crops), seed dealers tried to establish control over the market. In mid-nineteenth century England, some firms developed and promoted unique mixtures of grass seed 'over which they effectively asserted intellectual property rights' (Walton, 1999: 37). Seed companies were constantly on guard against the possibility that the farmers whom they contracted to multiply seed would save part of the harvest for their own sale (Kloppenburg, 1988). Lester Pfister, one of the early commercial maize seed growers in Illinois, was angered when he found that the Department of Agriculture was distributing one of his inbred lines (Fitzgerald, 1990). There were also occasional attempts to patent maize lines, but these were not successful.

The advent of hybrid technology opened new possibilities for the protection of plant breeding innovations. One of the early hybrid researchers argued that, if it was not possible to protect inbred lines, it might be possible to protect hybrid seed production methods (ibid.). As hybrid research advanced, it soon became obvious that the methods themselves allowed substantial protection of innovation. Writing in 1919, East and Jones, two of the pioneers in hybrid research, speculated on the potential:

> [I]t is the first time in agricultural history that a seedsman is enabled to gain the full benefit from a desirable origination of his own or something that he purchased. The man who originates devices to open our boxes of shoe polish or to autograph our camera negatives, is able to patent his product and gain the full reward for his inventiveness. The man who originates a new plant which may be of incalculable benefit to the whole country gets nothing – not even fame – for his pains, as the plants can be propagated by anyone. There is correspondingly less incentive for the production of improved types. (cited in Kloppenburg, 1988: 99)

Hybrid maize development was the stimulus for substantial investment in private plant breeding. The hybrids provided significant yield and other advantages to farmers throughout most of the Corn Belt, and their adoption proceeded at a remarkable rate. Although farmers began to grow hybrid maize only in the early 1930s, by 1945 approximately three-quarters of the US maize area was under hybrids (Duvick, 1998).[18]

The first major effort at plant variety protection through the legal system was initiated by nurserymen who had for many years been trying to protect their stocks from unauthorised propagation. Their efforts resulted in the US Plant Patent Act of 1930, which covered mainly fruits and flowers. Agricultural seeds (and crops like potatoes) were excluded from the Bill, in part because of opposition to the possible ownership of the parts of the plants used for food (Fowler, 1994). Similar legislation was enacted in a number of European countries in the ensuing decade.

The movement towards variety protection for field crops took several more decades. As Fowler explains, there were technical problems to be overcome; for most crops it was difficult to produce a sufficiently uniform variety that could be subject to precise

---

[18]It is certainly true that very little private money was invested in open pollinated maize research after the advent of hybrids, for understandable reasons. However, it is questionable whether this represents a conspiracy within science and industry to keep more accessible and productive seed technology from reaching farmers, as some authors argue (e.g. Kloppenburg, 1988; Levins and Lewontin, 1985).

identification and hence protection. In addition, the US seed industry faced a dilemma regarding the possibility of variety protection; on the one hand, this would allow greater control over the sale of private varieties, but, on the other hand, the registration procedures would open the door to government oversight and regulation. The issue was pursued more vigorously in Europe, and in 1961 six countries became the initial signatories in the creation of the Union for the Protection of New Varieties of Plants (UPOV). The convention came into force in 1968 and established forms of plant variety protection outside the patent system. These events stimulated further activity in the US, resulting in the passage of the Plant Variety Protection Act in 1970.

The UPOV Convention (amended in 1978) allowed plant breeders to register their varieties so that they could be protected from unauthorised use in seed production. Seed producers wishing to multiply and market seed of the protected variety had to negotiate royalties or other payments with the breeder. Other breeders were allowed to use the protected varieties for research purposes and farmers were allowed to save seed of the protected varieties for their own use (the so-called 'farmers' privilege'). A revision in the convention in 1991 significantly tightened some of these arrangements, in particular making it more difficult to use protected material in other breeding programmes and eliminating the farmers' privilege.

This latter restriction is one of the more contentious issues in the debate over variety protection. In the UK, for instance, farmers who wish to save seed of a protected variety must pay a royalty (collected through the British Society of Plant Breeders); farms below a certain size are currently exempt. Countries entering UPOV may be signatories to the 1978 or 1991 convention. Those following the earlier convention (e.g., several Latin American countries) allow farmers to save seed. In the US, farmers may save the seed of protected varieties but their ability to sell it to other farmers has been significantly curtailed by recent legislation.

There are several other methods for protecting seed. Certain companies in the US have begun to sell seed with purchase agreements (similar to those used for computer software) in which the farmer agrees that the harvested crop will not be used for seed (van Wijk, 1997). US law also allows the patenting of plant varieties (which usually precludes the possibility of saving seed). In the past decade, the growth of biotechnology in the US and Europe has stimulated the patenting of genes and processes used for the production of transgenic crops. In some cases, companies in North America have hired detective agencies to pursue farmers suspected of saving transgenic seed.

Perhaps the most notorious method for controlling property rights has been the proposal of a 'terminator technology', a genetic mechanism inserted in a plant variety that would render the progeny sterile. For industrial agriculture, where farmers rarely save seed and are used to using proprietary technology, this might prove acceptable, although even here the image of sterile seed might be difficult to sell. For developing countries, where a significant amount of seed is obtained from other farmers or from grain markets, such an innovation could cause serious problems.

There are several concerns regarding this expansion of plant variety protection. All members of the World Trade Organization (WTO) must provide a plant variety protection system, either through the 1978 or 1991 UPOV Conventions or by devising a *sui generis* system that provides acceptable protection. It is not clear what implications such legislation might have in the South with respect to seed-saving by farmers or the ability of local (public or private) plant breeders to compete with multinational companies. One of the most serious concerns relates to the increasing concentration in the global seed industry, as only the largest companies have the resources to protect their products.

Part of the impact of the corporate control of transgenic crops on industry concentration depends on the structure of the industry itself. In the US, although most of the transgenic technology is owned by a few large companies, it is licensed to many other companies, as well as to public organisations. For instance, although Monsanto has developed and patented the technology for herbicide-tolerant soybeans, there are about 300 different soybean varieties currently incorporating this gene (Traxler et al. 1999). The large companies have the resources to develop the technology, but many smaller seed companies control varieties adapted to particular environments and have a loyal clientele. This results in the technology-holder licensing its genes and techniques for incorporation in other companies' varieties. There is also a trend for the larger companies to buy up the more successful medium-sized firms, however.

In response to these changes in plant property rights many countries have taken steps to protect their own genetic resources, most notably through the Convention on Biological Diversity, established in 1992. An additional response has been the promotion of the concept of 'farmers' rights', particularly by FAO (Brush, 1992a), the basic idea being the establishment of a fund that channels compensation from seed companies to the countries or communities that have been the source of germplasm for commercial plant varieties. Some versions also envisage targeting royalties or other payments to specific farming communities that have provided germplasm used in commercial (or even public) breeding programmes.[19]

We have devoted considerable space to examining the evolution of plant variety protection because it illustrates some important institutional issues. We may recall that Demsetz (see p.14) argued that changes in the economy and in knowledge would lead to changes in property rights regimes. The growth of industrial agriculture, the demand for crop varieties with specific traits, the tremendous advances in biological science, and the increased capacity to monitor variety use and to enforce regulations all provide impetus for the redefinition of property rights related to seed. The identification of an appropriate protection framework is often presented in terms of the balance between providing incentives for innovation and protecting against the concentration of power.

Another perspective on plant variety protection that is relevant to institutional analysis is a reminder that debates on intellectual property rights utilise two radically different

[19]There are at least three problems with the pursuit of a full-blown approach to farmers' rights. First, it implies an exceptionally complex record-keeping system to track the contribution of particular varieties to the end products of formal breeding programmes. Second, it begs the question of defining and identifying the precise 'community' that should be credited with the ownership of the variety. Third, farmers' rights would appear to encourage the same restriction of germplasm exchange that their proponents (correctly) condemn in over-zealous plant variety protection legislation.

concepts of information (Boyle, 1996). Much of institutional economics is based on the assumption that development depends on the efficient provision and widespread availability of information. Intellectual property protection, on the other hand, is aimed precisely at the limitation of access to information in order to provide incentives for innovation and development. Society must decide how to balance the use of, and access to, information.[20]

Each country must utilise its legal and regulatory systems to identify the appropriate level of information management. The justification of intellectual property rights in order to provide incentives for research is a strong one, and there is general agreement that some type of plant variety protection is useful. Analyses of its impact over the past 20 years demonstrate increased commercial plant breeding and variety development, but the results are not as clearly delineated or overwhelmingly positive as might be expected (Lesser, 1997). The appropriate level of protection will depend on the specific situation. Argentina's protection laws prohibit grain millers from cleaning the wheat they buy from farmers and reselling it as seed. This has helped local private wheat breeding enterprises to survive. On the other hand, the law allows farmers to save the seed of protected varieties without paying royalties (van Wijk, 1997).

A balance must also be sought in the protection of germplasm for plant breeding purposes. The 1991 UPOV Convention protects breeders from the possibility of competitors selling an 'essentially derived' version of their variety (one which is equivalent except for minor cosmetic changes). But there is evidence from the US that overzealous restrictions on the exchange of germplasm can limit private plant breeding, and it is clear that excessive protection is detrimental to public plant breeding (Frisvold and Condon, 1998). The patenting of the various components and processes of biotechnology means that a particular transgenic variety may have several owners. When the development of such a variety requires the collaboration of several firms, or a partnership between public and private research, the high transaction costs of negotiating an acceptable division of compensation may discourage the effort.[21]

If we understand legal systems as institutions that respond to changing economic opportunities (Needham, 1983), then we have a better idea of the pressures and prospects that affect plant variety protection. The balance is between the public sanctioning of incentive systems that lead to technological innovation, on the one hand, and excessive corporate pressure to protect and concentrate access to resources, on the other. It is a choice regarding the degree to which information is freely available to innovators, and the justifications for the restriction of information with the promise of further progress. These factors have to be considered in the light of the benefits of seed saving and the progress that has been achieved to date through a relatively open system of germplasm exchange. The choice is a difficult one. It must be made in the context of

---

[20]Boyle (1996) argues that the intellectual property rights debate is dominated by the romantic image of the lone author, who must be protected and nurtured, rather than by consideration of the best public use of the author's products. The same argument could apply to the image of the 'lone breeder' or the innovating enterprise, as opposed to the public dimension of agricultural development.

[21]Such examples of this 'tragedy of the anticommons', caused by an excess rather than a lack of property rights, are already coming to light in the biomedical field (Heller and Eisenberg, 1998).

particular economic and social conditions and should not be based on ideology or be subject to undue political influence. The institution of law should not be considered as 'a system of abstract ideas but as a means to practical ends' (Cotterell, 1989: 185). The choice of plant variety protection regime is a pragmatic one, and it behoves each society to make its decision carefully.

Summary

This chapter has reviewed the growth of private seed provision. Although the examples were drawn from several countries and several points in history, they share a number of characteristics. Private seed provision tends to emerge in the context of commercial agriculture, although not all farmers who purchase seed will be marketing their production. The seed industries in England and in the US emerged at different times, but in each case they were part of dynamic change in the agricultural sector. Private seed provision will favour those crops for which there is demand for specific varieties or for product quality. Early vegetable seed producers in England and maize seed producers in the US often derived much of their demand from new varieties that they had developed or acquired. When seed represents a small proportion of the total costs of production (e.g. pearl millet), it is more likely to be purchased than when it represents a significant investment (e.g. potatoes). In many situations, the opportunity for hybrid seed production has been the most important initial stimulus for the private seed industry.

The organisation of commercial seed provision requires effective flow of information. Small-scale enterprises often integrate all of the operations, and family-run businesses often facilitate co-ordination. Once an enterprise reaches a certain size, it must decide whether to continue to manage all operations or to contract out. One of the key operations becomes marketing, as seed can no longer be sold exclusively at the farm. The establishment of trust between seed merchants and producers is crucial to the expansion of the trade. The concentration of wide-ranging seed production activity (as in examples in the US and India) allows for the development of various scales and complexity of operation. The clustering of the enterprises facilitates information flow, increases trust among the participants, and lowers transaction costs. In cases where there is significant public-private interaction, networks of acquaintance and employment facilitate interactions, as when former public employees establish seed businesses that utilise public varieties or other facilities.

Farmers must learn how to take advantage of the private seed sector. When the sector emerges, there are often instances of fraudulent sale and an environment of inadequate information and uncertain sanctions. Unless companies and merchants can establish good reputations, the nascent sector may founder. Small local enterprises often have an initial advantage, but they usually do not have the capacity to market large quantities of seed. More generalised mechanisms for trust and reputation are required. Markets do not necessarily provide all of the information that farmers need, as we have seen in the cases of confusion about variety names and company identities in India. It takes time for farmers and enterprises to develop sufficient experience to understand each other's requirements.

The most problematic feature of private seed enterprises is the definition of property rights for their varieties. In the early years of formal plant breeding, private individuals who developed new varieties often did so in order to participate in a rapidly expanding scientific endeavour, or to achieve local prestige. But as plant breeding produced more attractive varieties, increasing demand brought with it a desire for financial reward. Some form of protection is necessary in order to provide sufficient incentives and to ensure that competitors do not profit unfairly from the use of others' innovations. But current forms of variety protection have begun to impinge on farmers' ability to save seed and are threatening the system of public germplasm exchange upon which much plant breeding has been based. The transaction costs involved in protecting these property rights are now so high that only the largest firms can afford them, leading to possibilities of excessive concentration in the seed industry. The evolution of plant variety protection is a good example of how property rights institutions are affected by economic and technical change. Identification of the most appropriate balance between property rights and public access is an urgent priority for national seed policies. It has significant implications for the future of the public seed sector, to which we turn in the following chapter.

6 The Public Sector Role in Seed Systems

Public sector contributions

The previous two chapters have discussed the organisation of private (farm-level and commercial) seed provision. The public sector has been in the background of much of that discussion, providing the laws and contributing to the infrastructure that allows agricultural markets to develop, and supporting agricultural education and research. In this chapter we move the contributions of the public sector to the foreground. We examine the performance of public plant breeding; the delivery of information by state extension services, public seed production enterprises, and seed regulation.

Publicly funded agricultural research has supported plant breeding that has led to many of the new crop varieties developed in the past century. Although the contribution of private research has been growing steadily, spurred first by the development of hybrids and now by the advent of biotechnology, public breeding remains an important contributor to seed provision in both industrialised and developing countries. It is important that we examine the information exchange that takes place between public researchers and their clients, and that we understand the incentives for public plant breeders.

The products of public research (new varieties and crop management information) have traditionally been transmitted to farmers by government extension services. We shall want to look at the incentives and efficiency of such information exchange. We shall also examine the degree to which farmer organisations – groups and networks – contribute to this exchange of information.

In many countries the state has played a strong role in seed production as well. The importance of state seed enterprises has declined in recent years, but they remain a significant source of seed in a number of countries in the South. We shall examine the performance and incentives of these enterprises. There are also numerous examples of state encouragement of collective seed production, through co-operatives or other organisations, and we shall briefly review this experience.

Finally, one of the most prominent roles of the state in seed provision has been the establishment of seed regulation. We have seen that seed provision is subject to information failure because it is often difficult for farmers to assess the type or quality of seed that is available in the market. Government regulation is one answer to this type of information failure, and seed regulatory frameworks play a large role in determining the course of seed system evolution. We shall examine the experiences of public seed regulation.

Public agricultural research

The public sector's role in agricultural research can be justified on the grounds that most of its products have public good attributes; they are neither excludable nor subtractable. It is difficult to exclude farmers from the plant varieties produced by public research, and their use by one farmer does not diminish the supply for others. The previous chapter discussed how until recently it has been difficult to establish an effective system of property right protection for most agricultural technology, hence much of the research has been in the public sector. It might be possible for farmers to organise to carry out or to fund research themselves, but it would be very difficult to co-ordinate the activities of a large number of small farms facing a wide range of production conditions (Hayami and Ruttan, 1985). Such collective action for agricultural research is most likely for farmers growing specific commodities that are commercially remunerative. In addition, because of the low price elasticity of demand of most agricultural products, technological advance often results in lower prices, so that consumers derive a significant share of the benefit (ibid.). For these reasons, it is likely that public research will continue to play an important role in agricultural development. However, there are important questions about the incentives and the responsiveness of such research.

One of the earliest examples of public investment in agricultural research was the Land Grant College Act of 1862 in the United States. States were provided with land and resources to establish colleges that would promote the application of new knowledge in fields such as biology and chemistry for the development of more productive agricultural practices. Almost from the beginning, these colleges faced the question of what type of incentives should motivate public research. In particular, there was considerable debate over the relative emphasis to be given to providing farmers with practical advice versus organising original research (Busch and Lacy, 1983). The debate was carried on among members of the colleges, as well as between the colleges and the public. Some felt that the agricultural colleges existed mostly for the purpose of education and service, and should concentrate on dissemination of information, soil testing, variety trials and similar activities. Others felt that agriculture would not advance significantly unless more time and resources were available for basic research. A study of the contemporary public research system in the US reveals the complex mixture of motivations that determine the direction of a researcher's programme, including scientific curiosity, professional advancement, and response to the needs of various client groups (ibid.)

The issue of appropriate incentives for public research is related to the question of defining the clientele for that research. With respect to farmers' requirements, as long as the colleges' principal tasks were those of training and advising, they could address a wide range of farmers. But as research activities, and particularly variety development, came to assume increasing importance, success was measured by the utilisation and performance of the colleges' products. The tension between providing service and guidance to all farmers, on the one hand, and developing measurable research results, on the other, is well illustrated by the emergence of hybrid maize. Some researchers saw their primary role as helping to organise state 'corn contests' that allowed farmers to test a range of public and private maize varieties, including those they had developed themselves, in order to identify the best materials for each location. Others believed that more effort should be devoted to hybrid research which offered the possibility of significantly increasing maize yields across a wider range of environments (Fitzgerald, 1990).

The University of Illinois established a 'corn contest' in 1930. It involved planting yield trials of public and private varieties and hybrids in farmers' fields. The contest was an important means for exchanging information:

> The college, at almost no expense, received experimental information on the adaptability and yield of a wide variety of available corn types, information it had neither the fields nor the staff to acquire alone. The seed companies got free advertising for their corn seed, information about its merits relative to the competition, and a cheap and efficient means of testing new lines that were not yet in commercial production. And the farmers, who saved money buying seed corn from the college rather than a seed house, were able to determine which of the many corn varieties was best suited to their particular conditions (Fitzgerald, 1990: 127).

As hybrid development progressed and attracted more attention (and increasing competition and success from the private sector), there was added pressure to focus on this type of research. By 1937 the University of Illinois had developed over 100 maize hybrids, and a number of private companies were not far behind. But the majority of the maize breeding was centred on the northern part of the state, where production conditions were better. The south of the state, with poorer soils (and poorer, often tenant farmers) received very little attention from this research (ibid.). University staff often had to choose between providing support and advice to farmers with less political clout, or participating in research that was having a major impact for many farmers, although generally those with better resources.

The complexity of incentives for public agricultural research was affected by the power of other actors in the rural economy. As the land grant colleges grew, they also began to see the business and banking communities as their clients, from whom they increasingly sought support (Kloppenburg, 1988). This complexity has not diminished, and public researchers in the US describe how their decisions are influenced by the perceived demands of clients that include small and large farmers, agribusiness, rural residents, and the general public (Busch and Lacy, 1983). This diversity of incentives for research reminds us of the discussion of induced innovation in Chapter 1. The theory tells us that the development of agricultural technology responds to factor scarcities, but it begs the question of whose scarcities are addressed, and how this information is transmitted to public research.

The experience of public sector agricultural research in the South exhibits many of the same challenges of establishing incentives and identifying clients. The end of colonialism in Africa and Asia saw most countries establish public research services, some of which had significant antecedents in the colonial era. Substantial support for national research programmes has come from the international agricultural research centres (IARCs). The first of these, the International Rice Research Institute (IRRI) in the

Philippines, was established in 1960, and there are now 17 of these centres, funded by donations from bilateral and multilateral donors. Public sector research in the South has had mixed results and, except for brief periods, has been considerably underfunded, compared with public research in the North (Alston et al., 1998).

Our interests are confined largely to variety development, and here public research has had some notable successes. Certainly the best-known achievement has been the so-called Green Revolution, which has been a source of significant increases in agricultural productivity as well as of considerable controversy.[1] Although the term Green Revolution is now used to describe almost any instance of technological change in developing country agriculture, it originally referred to the development of short-straw, fertiliser-responsive varieties of wheat and rice beginning in the mid-1960s. These spread rapidly through many parts of Asia (as well as to a few other areas). This technology conforms well to the theory of induced innovation and responds to the needs of farming systems where land is the limiting factor. Hence it is particularly appropriate for much of Asia. Indeed, one can trace the history of experimentation with short-stature, fertiliser-responsive crops to mid-nineteenth century Japan (Francks, 1984).

However, considerable criticism has been directed at the Green Revolution strategy because it concentrated on areas with better resources. Most of the early success of the new varieties was in areas with adequate irrigation. Government attention was also given to the delivery (and often subsidisation) of inputs. These biases are partly explained by the strategy of directing technology to where the highest impact is expected and partly by national political decisions that favoured particular regions of a country (e.g., Hewitt de Alcantára, 1976; Byres, 1981).

Although the Green Revolution rice and wheat varieties had their initial impact in more favoured agricultural areas, subsequent research has helped provide varieties suitable for a wider range of farming conditions. For example, more than 70% of the wheat and rice, and nearly 60% of the maize, grown in developing countries is MVs (Byerlee, 1994). There have also been successes for public varieties of crops such as beans, groundnuts, pearl millet and sorghum in particular countries. Nevertheless, concern about the ability of public sector research to address the needs of more marginal farming areas remains. In Latin America, for instance, the use of modern maize varieties and hybrids is much higher among commercial than among subsistence farmers (Morris and López-Pereira, 1999). The bias of public research towards better environments is illustrated in Table 6.1, which shows that farmers in the higher rainfall and higher elevation zones in Kenya are more likely to use public maize varieties. Table 6.2 shows the slower rate of adoption of public varieties by smaller farmers in Kenya.

The successes of the Green Revolution gave a significant boost to the image of public agricultural research, and its shortcomings led to a number of efforts to direct research to the needs of other farmers. The challenges are the same as those described for the evolution of the US research system: scientists operating under a complex set of incentives; the necessity to respond to a range of clients, with the politically powerful often

[1]There is a very large literature on the Green Revolution. An exceptionally thorough analysis of its impact is presented in Lipton and Longhurst (1989). For a brief discussion of the varying interpretations of the term, see Tripp (1996).

Table 6.1 Farmers' use of public maize varieties, by agroclimatic zone, Kenya (%)

Agroclimatic zone	% of farmers who ever bought public seed	Use of public varieties and hybrids, 1992/93		
		% of farmers using	% of area planted	
Lowland tropics	43	16	16	
Dry midaltitude	67	38	32	
Moist midaltitude	79	41	51	
Dry transitional	91	21	12	
Moist transitional	98	85	94	
Highland tropics	98	86	95	
Total	87	68	73	

Source: Hassan et al. (1998)

Table 6.2 Adoption of public maize varieties, by farm size, Kenya

	Farm class	
	> 1 ha maize	< 1 ha maize
Year 10% of farmers in class adopted	1966	1972
Year 30% of farmers in class adopted	1969	1980
% of farmers who never received extension advice	27	41
% of farmers who use credit to buy seed	29	2

Source: Hassan et al. (1998).

first in line; and the difficulties of organising research to address a wide range of location-specific problems. In the mid-1970s many of these efforts began to coalesce into a movement called farming systems research (FSR).[2] FSR was a feature of many donor programmes to strengthen and support national agricultural research systems. It was characterised by more interdisciplinary research (which attempted to understand and diagnose the complex problems of particular farming systems), the organisation of small teams responsible for location-specific research, and a trend towards moving research activities from the experimental station to farmers' fields.

As might be expected, FSR ran into a number of organisational problems within national research institutes. In particular, there were conflicts over research goals, the definition of clients, and the identification of the production constraints that should be addressed. There were problems in organising and acting upon the information from many different environments. In addition, there were questions of the appropriate incentives for carrying out research in distant and often isolated locations.[3] The FSR movement contributed to some reorientation in a number of national research programmes, but the impact was limited by the magnitude of the organisational problems and a decline in donor

[2]Tripp (1991) reviews the farming systems movement and describes a number of successful applications. Collinson (2000) provides a comprehensive overview of the practice of FSR.
[3]See Merrill-Sands and McAllister (1988) for an overview of a comprehensive set of case studies addressing the management of FSR.

funding beginning in the mid-1980s. The decline in funding was part of a wider shift away from supporting government programmes, an increasing reliance on market solutions, and a move towards channelling more aid through NGOs. The relative shift towards NGOs was marked by greater emphasis on what came to be called participatory research methodologies, which are described in Chapter 7.

Extension: Transmitting information to farmers

Public sector research is usually seen as being complemented by extension. The theory is that an extension service delivers the information developed by research. In the early years of the US land grant system, the emphasis was heavily on extension. As research began to gain the upper hand, fewer resources were available for extension, but the two functions remained under the same organisational roof and, at least in theory, part of every staff member's mandate. In many developing countries, extension and research are part of separate organisations; extension tends to be under the ministry of agriculture while research is often the function of a semi-autonomous institute. This raises questions about the incentives that extension agents might have for spreading other organisations' research messages, and about extension's capacity and willingness to transmit demands and concerns from farmers to research. On the other hand, the transfer of technical information is only one among a very broad set of objectives for most extension agencies, and merging research and extension organisations is often not feasible (Kaimowitz, 1989).

The incentives for public extension agents are as complex as those for researchers. Promotion within the organisation and away from isolated postings is certainly as important in motivating agents as the satisfaction of delivering information to farmers (Leonard, 1977). It is usually the case that extension agents find it easier to work with larger 'progressive' farmers and those of their own class or ethnic group (ibid.; Crowder, 1988). There are few incentives for tailoring messages to farmers' circumstances or for providing feedback to research. Extension is often expected to promote a standard package of practices. In drought-prone areas of Guangxi Province, China, farmers prefer public OPV maize varieties to the hybrids promoted by the government. The director of extension explains the dilemma: '[A]s government officials we have to serve government. Hybrid is government's target and our task is to extend it. Besides, OPVs are not as profitable for us. Now we have to consider our own survival, although we know farmers need good OPVs rather than hybrids in this mountainous area' (cited in Song, 1998: 136).

Government extension campaigns are part of the history of the Green Revolution. As the productive potential of the new varieties became evident, governments invested resources in promotion and publicity. In some cases farmers were encouraged to 'trade in' seed of local varieties to receive seed of the new varieties. Fertiliser was usually subsidised, as well as the pesticides that were used for rice production. These government campaigns were sometimes run by unpopular governments, and political resistance included opposition to the technology that was being promoted. In the

Philippines, for instance, the Marcos regime was strongly identified with support for the Green Revolution (Anderson et al., 1991), and it is not surprising that rural opposition included NGO seed activities emphasising independence from government organisations (Miclat-Teves and Lewis, 1993).[4]

It is unreasonable to expect public extension to do an efficient job of transferring information to farmers unless there is some mechanism that allows farmers to express their demands and concerns. One of the most frequently discussed methods for channelling farmer demand is through groups or organisations. There are numerous examples of the effectiveness of this strategy. In the US, agricultural colleges were active in organising farmer associations. The Wisconsin Experiment Association was formed in 1901 with 181 members in order to 'carry on experiments that shall be beneficial to all parties interested in progressive farming' (cited in Norskog, 1995: 234). The members tested new crop varieties produced by the college and the association expanded rapidly. By 1907 over 400 members were offering seed of the college's maize varieties for sale, and by 1920 branches of the state association were established in 50 counties. Such associations served to transmit farmer demand, but as they tended to represent the wealthier farmers, there was also a potential conflict with the college's mission. As one extension official observed in 1915, 'I can see great value in a body of men organised to promote agricultural development in the county…; but I also see grave danger that this body of progressive farmers will monopolise the services of the county [extension] agent' (cited in Fitzgerald, 1990: 96).

In mid-nineteenth-century England, farmers' clubs often engaged in experimentation. However, there were definite limits to the utility of this type of research. Significant variation among the conditions of the participating farmers meant that selecting varieties for recommendation could be difficult. Walton (1999: 47) cites one farmers' club report from 1840 that summarised trials, where 'the results of the same variety of wheat upon different soils seemed so much at variance, that it was impossible to decide on the merits of any one kind for universal adoption'.

Farmer organisations also played an important role in agricultural development in Japan after the Meiji Restoration. Under the influence of a growing market economy agricultural discussion groups and seed exchange societies were formed (Francks, 1984). Local governments began to sponsor agricultural associations, which were linked with a network of experimental stations. The associations were informed of the availability of new varieties from the government and given the opportunity to test them.[5]

Although farmer organisations can significantly improve the flow of information between farmers and the state agricultural apparatus, there seem to be a number of preconditions for their emergence. First, they tend to thrive where there is a strong

---

[4]The promotion of a uniform crop technology to increase food supply and support the state did not begin with the Green Revolution. In fifteenth-century Peru the Inca Empire transformed the agricultural landscape with intricate systems of terracing and irrigation. Agricultural diversity was radically reduced as the state concentrated on a single crop (maize) that fed the military and supplemented the diets of subject populations, as well as serving ritual purposes. The system required concentration on a relatively few varieties of maize that had required characteristics for production, storage and food preparation (Zimmerer, 1996).

[5]In the mid-twentieth century, Taiwan also relied heavily on collaboration between local farmers' associations and extension (Lionberger and Chang, 1970).

agricultural economy. In England, the number of local farmers' associations grew from just 35 in 1800 to about 600 in 1870 (Fox, 1979), corresponding to the period when England was experiencing its most rapid agricultural transformation. These associations arranged for lectures from agricultural experts and organised experimental programmes and shows. Secondly, it is often the wealthier farmers who have the time and resources to participate actively (Sims and Leonard, 1990). Finally, farmers must have clear incentives for participation. Groups are often formed around particular commodities that contribute an important part of farmers' incomes and for which it is worthwhile to organise to obtain technical information and to press for the delivery of other services or economic concessions.

The availability of information and farmer utilisation of public varieties

Critics of the Green Revolution often portray it as the imposition of a high external input technology on previously self-sufficient farmers. This is an oversimplification on several counts. First is the notion that the MVs are necessarily dependent on fertilisers and other chemicals. This confuses fertiliser efficiency with fertiliser dependence. Many MVs are more efficient than local varieties at utilising fertiliser, but may also outyield the local varieties without fertiliser. Use of fertiliser is often determined more by price than by the type of variety grown. Byerlee and López-Pereira (1994) provide data showing a lack of correlation between MV use and fertiliser use for maize; in some countries (such as Zimbabwe and Thailand) MV use is high but fertiliser use is low, while in other countries (such as Malawi or Mexico) the reverse is the case. An associated, and more complex, issue relates to pesticide use. The uniform growth habits of rice MVs and their role in the expansion of continuous cropping (because their earlier maturity allowed more than one crop per year) contributed to an increase in pest problems. This was met with a large rise in insecticide use, usually exacerbated by high pesticide subsidies. The problem has yet to be resolved, but the experience of Indonesia has shown that when the subsidies are removed and a comprehensive programme of integrated pest management (IPM) is instituted, pesticide use in rice drops precipitously, with no effect on yields (Whitten et al., 1996). In short, government subsidies certainly provide incentives for farmers to use inputs, and to choose varieties that respond best to those inputs. But changes in input prices rapidly bring about changes in input use and, to the extent that other varieties perform better with lower input levels, changes in variety.

Another problem with the portrayal of the Green Revolution as the triumph of government promotion over farmer rationality is the pattern of MV adoption. Table 6.3 summarises data from a number of studies on farmers' source of information about the MVs they are using. In relatively few cases is extension a very important source of information and in almost all cases information from other farmers is predominant. In addition, a significant proportion of the seed of MVs that these farmers are using comes from other farmers rather than from official sources. This is evidence of the importance of communication among farmers about the new varieties and their characteristics.

Table 6.3 Farmers' sources of information and seed, and knowledge of variety names for MVs (%)

| Location | Crop and MVs | Source of information about MV planted | | | % of MV seed obtained from other farmers | % of farmers growing MVs who cannot name the variety |
		Another Farmer	Extension	Other		
Ghana[a]	Maize. About 6 OPVs released in past 15 years.	48	49	4	19–33	34
Punjab, Pakistan[b]	Wheat. More than 10 MVs grown by farmers, although a few predominate.	48–69	14–30	17–22	47	5–20
Mardan, Pakistan[b]	Wheat. More than 10 MVs grown by farmers, although a few predominate.	57	28	15	66	33–50
Nepal[c]	Wheat. Two major MVs and several minor ones.	*	*	*	*	50
Rajasthan, India[d]	Pearl millet. Approximately 15 private and public hybrids available.	39–48	12–15	40–46	*	59–89
Andhra Pradesh, India[e]	Rice. Approximately 40 MVs grown by farmers.	72–86	6–26	2–8	34–61	<5
Western Province, Zambia[f]	Sorghum. Two early-maturing MVs.	60	21	19	48	42
Eastern Kenya[g]	Pigeonpeas. One MV.	84	16	0	67	*

Sources:

a) Morris et al. (1999).
b) Heisey (1990)
c) Morris et al. (1992).
d) Tripp and Pal (2000).
e) Pal et al. (forthcoming).
f) Lyoba and Tripp (1999).
g) Audi et al. (1999).
* no information or not applicable.

Table 6.4 Farmers' criteria and opinions about pearl millet varieties, Eastern Rajasthan

Criteria	Opinion	Farmers' Choice	
		Hybrid	Local Variety
Grain yield. When there is adequate moisture, hybrids tend to outyield local varieties.	Yields better in good rains.	72%	28%
	Yields better in poor rains.	58%	42%
Grain quality. Local varieties are generally preferred for food preparation, although some hybrids are appreciated for attractive grain.	Has better food quality.	11%	89%
Fodder quality. The fodder must be palatable for animals and local varieties are generally superior.	Has better fodder quality.	26%	74%
Resistance to striga. The parasitic weed striga causes significant yield loss and the hybrids are more resistant.	Resists striga.	97%	3%

Source: Tripp and Pal, 1998.

Perhaps the most prominent thread running through the many studies on the adoption of MVs is the fact that farmers use these varieties when they are appropriate to their circumstances and reject them when they are not.[6] Access to extension may provide an added source of information, but it is never a sufficient reason for adoption in the absence of compelling agronomic or economic advantages.

Table 6.4 summarises farmers' opinions about pearl millet varieties in eastern Rajasthan. The table shows how farmers choose between planting local varieties and the public and private hybrids that have recently become available. Neither type of variety fulfils all the criteria, and farmers must base their choice on their perceptions and priorities. One of the strengths of the hybrids is their ability to withstand the parasitic weed, striga, which is more prevalent in sandier, unirrigated fields. This leads to a pattern that is the reverse of the conventional wisdom about MVs; farmers in more marginal environments are more likely to plant the MVs, while in many cases when farmers acquire access to irrigation (which helps control the striga) they revert to local varieties, which they find taste better (Tripp and Pal, 1998).

The Rajasthan example illustrates another feature of information flow regarding public crop varieties. Although there are several local varieties and more than a dozen

---

[6]One of the earliest analyses to recognise this was Perrin and Winkelmann (1976).

pearl millet MVs available, farmers' discussions tend to be based on the two general classes. This is not to say that farmers are unable to distinguish among the MVs (or the local varieties), but their knowledge of the differences is far from perfect. This is perhaps a difficult case, because many of the pearl millet MVs are quite similar. But the problem is not unique, as shown in the last column of Table 6.3. A significant number of farmers using an MV are unable to give a name that distinguishes it from other MVs. The official names of MVs are sometimes not significant in the local language, or are composed of letter and number codes, so farmers often devise nicknames to distinguish among MVs. But often even the nicknames are inadequate, as the data in the table illustrate.[7]

The problem is particularly relevant to the more recent MVs that have been produced by public research. For a number of crops, MVs are clearly distinguishable as a class from local varieties. In the case of the first generation of Green Revolution wheat and rice varieties, their short stature and growth habit easily distinguished them from all other varieties. In those areas where they offered significant advantages, farmers learned how to manage them and began to use them. Further efforts by public research have resulted in additional MVs, often with characteristics such as disease resistance. In the case of wheat, rust diseases are a major problem, and the pathogens are able to mutate in response to varieties that initially offer resistance. Although the majority of Pakistani wheat farmers recognise rusts as a problem, relatively few of them appreciate differences in varietal susceptibility. Campaigns to get farmers to adopt newer rust-resistant MVs (accompanied by the official banning of the older varieties) are usually unsuccessful unless a serious rust epidemic occurs (Heisey, 1990). This is an example of the failure of the public research and extension system to transmit adequate information about new varieties, and the limitations of farmers' own systems of distinguishing and choosing among varieties.

These weaknesses in the transmission of information about public varieties have serious implications for the prospects of public sector biotechnology. Although most of the attention has been focused on the private introduction of transgenic crops, there is also considerable public sector investment in biotechnology research (Cohen, 1999), which it is hoped can be used to address some of the problems of resource-poor farmers who have been neglected by the Green Revolution and who are not the primary clientele of commercial seed companies (Nuffield Council on Bioethics, 1999). But once again, information is the key. If a public transgenic variety incorporates disease resistance or superior nutrition, for instance, but is otherwise indistinguishable from conventional varieties, farmers need to have access to adequate information to help them recognise and identify the new variety (Tripp, forthcoming).

Chapter 4 discussed examples of inadequacies in farmers' abilities to distinguish among local varieties, so it is not surprising that similar problems occur with MVs.

---

[7]Table 6.3 does not pretend to cover a representative sample of areas using MVs, and the majority of studies do not report the proportion of farmers unable to identify the MV they are using. But these examples span a wide enough range to indicate that it is not an isolated problem. See Morin et al. (1999) for a discussion of Philippine rice farmers' classification of local and modern varieties and a description of the various names used for a single variety.

However, the amount of effort that farmers invest in identifying and pursuing new crop varieties varies considerably. In some areas they are very aware of the existence and characteristics of new MVs. One example is illustrated in Table 6.5, which demonstrates how new rice MVs spread among farmers in Andhra Pradesh. It shows that the proportion of new varieties (those released within the previous 10 years) is higher in farmers' fields than it is in the commercial seed market (where the state seed corporation and private firms both participate). The last two columns of the table show that the source of much of the seed of the new varieties is other farmers and that farmers are more likely to go to their neighbours to acquire seed of new MVs rather than of older ones.

One of the major contributors to the dynamic of the rice seed system in Andhra Pradesh is the crop's commercial importance. Rice is a major cash crop and farmers pay close attention to the demands of the market. In one part of the state, for instance, farmers may grow three MVs: that with highest grain quality (and highest price) is grown mostly for sale; a variety of intermediate quality is often grown for home consumption; and a low quality (but high yield) variety is grown for the market (where it is in demand for government subsidised food programmes) (Pal et al., forthcoming).

The market acceptability of MVs often affects adoption patterns. Ashby (1982) describes the introduction of one of the first rice MVs in Nepal. The variety had exceptionally high yield, but its grain quality attracted a lower market price than many of the local varieties. Although larger farmers were the first to begin using the MV, smaller subsistence-oriented farmers eventually dedicated a higher proportion of their fields to the variety because it helped meet household food requirements. The larger commercially-oriented farmers, on the other hand, found they could earn more by selling the local varieties.[8] Market characteristics are a particularly important determinant in the

Table 6.5 The diffusion of new rice varities[a], Andhra Pradash, 1998

District	*% of new varieties in public seed sale[b]*	*% of new varieties in farmers' fields*	*% of new varieties that farmers acquired from other farmers*	*% of old varieties that farmers acquired from other farmers*
Srikakulum	27	42	73	48
East Godavari	20	41	40	25
Mahboobnagar	3	3	64	34

a) 'New varieties' are those released after 1990.
b) District figures for private seed sale are not available, but state-wide data show a proportion of new varieties similar to that of the public sector.

Source: Pal et al. (forthcoming)

[8]The opposite pattern obtained for a maize MV in the same region of Nepal. Although high yielding, its greater height and longer maturity interfered with small farmers' intercropping and rotation practices, so it was the larger farmers (with more land and less labour) who tended to be the most enthusiastic adopters (ibid.).

dynamics of variety diffusion. Chapter 4 discussed how local varieties are spread by farmer-to-farmer interchange. We have seen here that a major source of seed for MVs is neighbouring farmers, even in the presence of strong public seed production programmes. 'Unofficial' MVs are a particularly interesting example of farmer-to-farmer diffusion. There are cases of public plant breeding products that fail to gain official approval or promotion but nevertheless spread rapidly through informal interchange among farmers, and are often cited as examples of the strength of local seed systems. Four prominent examples are summarised in Table 6.6. Although each case is complex, and the diffusion of the variety depends on a number of factors, it is interesting that all of these 'unofficial' MVs share one important quality: a high market price. This is strong evidence of the important role played by market demand, even in cases of informal variety diffusion, where farmers contradict the judgements and advice of public officials.

The importance of the market also has a bearing on the diversity of varieties in farmers' fields. The Green Revolution is regularly blamed for reducing variety diversity, and there is no doubt that the past several decades have witnessed a significant reduction in the numbers and cultivation of local crop varieties, particularly in areas where MVs have been introduced.[9] But the causality is complex, and it must be remembered that during the

Table 6.6 'Unofficial' rice varieties that have spread from farmer to farmer

Location and variety		*Positive characteristics*
Nepal[a]	Pokhreli masino, a variety of uncertain origin, was included in the extension distribution of seed kits, and spread rapidly from farmer to farmer.	High yield under good management, early maturing, good cooking quality, high market price.
Philippines[b]	Bordagol, discovered by a farmer in a field of MV rice. After several cycles of selection by the farmer, the variety spread to cover 10,000 ha.	Yield equivalent to MVs, good palatability, 5–7% higher market price.
Western India[c]	Kalinga III, a variety released in eastern India but unknown elsewhere. A rural development programme included it in on-farm tests and it became very popular.	Early maturity, high grain quality, high market price.
India[d]	Mahsuri, a variety introduced from Malaysia in 1967 but rejected by rice breeders because of lodging. A farm labourer carried seed to his village and it soon spread. It, and several related varieties, have since been officially released, and are among the most popular varieties in India.	Very high grain quality and market price.

Sources: a) Green, 1987; b) R. Salazar (personal communication); c) Witcombe et al., 1999; d) Maurya, 1989.

[9]The extent to which genetic diversity has been affected by modern plant breeding is an exceptionally complex question, for which no easy answers (and precious little data) are available. For an interesting exploration of the issue applied to wheat breeding, see Smale (1997).

same period the provision of irrigation and access to fertiliser and other inputs also increased (all of which make growing conditions more uniform and obviate the need for a range of varieties adapted to specific environments). Despite these factors, local varieties are often maintained, even in areas of high MV use. Brush (1992b) reviews evidence from three centres of crop diversity (potatoes in the Peruvian Andes, maize in Mexico, and wheat in Turkey), and finds evidence of the persistence of local varieties despite the introduction of MVs. In the Peruvian case, MV potatoes are grown for their high productivity, but local varieties are prized for their taste and high market price.

Nevertheless, the expansion of commercial agriculture certainly has a strong influence on the diversity of crop varieties grown. As farmers shift to meeting market demands they must use varieties that fulfil processing and handling requirements, and as their operations become more mechanised factors such as plant height or seed size become important. The concentration of variety use is evident even in areas with very productive public plant breeding systems. In Andhra Pradesh, public and private seed enterprises produce seed of over 50 rice varieties. Nevertheless, in any given district, 3 MVs (although not necessarily the same three) occupy between 77 and 95% of the rice area each season (Pal et al., forthcoming).

The adequacy of information exchange also plays a role in this pattern of concentration. We have seen that farmers are often not well informed about what modern (or local) varieties are available. When they rely heavily on their neighbours for information on variety choice, the probability of concentration increases. It is also risky to experiment and time-consuming to obtain information about different varieties, especially if there are well-established markets for a few standard ones. The concentration contributes to risks of loss from disease (as pathogens can more easily build resistance if they have only a few varieties to contend with). However, the social value of planting a more diverse array of varieties is lower than the private value of concentrating on varieties of proven agronomic and market performance (Heisey et al., 1997).

Although much of this concentration may be blamed on markets, it is also possible that markets, and increasingly efficient means of information exchange, can promote diversity. There is some evidence that the situation may be less acute than it was during the earlier years of public plant breeding. A single wheat variety occupied 60% of Northern and Central Italy in the 1920s, for instance, and one variety occupied 80% of the Indian Punjab in the 1950s (before the Green Revolution) (Smale, 1997).[10] As plant breeding programmes expand and produce a wider range of varieties, these extremely high levels of concentration have been reduced, although there is still cause for concern. A telling comparison is provided by two areas of Rajasthan, one with long experience using commercial pearl millet seed and the other more recently introduced to seed markets. Although the range of companies and varieties available is roughly equivalent in the two areas, the farmers in the area with more experience utilise a wider range of varieties and exhibit a much less concentrated pattern of use (Tripp and Pal, 2000) – a difference due in part to wider access to information.

[10]It is not generally appreciated that a significant use of MVs in the Punjab predates the Green Revolution. In 1945, 2.8 million hectares of the Punjab were planted in public wheat varieties (Gill (1978) cited in Wood and Lenné, 1997).

In summary, farmers' use of MVs depends to a considerable degree on the information that is available. Farmers experiment with MVs and exchange information among themselves. Information from extension services is also used, but is often not particularly important. The availability and subsidisation of complementary inputs also influence farmers' choice of varieties. However, the major factors determining the decision to grow a new variety are agronomic performance under particular farming conditions and market acceptability. Nevertheless, it is clear that the information available about MVs is often inadequate. The public sector has not been very effective in providing information that would help farmers distinguish among MVs, and there is often confusion about the names and characteristics of different varieties. Although many MVs are grown by farmers who market little or none of their harvest, the market is a particularly important means of transferring information about new varieties. On the other hand, the market plays a significant part in reducing the incentives for growing diverse varieties and tends to exacerbate the tendency to rely on a relatively few MVs.

Public seed production

The public sector has also played an important role in seed production.[11] Although there are few contemporary instances of public seed enterprises in the industrialised countries, parastatal seed companies are still important in many developing countries. Their existence was originally justified as being a logical conduit for the delivery of public varieties. In most of these countries there was little or no private seed production when the public research institutes became established, and hence few immediate alternatives. The performance of these enterprises has varied greatly between countries, and their continued existence is often difficult to defend with the growth of private seed production capacity.

In India, the National Seeds Corporation was established in 1963, followed by 13 state-level corporations. These public corporations provide well over 100,000 tonnes of rice and wheat seed each year, as well as seed of many other crops (Turner, 1994). Some of India's state seed corporations are self-sustaining, while others are in considerable financial difficulty. In the past decade they have encountered growing competition from the private seed sector, especially for hybrids and other commercially attractive seed (see Table 3.3). Public sector seed companies are the principal suppliers of rice and wheat seed in most other Asian countries as well.

Most of the formal seed activity in sub-Saharan Africa has been through parastatals. The Kenya Seed Company was founded as a private company but the government acquired a controlling interest in 1980 (Rusike, 1995). One of the major exceptions to government control has been the private Seed Co-op of Zimbabwe but, until recently, agreements between the government and the company effectively gave it monopoly

---

[11]There are early examples of state interest in seed supply. In seventeenth-century Mughal India revenue assessors were advised to provide seed loans to needy cultivators in order to promote agricultural production (which was taxed at exceptionally high rates) (Habib, 1999: 295).

status (ibid.). A number of national seed companies in Africa have been closed (e.g., Ghana), sold to private interests (e.g., Malawi) or are on the selling block.

There are several problems with public seed enterprises, one of the most obvious being that their monopoly status seriously detracts from incentives to provide good service. In Mexico, mentioning the name of the state seed company (PRONASE) to farmers often elicited the rhyming reply, *'No nace!'* ('Doesn't germinate!'). This is certainly not to say that all public seed is of low quality, but some employees' opportunities for shirking often gain the upper hand over the public service motivations of others. Not only is the seed quality often low, but state companies are often unable to produce and deliver the seed of crops and varieties suitable for smaller farmers or more marginal growing conditions, although this is one of the main justifications for the public enterprise. In Eastern and Southern Africa, for instance, the public seed companies concentrate most of their efforts on hybrid maize, which could be provided just as well by the private sector.

Public enterprises have often been part of campaigns to promote new varieties. As such, they often benefited from price subsidies. When parastatals were newly established and farmers were being introduced to new varieties, there may have been some justification for subsidies. But those arguments cannot be made today, although there are still many instances of state price support. The market share of the Mexican state seed company rose and fell in the 1980s according to the level of government subsidy (McMullen, 1987). A further disincentive to private seed development is the privileged role accorded state seed enterprises in government extension and rural development activities which, for instance, often specify the use of public sector seed in credit programmes.

It is probably significant that some of the most viable public seed companies exist in India, in the midst of growing competition from the private sector. One of the most successful, the Andhra Pradesh State Seed Corporation (APSSDC), operates in a state with one of the highest concentrations of private seed enterprises. The reasons for its success are complex, and include good management and high demand from the state's farmers . However, the APSSDC is losing ground to the private sector, which is gaining a growing market share of even the corporation's principal product, rice seed. The APSSDC will continue to be an important part of the government's seed provision policy for the foreseeable future, but its strategy of maintaining many production facilities throughout the state (partly in response to political exigencies) is a serious impediment to becoming truly competitive with the private companies (Pal et al., forthcoming). The fate of other public seed companies that are less productive and not so well managed is even more in doubt.

The performance and survival of public enterprises are also tied to political factors. Bates (1995) compares the relative success and efficiency of the Kenyan Coffee Marketing Board with the much poorer performance of the Coffee Marketing Board of Tanzania. He believes the difference can largely be explained by the fact that in Kenya many politicians owned coffee farms and thus had the incentive to ensure that the industry performed efficiently. Tanzania's political base, on the other hand, was not in the coffee-growing regions. Precisely the same set of factors can be used to explain the relative success of the Kenya Seed Company (whose clients and seed growers include important political figures) compared with the dismal performance of the Tanzanian parastatal TanSeed, which has been exceptionally ineffective (Rusike, 1995).

Seed Co-operatives
There are also many instances of public plant breeders attempting to organise farmers to produce seed of public varieties. In the US in the early twentieth century, crop growers' associations were formed to multiply the seed of public varieties, for which the universities often provided quality control and certification services (Kloppenburg, 1988). Even when hybrid maize came to be dominant there was an assumption in some state universities that farmers would still play the leading role in seed production, and they established administrative systems, training programmes and certification services to support farm-level hybrid seed production. In 1939 the state of Wisconsin had 436 farmers producing hybrid maize seed (ibid.). However, these small-scale producers were soon overtaken by larger seed companies that were better able to market their products.

Seed producer co-operatives have been an important part of seed system development in a number of countries. They played an important role in the emergence of the commercial seed sector in France (McMullen, 1987) and Zimbabwe (Rusike, 1995). In El Salvador, the initial development of maize seed production featured small growers; co-operatives then came to the fore, but they have since been overtaken by several local seed companies (Choto et al., 1996).

There are serious limitations to promoting co-operative seed production, however. The majority of instances of successful co-operative production have developed from well-established co-operatives that are either able to produce seed for their members or can exploit particular resources to enter seed production. A number of examples from India illustrate these factors. The National Dairy Development Board has been able to organise its members to produce seeds of fodder crops that are difficult to obtain elsewhere (Baumann and Turton, 1998). A number of co-operatives in Andhra Pradesh produce and sell rice seed as a commercial activity. In virtually all of these cases the co-operatives were already well-established enterprises, with widespread input marketing activities and warehouses and other facilities needed for seed marketing (Tripp and Pal, 2001). In Himachal Pradesh, farmers in a high-altitude zone with strong advantages for seed potato production were able to develop a co-operative that produces and markets seed potato in other parts of the country (Baumann and Singh, 2000).

However, there have been many failures in attempting to establish seed growing co-operatives. Crissman (1989) describes the top-down formation of seed producer associations that were registered as co-operatives in the Philippines. They were unsuccessful because they did not respond to the needs of their members; indeed the main incentive for joining them was to take advantage of subsidised credit. Seed producer co-operatives are subject to many of the problems that affect co-operative development in general. Most important, co-operative formation and activities must be the products of clear demands from the members (Braverman et al., 1991). In too many cases, co-operatives are formed on the initiative of government or donor projects, with little evidence of grass-roots support or understanding.

Regulation

In addition to public sector activities in plant breeding and seed production, the state often plays a prominent role in seed regulation.[12] Before discussing the conduct of seed regulation, we should examine the nature of regulation in general. Regulation is a response to inadequacies in information provision. Although regulation has a range of meanings, a useful one for our purposes is 'the public administrative policing of a private activity with respect to a rule prescribed in the public interest' (Mitnick, 1980: 7). Regulation is justified when conventional legal and market mechanisms are insufficient to ensure a flow of information that affords enough certainty for potential parties in transactions. In such situations, the government establishes special regulatory bodies (e.g., review boards or certification agencies) to provide additional information in order to facilitate commerce.

As with many government activities, however, the motivations and incentives for regulation are more diverse than theory might suggest. Bernstein's (1955) analysis of the history of several US regulatory commissions established during the 1930s provides a useful introduction to the complexities of regulation. The analysis posits a life-cycle for regulatory agencies that includes four stages. In the 'gestation' stage, the agency is established in response to strong public pressure in the face of a crisis in information management. The 'youth' stage is characterised by a crusading attitude in the public interest, although the public may begin to lack comprehension of the need for regulation. The 'maturity' stage sees a regulatory agency performing increasingly routinised duties that feature growing links with the regulated industry. In the final stage, 'old age', the agency is the victim of excessive bureaucracy and may begin to protect the interests of the regulated industry rather than those of the public.

Although this scheme is oversimplified and does not accurately portray the evolution of many regulatory agencies, it is useful for reminding us that the incentives for regulation are complex, and that they may change over time. The staff of government regulatory agencies are often motivated by a desire to serve the public interest and to ensure that adequate information about the regulated industry is available. But government agencies also have an instinct for self-preservation, and regulatory bodies can easily fall into bureaucratic routines that perpetuate and justify their own existence rather than contributing to efficient provision of information. In addition, a regulatory agency must necessarily depend on the regulated industry for much of its information, and relationships often develop that lead to a shift in agency priorities; the agency may end up being 'captured' by the industry and devoting itself to protecting the status quo rather than providing an information environment that promotes productive interchange. Indeed, some theories of regulation argue that its origin is in fact political pressure on government from an industry that wishes to limit competition and to control access to the market (e.g., Stigler, 1971).

---

[12]A more detailed discussion of the origins of seed regulation is to be found in Tripp (1997).

The contributions and inadequacies of government regulation need to be seen against a background of alternative mechanisms for addressing information deficiencies. For instance, procedures for self-regulation can be established in which standards and enforcement are managed by an industry association, the justification for this type of self-regulation being that it enhances consumer confidence and promotes industry growth. On the other hand, such activities may be used to control or limit new entrants to the industry. Independent private regulatory bodies, such as certification authorities, can also be established, and a firm can decide whether to have its products regulated in this way. In cases of voluntary certification (by private or public bodies) it is assumed that the consumer will seek out information about the value of the certification.

In addition to formal regulation, certainly the most important means of overcoming these information deficiencies in formal markets is through the development of reputations, the establishment of brands, and the provision of guarantees (Akerlof, 1970; Klein and Leffler, 1981). If an enterprise invests significant resources in establishing its reputation, consumers perceive that it is unlikely to jeopardise this investment by providing unacceptable products. Brand names have become an important tool for promoting reputations and a means of communicating information about product quality. In a competitive market where consumers have clear choices and products are adequately identified, the need for government regulation is significantly diminished. We now turn to examine how these alternatives for information management are related to the development of seed regulation.

We have seen that seed markets have a number of characteristics that may lead to information asymmetry, with the seed provider having more information than the buyer. First, the farmer may be unfamiliar with the characteristics of the variety on offer. The regulatory response is the establishment of variety release and registration procedures which mandate the description, and often the performance testing, of a variety before it can be sold as seed. Secondly, even if the variety is well known, it may be difficult to ascertain its identity simply by inspecting the seed. A seed certification agency verifies the origin of the source seed used for multiplication and makes field visits to ensure the purity of the seed being grown. Finally, the physical quality of the seed (such as its germination potential and cleanliness) is often impossible to judge until it has been planted. Physical seed quality control is carried out through inspections and laboratory testing, the results of which are used in issuing a certification label.

The development of the formal seed industry in the industrialised countries included many instances of these types of information asymmetry. Early efforts to address the confusion in variety identification were often organised by private bodies. For instance, by 1905 the German Agricultural Society had established a register of commercial crop varieties, which included the morphological characterisation of the varieties and the results of performance testing (Rutz, 1990). Confusion in varietal nomenclature was a problem in the US as well; by the late nineteenth century a single variety of wheat was being traded under 24 different names and an oat variety was known by 18 different names (Parsons, 1985). By the early twentieth century, state crop improvement associations (private organisations affiliated with the agricultural universities) offered inspection services for seed crops. In many European countries the private voluntary efforts at variety registration became part of mandatory government regulation that included performance testing. Current EU seed regulations require that any new field crop variety pass performance tests in at least one member country and be registered in a Common Catalogue of varieties that are eligible for sale. In the US, on the other hand, the seed industry was able to thwart several attempts to establish mandatory variety registration (Kloppenburg, 1988). As a result, varieties may be sold without any type of registration.

If varieties are registered and their distinguishing morphological characteristics are recorded, they are then eligible for certification. In many European countries, voluntary testing schemes were introduced early in the development of the commercial seed industry. The Netherlands Government began providing seed testing services in 1877. A seed certification system was established in Sweden in 1888, under the management of the Royal Swedish Academy of Agriculture (Tripp and van der Burg, 1997). These voluntary schemes eventually led to the mandatory certification system now in force in the EU.

In the UK, we have seen that the rise of commercial seed dealers in the nineteenth century was accompanied by increasing investment in their reputations. They joined an effort to eliminate the sale of fraudulent seed through the passage of the Adulteration of Seeds Act in 1869 (Walton, 1999). However, as the seed trade developed in the early twentieth century, and as public plant breeding began to provide new varieties, there was often confusion in nomenclature, as various traders would offer different names for their selections of the same variety. In the 1920s the National Institute of Agricultural Botany (NIAB) began to establish 'Synonym Committees' for various crops. Although they had no legal status, these were largely successful in enlisting the co-operation of the seed trade to establish a uniform nomenclature for the varieties in use (Kelly and Bowring, 1990). In the late 1940s, the NIAB established a Cereal Field Approval Scheme with seed growers and merchants; participants were required to employ a trained seed crop inspector. In 1964, a Seeds Act established an index of variety names that included penalties for selling seed that was incorrectly labelled (ibid.). When the UK joined the EU, its seed regulations became mandatory.

In the US, most of the early activities in seed certification were managed by the state crop improvement associations. Fitzgerald (1990) describes the activities of the Illinois Crop Improvement Association (ICIA) which had been formed in 1921 to promote 'pure seed' and address farmers' problems of maintaining varietal purity and distinguishing among variety names and synonyms. This was a voluntary activity, but seed growers 'who did not participate in the certification programme found that farmers discriminated against their seed' (ibid.: 123). There were other incentives for companies to support this early certification scheme:

> For the big companies, who had built up a loyal clientele and did not need certification to succeed, membership in the ICIA was both symbolic and strategic. First, in a community of seed producers as fraternal as those in Illinois, the large companies did not want to seem

uncooperative in the pure-seed campaign. Indeed, it was to their advantage to appear magnanimous toward the smaller companies, some of which acted as sellers for them. Second, by participating in the ICIA and in particular by sitting on the board, large companies were able to help design and guide policies to further their own interests (ibid.: 124).

The almost universal participation in the certification programme of the ICIA began to decline in the 1930s. The Depression seriously affected farm incomes, and farmers were less interested in seeking, and paying extra for, certified seed. As hybrid maize became popular, private hybrids began to claim an increasing share of the seed market. The private companies, particularly the larger ones, found that their own quality control procedures and their investment in brand image and reputation were sufficient to attract customer loyalty. Seed certification in the US is voluntary. Much of it is still in the hands of the state crop improvement associations, now organised under the umbrella of the Association of Official Seed Certifying Agencies (AOSCA). Very little private hybrid seed is certified, but much of the commercial seed of crops such as wheat and soybeans is certified by these agencies.[13]

The most obvious feature of the evolution of European and US seed regulatory management is the contrast between mandatory and voluntary strategies. But this is not the most important characteristic from an institutional perspective. Indeed, it is the similarities rather than the differences between these histories that should draw our attention. In both cases, regulation emerged from farmers' concerns about quality during a period of rapidly expanding seed markets. The initial responses were sometimes privately organised, but had the support of state agricultural departments and universities, or grew out of publicly sponsored research or farm support organisations. The battle for regulatory authority between the seed industry and the state has been waged in a relatively transparent political arena. In all cases the private industry played a strong role in determining the shape of regulatory frameworks and a range of mechanisms offered possibilities for farmer representation in the debate.

In addition, the competition between the public and private sectors for regulatory control should not obscure the significant amount of collaboration between them in developing adequate regulation. Although the US has no mandatory variety regulations, varieties of many field crops are regularly submitted to National Variety Review Boards that include representatives of the private certification agencies, scientific societies, private plant breeders, and the US Department of Agriculture (Otto, 1985). On the other hand, EU variety release procedures and certification schemes entrust significant responsibilities and management to private seed companies. It is the similarities in institutional richness and breadth of participation, rather than the differences in authority, that should highlight any comparison of US and European seed regulation.

The evolution of seed regulation in developing countries has tended to follow a different course. The major impetus has come from public sector plant breeding

---

[13]Seed laws are established by the states, rather than the federal government. There is some variation between state laws. For instance, Makus et al. (1992) discuss instances in which certain states have adopted mandatory certification of potatoes, in response to pressure from producer associations, in order to control seed-borne disease and to enhance the reputation of the state's products.

programmes. As these began to develop new varieties, official testing and approval procedures were established. All public varieties were required to pass performance tests before they could be sold as seed. As other varieties became available (from private sources or other public research programmes) 'internal' procedures were adopted for approval of these 'external' varieties. This pattern is common to most developing countries, where private varieties (or indeed any variety from outside the state research establishment) often face lengthy, and at times unclear, testing and registration requirements. The common justification is that this protects farmers from inferior varieties, but there is ample evidence that these testing procedures often ignore conditions and criteria of importance to farmers.[14] These regulations also serve as convenient barriers to foreign varieties that may compete with public ones.[15] With the rapid expansion of the private seed sector some countries are beginning to change their variety regulations. India, for instance, allows the sale of private crop varieties without official testing or registration.

In the early years of public breeding programmes in developing countries seed of new varieties was often produced and sold by parastatal companies. Almost without exception, state certification authorities were also established. The regulatory procedures were usually based on foreign models; Kimenye and Nyangito (1996: 14) describe Kenya's regulations as 'a blend of British law and Dutch regulations', reflecting the country's colonial history and several Dutch seed projects. Despite the demise of the parastatal enterprises, mandatory seed certification remains in place in many countries. Many of the inadequacies in government certification can be described as incentive problems. The government certification agency serves a small number of seed enterprises (often only the parastatal) and is funded from a limited budget. It has little direct communication with farmers, and thus little motivation or opportunity to improve its service. A study in Zambia showed that only 6% of farmers could understand the information on a certification label, even though most of them had experience in buying certified seed (Andren et al., 1991).[16]

Changes are beginning to appear in seed regulation, however, and some countries are beginning to allow the sale of 'truthfully labelled' seed (the label of which describes legally enforceable minimum standards for germination, purity and other qualities). In these cases, responsibility for quality shifts to the seed enterprises. The reform of the Peruvian seed sector, described in Chapter 5, included the establishment of voluntary, decentralised, seed certification agencies (CODESEs). In India, which allows truthful labelling, seed of private varieties is not certified, but private companies or co-operatives may certify the seed of public varieties that they sell. If the enterprise is not well known, government certification may help it gain legitimacy. Most co-operatives that sell rice seed try to have their seed certified (Pal et al., forthcoming). Certified seed is sometimes eligible for government subsidies or other preferential treatment, and this is a further

---

[14]See, for instance, the discussion of the variety testing system in India in Witcombe et al. (1998).

[15]Seed regulations in Pakistan allow the sale of foreign rice or wheat varieties, but they must enter national performance trials and yield at least 20% and 12% (respectively) more than the best local public varieties (Alam and Saleemi, 1996).

[16]Evidence of farmer lack of familiarity with the information on certification tags in India is presented in Tripp and Pal (2000) and Pal et al. (forthcoming).

incentive. On the other hand, the expense and effort required for official certification may be judged unnecessary; one well-known co-operative pointedly avoids the certification agency and uses its reputation to ensure seed sale (ibid.).[17]

As long as strict government regulation is in place, there is little chance of encouraging diversification of national seed systems. Table 6.7 summarises current seed regulations for four African countries. The variety release procedures favour the varieties of the national research programme (and make few concessions for public varieties released in neighbouring countries). Although private varieties can be approved for sale in Malawi and Zambia, only the larger companies are likely to be able to pay the testing fees. In Kenya and Zambia, the formal sale of seed of (unregistered) local varieties would not be permitted. Certification requirements have been relaxed for certain crops in Malawi and Zimbabwe, but all seed must still undergo official government testing for purity and germination. This means that a small seed enterprise, or a grain merchant who wishes to clean and sell grain for seed, must arrange for testing. In Zambia, a simplified scheme of certification and testing has been introduced for the many NGO and donor seed projects found in the country. Although such projects are allowed to operate in the other countries as well, they are illegal under a strict interpretation of the regulations. Finally, there is little provision for point-of-sale inspection (with the exception of Zambia), despite the fact that this is the place where most seed quality problems occur (because of improper handling or storage by inexperienced merchants, or fraud by unscrupulous ones). It is also the place where the agency would have the most direct interaction with farmers, but current regulatory regimes do not give priority to consumer participation or education.

These African cases illustrate the regulatory dilemma faced by many countries. Strict government regulation is a strong disincentive for the emergence of commercial seed enterprises. On the other hand, the absence of regulation could lead to unscrupulous or inexperienced operators providing low quality seed, which would discourage farmers from using the seed market. This is especially a problem in countries where consumer law and protection are weak. The experience of industrialised countries indicates that the best solution may be to break up the current regulatory system, allow more entrepreneurial activity to emerge, and then use the experience of the diversifying seed system to establish new regulatory institutions, based on the equitable participation of farmers, seed enterprises and government.

Summary

The public sector plays a number of important roles in seed system development, one of the most important being support for agricultural research, which has many of the characteristics of a public good. Public plant breeding has been responsible for developing

---

[17]Compare this situation with that of a co-operative in Bolivia selling bean seed. It found that it could sell seed locally without certification because it was well known to nearby farmers; but it realises that it will need to contract the (private) certification service to help it get established in more distant markets (Rosales, 1995).

Table 6.7 National seed regulations

Function	Kenya	Malawi	Zambia	Zimbabwe
Variety release	Varieties must pass through National Performance Trials, but these are not established for all crops	Varieties must be tested in nationwide trials for two years	Varieties must pass mandatory 2 years of testing	Usually 3 years of testing required. Approval required by Varietal Release Committee
	Approval required by National Variety Release Committee. Status of foreign and private varieties not clear	Approval required by Variety Release Committee	Approval required by Variety Release Committee	Procedures for foreign or private varieties not well established
		Private or foreign varieties pay fee for testing	Private or foreign varieties pay for testing	
Seed certification	Mandatory certification for most food crops	Mandatory certification for hybrid maize and tobacco	Only seed of regulated varieties may be produced	Mandatory certification for 7 crops, including maize
		Other crops must pass germination and purity tests	Seed certification and testing are mandatory. In small-scale seed projects, an alternative scheme is being established	From August 1998 seed of groundnut, pearl millet, sorghum may be sold as standard seed but must be tested for purity and germination
		No provision for truthfully labelled seed		
Point-of-sale inspection	Inspection done by National Seed Quality Control Service, but not included in seed legislation.	Inspections provided for by Seed Act. Seed Services conducts annual inspections, but funding is not adequate	Routine inspections managed by Seed Control and Certification Institute	No funding for Seed Services to carry out inspections at point of sale
	No ability to enforce 'stop sale' orders		Approximately 4,000 samples per year	
	Inadequate funds for inspection		Inadequate funding.	

Source: Tripp (2000).

111

many of the crop varieties currently used by farmers. However, the incentives for public sector research are exceptionally complex. There are almost always conflicts with regard to the types of farmers to serve, the orientation of the organisation (practical training versus research), and the degree to which public research should support, compete with, or give way to, the private sector. Public choice theory warns us to pay close attention to the possibilities that public agencies will further their own interests. The likelihood that public research will respond to the problems of particular groups of farmers is highly dependent on those farmers' capacity to make demands on the research organisation.

Information about public varieties is supposed to be transmitted to farmers by extension services. These organisations have had variable success, and there is much evidence to show that farmers often obtain most of their information about public varieties from other farmers. Farmers' organisations can also be important sources of information (and vehicles for interaction with extension and research), but such organisations are most likely to be viable when they address issues that make a significant contribution to farming incomes. Information about new varieties is also transmitted through grain markets. Nevertheless, there is good evidence to show that farmers' current access to information about public varieties is often inadequate.

Although there is little state seed production in industrialised countries, this is still an important public activity in many developing countries. The incentives for state seed monopolies are such that these enterprises rarely provide satisfactory service. There are also examples of co-operatives having been organised for commercial seed production. In almost all successful cases, these co-operatives had already been established for other purposes. Either the seed production responded to the requirements of the co-operative members themselves, or the co-operative had the facilities and commercial contacts that enabled it to expand into seed production. Although most farmers would value a local source of quality seed, successful co-operative production requires strong commercial incentives and cannot be expected to elicit collective action in the absence of clear commercial benefit.

Finally, an important example of public sector participation in seed systems is regulation. The evolution of seed regulatory regimes is an excellent example of institutional development. The major lesson from the history of seed regulation in industrialised countries is that responsibilities must be shared between governments, seed producers and farmers. Regulation should be a response to farmer concerns about information deficiencies in seed markets. The standards and procedures that guide public plant breeding and public seed enterprises cannot simply be transformed into adequate regulatory frameworks for an expanding and diverse seed market. Adequate solutions to information deficiencies in seed markets may include public or private regulatory bodies; consumer law and education; and the establishment of enterprise reputations, brand identities and guarantees. In any event, these regulatory solutions must emerge from open political debate, and they must transmit information that is comprehensible and useful to all parties. Regulation should be the outcome of negotiation between farmers, the seed industry, and the state. As economies and technologies change, further negotiations will modify the evolving institutions of regulation.

7 The Experience of Seed Development Projects

Introduction

The previous chapter described the roles of the public sector in the evolution of national seed systems. In many developing countries the actions of the national government have been augmented by bilateral and multilateral donor assistance. In agricultural research, for instance, donors contribute a significant proportion of the resources available for public research; by 1991, 43% of the funding for public agricultural research for a group of 22 African countries was provided by donors (Pardey et al., 1997). The CGIAR system has also had a significant influence on the course of public agricultural research, although the system's total budget represents less than 2% of total public agricultural research expenditure in developing countries. A large number of donor projects have been established to support agricultural extension systems; the World Bank's efforts at introducing the Training and Visit (T&V) system in many countries is among the best known examples. In addition, many of the parastatal seed companies have been established with donor assistance.

There have been an exceptionally large number of donor seed projects in developing countries. In the 1980s and early 1990s FAO invested US$80 million in 120 seed projects in 60 countries; the World Bank funded over 100 seed projects between 1975 and 1985; and USAID had seed projects in 57 countries between 1958 and 1987 (Maredia et al., 1999).

Most of these donor projects have had a significant influence on the direction and priorities of public seed activities. Donor conceptions of government responsibilities, administrative organisation, and intended clientele have all influenced the performance of the public seed sector. It is thus difficult to draw a line between the public activities described in the previous chapter and the experience of donor seed projects, which is the subject of the present one. The chapter focuses on three types of donor seed activities that have all gained prominence within the past decade or so. They represent a major reorientation of donor strategies towards supporting the public seed system. The three types of projects to be examined include: decentralised or participatory plant breeding, aimed particularly at developing crop varieties more suitable for marginal environments; local-level seed projects that attempt to develop small-scale seed enterprises; and the emergency provision of seed to farmers facing hardships caused by natural disasters or civil conflict.

Although these are three quite different sets of activities, their rise to prominence is related to a common set of factors. Primary among these is the adoption of liberalisation strategies by donors and the imposition of these policies on many recipient governments. Support for public agricultural research and extension has decelerated, and donors and governments are less likely to fund conventional research or extension activities. Donors have become much more interested in encouraging private initiative in agriculture. There is very little sympathy for public seed production, and even research and extension are encouraged to exploit market incentives (Pray and Umali-Deininger, 1998; Rivera, 1996). At the same time, donors have increasingly turned to the NGO sector as an alternative for stimulating agricultural development.[1] NGOs are seen as being more efficient and accountable in their use of donor funds, more willing to innovate, and more in touch with the rural poor than most public agencies (Meyer, 1992). This shift in donor support has been marked by a significant movement of personnel, and as the public research and extension agencies cut back on staff or become less attractive places to work because of funding problems, many former public employees gravitate to the NGOs (Farrington and Bebbington, 1993). In some countries, NGOs now control a significant proportion of the aid budget for agricultural technology development (e.g., Woodhouse, 1997). Finally, the problems of structural adjustment and the rise of the NGO sector, combined with a series of droughts and civil wars, particularly in Africa, have led to the 'institutionalisation and professionalisation of fighting famine' (de Waal, 1997: 23) which includes an increasing capacity to mount localised relief schemes, mostly by NGOs.

These factors have all had a significant influence on the structure of aid to national seed systems. An increasing number of projects for crop variety development adopt a decentralised approach and attempt to shift an increasing amount of the plant breeding and selection on to farming communities. Similarly, relatively little aid now goes to state seed production. Instead, a large number of projects attempt to foster the emergence of local self-help or entrepreneurial production, the theory being that neither public nor conventional private seed enterprises will reach isolated communities and marginal farming systems, and so the organisation of grass-roots production is required. In addition, as NGOs and other agencies develop experience and infrastructure for relief programmes that respond to civil disorder and natural disasters, seed provision has become an increasingly prominent part of their strategies.

This chapter will examine these examples of significant reorientation in donor seed policy. We shall briefly review the performance of these types of project, but our main concern will be the institutional implications. Do these new strategies help establish mechanisms that increase access to the various types of information required for seed system development? Do they contribute to and strengthen local networks of information flow? Do they include appropriate incentive structures that will ensure sustainable performance after project support is ended?

---

[1]No attempt will be made here to provide an inventory of the various types of NGOs. See discussions in Farrington and Bebbington (1993) and Vakil (1997).

Decentralised plant breeding

Critics of the Green Revolution, and of other efforts at agricultural technology development, have pointed out that many farmers have not yet benefited from new crop varieties. An increasingly common response has been to decentralise public plant breeding efforts. This strategy has given rise to a wide range of approaches, including efforts at collecting more relevant information about farmers' conditions and priorities; developing better contacts with client farmers and giving them more responsibilities in setting research directions; organising local seed fairs; bringing plant breeding and variety selection activities to farmers' fields; and organising independent networks of farmer plant breeding and variety selection. We shall briefly review each of these approaches.

Chapter 6 referred to the development of movements such as Farming Systems Research (FSR) that have attempted to provide better information about farmers' circumstances in order to orient public plant breeding priorities. In many cases, public plant breeding has been carried out in isolation from the realities of small farm management. A single example will suffice to illustrate this. In Pakistan, as in most other countries, public maize improvement programmes have emphasised the selection of varieties for high grain yield and resistance to pests and diseases. The research assumes that the crop will be planted under conventional planting densities and crop management. However, the maize management of many Pakistani farmers responds to other priorities. Maize is valued as much for its fodder production as for its grain. It is planted at densities 3 to 4 times as high as the official recommendation and plants are continually removed during the growing season to feed to animals. The failure of many public maize varieties to gain acceptance under these conditions owes much to the fact that breeders pay little attention to selecting for varieties that can thrive under high densities and that have a high green matter production (Byerlee et al., 1989). The ability of a public research system to respond to the needs of its clients depends on its capacity to obtain such information about farmers' priorities and its willingness to use the information to orient breeding programmes.

Most of the early examples of FSR concentrated on obtaining information from farmers through various types of formal and informal interview techniques. As the FSR movement progressed, increasing attention was given to the concept of participation and to the importance of delineating a more proactive role for farmers in the research process. These interests were linked to a broader interest in participatory methodologies for development activities in general, most notably the techniques that have come to be known as 'participatory rural appraisal' (PRA) (Chambers, 1997). With respect to agricultural research, various levels of farmer participation were delineated. One classification (Biggs, 1989) proposes four types of participation: contractual (in which farmers simply agree to provide land for formal experiments); consultative (where farmers and researchers discuss farming problems and potential solutions); collaborative (where farmers and scientists participate as equal partners in research); and collegial (in which scientists concentrate on strengthening farmers' own research capacities).[2]

[2]For a similar taxonomy of levels of participation in political processes see Arnstein (1969).

The growing interest in participatory research led to considerable debate about the meaning and limitations of farmer participation, and the term was sometimes applied to activities that did not represent any real change in the ways researchers communicated with farmers.[3] However, a number of innovations genuinely attempted to place more authority in the hands of farmers. One example is the formation of community committees for agricultural research (known by their Spanish acronym CIAL) in Colombia and several other countries in Latin America (Ashby et al., 1995). These CIALs are supported by donor project funds. The process begins with discussions between farmers and research and extension personnel. In villages where interest is shown, a committee is formed and leaders are elected. The CIAL is then given support in organising its own diagnostic activities and deciding what types of experiments it wishes to undertake. The project helps provide inputs and other support for the experimentation. Farmers are then free to decide how to act on or carry forward the results of their experiments, which may cover a wide range of activities, including testing new crop varieties.

A related activity that is gaining popularity in donor and NGO seed projects is the organisation of local seed fairs (Tapia and Rosa, 1993; Biggs and Matsaert, 1999). These fairs usually feature the display of local varieties of as wide a range of crops as possible, with prizes awarded to farmers displaying the greatest diversity. Such fairs can serve to increase local awareness of genetic resources and can help identify varieties that might be the focus of future breeding or selection efforts.

Much of the initiative in these participatory research activities came from social scientists, but a growing number of examples feature decentralisation strategies managed by plant breeders. There has always been debate about the strategy of plant breeding for wide adaptation. The Green Revolution featured day-length insensitive varieties that were responsive to fertiliser and could be planted in a range of environments; but there are limits to this strategy, and many breeders believe that more effort should go into location-specific plant breeding (Ceccarelli, 1989; Simmonds, 1991). Although the potential of decentralised breeding is easy to appreciate, it does not obviate the need to address many of the challenges of conventional plant breeding: the choice of environments to be targeted, the degree of control to be exercised over the breeding environment, the degree of farmer management, and the criteria to be used for selection. The various answers to these concerns have led to a range of decentralised plant breeding methods.

Witcombe et al. (1996) make the useful distinction between participatory variety selection (PVS), in which farmers participate in testing and choosing among varieties or lines provided by the research service, and participatory plant breeding (PPB), in which farmers make selections among unfinished breeding lines and may even make their own crosses. PVS has much in common with many of the on-farm variety testing activities of FSR and participatory methods. PPB, on the other hand, implies the contribution of farmers at a much earlier stage in the breeding process. Although most examples of PVS and PPB involve the testing and development of public varieties, farmers' local varieties or landraces may also feature in these activities.

[3]For a review of the problems associated with the use of the term 'farmer participation' see Tripp (1989).

A final example of decentralised plant breeding can be distinguished not so much by its technical procedures as by its political stance. There are a number of plant breeding activities, mostly run by local NGOs, that emphasise the establishment of farmer-managed variety development as an alternative to public sector research. Some of these efforts may maintain relations with the public research or university service, but a primary goal is farmer empowerment. One of the older examples is MASIPAG, a programme in the Philippines that emphasises: the selection of varieties that require few external inputs, the use of local varieties, the organisation of plant breeding to address farmers' perceived needs, and the capacity of farmers 'to gain control of their seeds' (Salazar, 1992: 25). Such activities are tied closely to NGO activities that oppose the current political regime and attempt to gain more voice for the rural poor. The organisation of an alternative breeding programme to the Green Revolution 'machine' managed by the government offers both symbolic and material advantages to participants.[4]

Most of these approaches to the decentralisation of plant breeding either feature a shift in the way donor funds support public plant breeding or abandon public research altogether for alternative strategies in the hands of local or Northern NGOs. They do not, however, escape the dilemma of defining the incentives for research that were discussed in Chapter 6. In particular, the question of identifying which clients to serve, the choice between building up farmer capacity and advancing research, and the influence of professional goals all contribute to the complexity of the incentive systems for decentralised schemes. Decentralised plant breeding may make it possible to address location-specific problems better, but precisely which farmers participate is still largely determined by the agency or the NGO in charge of the programme. Within agricultural research organisations, 'objective' science cannot be disentangled from political positions, and there is still considerable scope for scientists to choose research problems and methods that correspond to their own political visions. The decentralised breeding methods also exhibit a wide range of philosophies on the prospects and limitations of building up farmers' own capacities. Finally, shifts in funding priorities now make this type of local-level research a more attractive career path for professional breeders.

Most of the efforts at decentralised plant breeding are less than a decade old and it is difficult to present any firm conclusions about their performance. But it is worth asking how they have affected the flow of information between breeders and farmers, and among farmers themselves; what incentives are in place to ensure that such efforts are sustainable; and what impact these strategies might have.

Decentralised plant breeding projects have demonstrated that farmers are able to choose from among a range of varieties or breeding lines that are grown in on-farm or experimental station plots (Thiele et al., 1997; Sperling et al., 1993). The farmers' choices may differ from those of the breeders because of different priorities, and this information should be useful to breeders in adjusting their selection criteria. However, all varieties embody a range of characteristics, so trade-offs and compromises have to be

---

[4]Similar movements include a network of NGOs in Brazil working with groups of small farmers and unions of rural labourers, and the Save the Seeds Movement in Uttar Pradesh, which includes an emphasis on strengthening traditional agriculture as part of a range of self-help activities (McGuire et al., 1999).

made. It is interesting to note the importance of market characteristics in the criteria that farmers often emphasise in PVS (e.g., Thiele et al., 1997) or PPB (Sthapit et al., 1996). On the one hand, it underlines once again the importance of markets as determinants of farmers' choice of varieties.[5] On the other hand, it raises questions about the possibility that these projects may be biased towards farmers with greater market orientation. A relevant example is described by Ashby et al. (1987), where male and female farmers in Colombia were asked to evaluate new bean varieties; men's choices emphasised marketability, while women's choices featured food-preparation characteristics.

These instances of decentralised plant breeding can undoubtedly provide information to help orient crop research programmes, but what are the incentives for farmers to participate? The concept of public goods tells us that the costs of organising research among a large number of farmers, the slow progress to be expected, and the difficulty of excluding non-participants from the benefits, all justify the existence of a public agricultural research programme. In a sense, many participatory research activities would seem to challenge these assumptions. Granted that many of the activities are meant to be complementary to a formal public programme, it is still important to assess the costs and benefits to the participants.

Participation in variety selection activities may demand considerable time from farmers (Thiele et al., 1997), and this has a high opportunity cost for the poor, who hope to see immediate results from their investments (Farrington and Bebbington, 1993). A description of a participatory research programme in the Philippines lists a range of activities, including exploratory surveys, consultative meetings, validation workshops, planning workshops, technology trials, monitoring visits and field days (Campilan et al., 1999). One wonders how many farmers are able to contribute to these types of activities on a regular basis. A description of formally organised communal variety development in China gives an idea of the resource requirements for the successful pursuit of this strategy. A large number of farmers participate in the experiments, between 5 and 10% of the land of each brigade is set aside for experimentation, and the results are regularly published and distributed (Sheridan, 1981).

A recent analysis of the CIALs established in Honduras provides useful insights into the prerequisites for successful farmer participatory activity (Humphries et al., 2000). More than 50 CIALs have been established in Honduras. Although they are encouraged to carry out all types of relevant experimentation, the major part of their activities has been related to variety testing. Those that have been more successful tend to be found in communities that show evidence of a high degree of pre-existing social capital, i.e., where there is experience of previous community organisation and collective action, and the original members tend to have more resources than other community members and to have had experience of other projects. The management of the project had to address this problem and ensure wider participation in the CIAL activities and wider access to its

---

[5]The importance of markets may also be underappreciated in industrialised countries. A review of public potato research notes that '[a]lthough market preferences have ultimately shaped the consequences of potato breeding in North America, some would contend that even more attention could be paid to market demand to enhance the effectiveness of public-sector breeding programmes' (Walker, 1994: 25).

results (S. Humphries, personal communication). These observations echo experiences from the development of farmer groups in the industrialised countries, where farmers with more resources and broader networks are more likely to see returns from investing in group membership.

The major incentive for a farmer to invest in participatory activities is the possibility of gaining access to productive innovations. As progress is generally slow, farmers are likely to lose interest in group activities focused exclusively on agricultural experimentation. The CIALs in Honduras have found that the establishment of commercial production plots (to compensate members for voluntary work) and access to credit or community stores are often necessary to maintain participation. This is similar to experience in Mali, where Gubbels (1997) questions whether community experimentation and extension activities are a sufficient basis for the development of sustainable farmer organisations.

There is good evidence that innovations in decentralised plant breeding help build up farmers' capacity to experiment and to interact with formal research organisations. However, their sustainability without external support is open to question. We have seen that farmer groups and associations are most likely to form during periods of rapid growth in the agricultural sector, when group membership provides access to valuable information about new technologies. In addition, farmer associations are more likely to form around specific commodities with strong commercial demand. As Chapter 4 made clear, commercial incentives are not the only motivation for farmer experimentation, but farmers must have the time and the curiosity to devote to this activity, and be able to derive at least some type of community recognition or prestige from the results.

In any case, clear incentives for long-term involvement in local plant breeding must be evident. Discussions of participatory plant breeding in developing countries sometimes use the example of Dutch 'hobby breeders' as a potential model. These are usually retired farmers who volunteer to carry out selections on potato breeding material provided by public research or private companies. A small number of these farmers have made significant contributions to the development of commercially successful varieties. What is often overlooked is the fact that the identification of a successful variety entitles the selector to a share of the royalties, which could be as much as £20,000 per year (Lamont, 1993).

No matter how successful decentralised plant breeding may be in identifying useful new varieties, a number of questions still remain to be answered. First is the issue of impact. As yet we have little information on whether participatory plant breeding for many isolated and presumably distinct environments will yield a significant number of varieties with superior productivity. And, even if the results are positive, it is not clear how such processes can be scaled up to meet the needs of hundreds of other environments (Almekinders and Louwaaars, 1999). In addition, the identification of a new variety is of little use unless there is a mechanism for seed diffusion. We have seen that farmer-to-farmer movement of seed is often responsible for significant diffusion of new varieties, but whether such a system is capable of providing effective access to, and information about, location-specific varieties from participatory programmes is much in doubt. These questions will not be answered, however, until there is documentation on the adoption of varieties developed through these techniques and analysis of their costs.

Local-level seed production

The failure of many state seed enterprises in developing countries to deliver an adequate range or supply of seed, coupled with the slow growth and limited focus of the commercial seed sector, has led to a search for alternative methods of seed provision. One of the most common responses has been the organisation of local-level seed production projects by donors, NGOs, and national governments. These projects take various forms, but have a common strategy of providing training and incentives for farmers to produce and sell seed in their local area. There are certainly precedents for this type of development. Chapter 5 described several examples of farmers acquiring seed production skills and developing their own seed businesses. However, the experience of these local production projects has so far provided few examples of successful and sustainable commercial activity. This section explores the performance and the problems of these projects.

Many local-level seed projects require the formation of farmer groups. Individual farmers rarely have enough land to support a viable seed enterprise, and even those who do may not want to risk concentrating their resources on a new activity. The seed production is usually carried out on individual group members' land, although occasionally the group may acquire access to a plot that they manage jointly. Even if formal groups are not established, the NGO or project staff usually co-ordinate the activities of individual farmer growers. The projects are usually regarded as a way of meeting seed requirements in a local area. The majority of projects organise the multiplication of MV seed, but some promote the use of local crop varieties. (In many cases, the projects confuse the goal of introducing seed of a new MV with that of establishing a sustainable seed enterprise.)

In most cases the source seed is obtained through project staff. If it is seed of MVs, it is often acquired from the government research stations. In some cases the varieties to be multiplied have been identified by participatory variety selection. (For example, a few CIALs in Colombia have selected promising varieties from their experiments and have been assisted in establishing small enterprises that multiply this seed for sale to neighbouring farmers (Ashby et al., 1995).) The projects usually provide technical training to the participating farmers on seed production and storage methods. Arrangements are often made for some type of quality control (and occasionally for official certification). In some cases the project purchases the seed from the farmers for sale or distribution, but in many other cases the farmers are encouraged to sell the seed themselves.

There have been an extraordinarily large number of these local-level seed projects in the past decade or so. The model appeals to NGOs as well as to bilateral and multilateral donors.[6] In some cases local governments also follow this strategy.[7] Wiggins and Cromwell (1995) assessed the performance of some NGO seed projects in Latin America, Africa, and Asia and found that most had not achieved financial or organisational stability.

Table 7.1 summarises the range of seed multiplication projects found in Zambia in 1999. It shows the various models used for organising local-level seed production and illustrates the wide range of donor and government interest in this type of activity. These projects are funded by international and local sources; some have nationwide coverage while others are confined to one part of a province. Many of these projects involve the participation of government extension and seed regulatory personnel.

Local-level seed projects are subject to a number of problems. There is often confusion about goals and target participants and a lack of clarity about whether the principal objective is to increase the incomes of the participants or to develop a sustainable source of high quality seed. Some projects view seed production as a means of providing a source of income for even the most poverty-stricken farmers. However, simply because farmers are able to multiply and save seed for their own use does not mean that they can become successful commercial seed growers. Like other forms of contract farming, seed growing requires a certain level of skill and resources. In cases where small farmers have become successful commercial contract growers, an initial investment in training, organisation and credit has often been necessary (Benziger, 1996). Projects that have attempted to target their seed multiplication activities to the poorest sectors of the farming community usually have not been successful, and have often been unable to make any useful improvement to local seed supply.

There are some exceptions where the poorest members of a community can earn income as seed producers. These usually involve cases where the production process is exceptionally time-consuming. Baumann and Turton (1998) describe how some landless women in India have been able to earn a living by collecting fodder grass and processing and selling the seed. The high labour requirements, and the fact that the grasses are collected from common land, give these women a comparative advantage in this seed production activity. Much of the demand for this seed comes from government-sponsored wasteland rehabilitation programmes. Similarly, Lyon (1997) describes how older women in Ghanaian villages may specialise in growing tomato seedlings (which requires considerable time but very little land) for sale to their commercial tomato-growing neighbours.

One of the major failings of most local-level seed projects has been to ignore the importance of transaction costs in the process. The projects often confuse seed multiplication with seed provision, overlooking the fact that seed multiplication is only one part of the process. Source seed is usually provided by the project, and it is usually project staff who make the arrangements for its delivery. Thus the participating farmers do not

---

[6]Examples of the latter include the Inter-American Development Bank in Guatemala (Ortiz et al., 1991).

[7]In India, for instance, the Andhra Pradesh Department of Agriculture has initiated a 'Seed Village Programme' in which selected farmers are provided with access to source seed of rice and groundnuts. They receive advice on seed production methods and are then expected to sell the seed to other farmers in their village (Pal et al., forthcoming).

Table 7.1 Local-level seed projects in Zambia

Project	Donor	Coverage	Crops	Type of project
Southern Province Household Food Security Program	IFAD	Southern Province	Bambara nut, cowpea, groundnut, sesame, sorghum, sunflower, sweet potato	Seed growers trained in each district. Project buys seed from them, distributes to village seed committees
Luapula Livelihood and Food Security Program	FINNIDA	Luapula Province	Beans, cassava, finger millet, groundnut, rice, sorghum, sweet potato	Farmers loaned seed for multiplication, and encouraged to sell seed
Multiplication and Distribution of Seed/ Planting Materials	SIDA	Northern, North-western, Southern and Western Provinces	Cowpea, finger millet, groundnut, pearl millet, sorghum	156 farmers trained in seed production; expected to become seed producers
Smallholder Farm Systems Diversification Program	UNDP	Eastern, Lusaka, Central, Northern, Copperbelt and Luapula Provinces	Beans, cassava, cowpeas, finger millet, groundnuts, maize, pearl millet, rice, sunflower, sorghum, soybean, sweet potato	164 farmers trained in seed production; expected to sell to other farmers or to merchants
Drought Rehabilitation Program	SIDA	Southern, Lusaka, Eastern, Western and North-western Provinces	Cassava, cowpea, groundnut, pearl millet, sorghum, sweet potato	Farmers trained as seed entrepreneurs; project also helps move seed between areas
Livingstone Food Security Program (CARE)	USAID	3 districts in Southern Province	Bambara nut, green gram, groundnut, maize, millet, sorghum, sunflower	Farmers being trained to be seed entrepreneurs
Bulima Seed Growers Association	EU	Mpongwe District, Western Province	Groundnut	Group has sold seed to various donor projects; also attempts its own marketing
International Union for Conservation of Nature (IUCN) Seed Multiplication Program	World Bank	Lukulo District, Western Province	Cowpea, maize, rice, sorghum	Farmers are loaned seed to multiply. Repay loan to project, which distributes to other farmers
Chipata Diocese Development Project	Miserio (Catholic Church)	Several districts in Eastern Province	Groundnuts, maize, sunflower	As above
Farming Systems Research Team	Govt of Zambia	Kaloma District, Southern Province	Cassava, cowpea, groundnut, maize, pearl millet, sorghum	Farmers multiply seed and are expected to sell it to others
Rural Community Development and Motivation Project	Lutheran World Federation	Several districts in Eastern Province	Several crops	Seed is loaned to farmers and farmer groups for multiplication

Source: Zulu and Miti (1999)

acquire the skills or contacts to obtain source seed on their own, when the project comes to an end. Project staff also take upon themselves the costs of co-ordinating and monitoring the activities of the participating growers. Arrangements for external quality control are usually made by project staff, and again the participating farmers have little say in determining the regulation of their production.[8] Finally, the project staff often play an important role in arranging for the sale of the seed.

[8]The government seed certification agency in Zambia has instituted a separate, simplified system of seed certification for the many seed projects operating in the country (Zulu and Miti, 1999).

Seed marketing is a particularly glaring weakness in most local-level projects. When projects leave marketing responsibilities to the farmers, they are rarely able to sell significant amounts of seed; they have little experience in promoting their seed and few have commercial contacts that might help. We saw in Chapter 4 that much of the seed that is exchanged at community level moves through ties of kinship or friendship, and the project's farmers usually have difficulty expanding beyond these networks. In addition, most seed sold from one farmer to another attracts only the price of grain, and it is difficult for project farmers to charge the premium required to compensate for their extra investment and time. Although the 'seed' price often rises close to planting time, this usually reflects the scarcity of seed and grain at this time. Farmers who obtain a higher price for their seed are often being rewarded for the cost of grain storage rather than for seed quality.

A review of several such projects in southern Africa showed that, although they are often effective at helping to multiply and diffuse seed of new crop varieties, they are not appropriate to set the stage for sustainable enterprise development (Tripp, 2000). In one NGO project in Malawi (Msimuko, 1997), more than 300 farmer groups were formed to multiply and sell seed of new crop varieties. The vast majority of these groups chose to concentrate on multiplying seed of a new groundnut variety. Although many groups were able to multiply the seed, only a minority were able to sell a significant quantity to other farmers. The successful groups were able to sell up to 500 kg of the seed in one season. Some initiated ingenious promotion campaigns, announcing their seed at church meetings or posting hand-written slips of paper at market places. The seed selling price was usually no more than the grain price; in some cases group members sold the seed for less than the grain price to pay off their loan from the project. The sale of 500 kg of groundnut seed (by a group of 10–20 farmers) to neighbouring farmers who are purchasing on average 10 kg of seed each (enough for a tenth of a hectare) was useful for helping to diffuse the new variety, but was no basis for a viable enterprise (Phiri et al., 1999).

Not only do the projects usually cover many of the important transaction costs associated with developing a seed enterprise, but they also cover other costs as well, such as the provision of credit, inputs, and storage facilities. These provide added incentives for farmer participation, but do not contribute to financial sustainability. There is little evidence that these projects establish local enterprises with a viable financial structure (Wiggins and Cromwell, 1995). Projects may also arrange to buy the farmers' seed, contributing to the illusion of commercial success.[9] Table 7.2 summarises information about a donor project in Bolivia that organises PESEMs (the Spanish acronym for 'small seed enterprises') to produce seed potato. Each PESEM includes up to 30 farmers who manage seed production on their own plots. The PESEMs are quite popular because the price they receive for their seed potato is well above what they could get in the local market. The catch is that most of this seed is sold through the project itself or directly to NGOs which use the seed to distribute to their own farmers. The table illustrates the

[9]The most successful seed-producing CIAL in Colombia sells about half of its seed to the local extension agency, which uses it for other projects (J. Roa, personal communication).

Table 7.2 Donor support for small seed enterprises (PESEMs) in Bolivia

Activity	Support
Source seed	Purchased from state agency responsible for source seed. Agency is attempting to achieve financial autonomy but still receives some Swiss funds.
Credit	PESEMs receive some credit from Dutch project (PROSEMPA).
Seed Quality Control	Certification agency is supposed to be self-financing, but receives 50% of budget from donor (USAID) and 20% from Bolivian government.
Technical advice	Advice provided to seed groups by PROSEMPA.
Storage	Some communal seed stores provided by PROSEMPA.
Seed marketing	Most seed sold to potato producer groups sponsored by PROSEMPA or to NGOs that distribute seed to farmers.

Source: Bentley and Vasques (1998)

degree to which these 'enterprises' depend on the support of various donor activities in the Bolivian seed sector. One of the few PESEMs with any chance of long-term sustainability is a group of 10 women ('Las Juanas') that was formed long before the project began (by the current members' mothers) to produce and market handicrafts. They have since expanded into other economic activities, including seed. They avoid selling their seed to institutional buyers and instead display their produce at weekly markets and organise promotional demonstrations in neighbouring communities (Bentley and Vasques, 1998). It is the group's previous organisational and marketing experience that determines their success.

Another country that has had several small-scale seed projects is Nepal. Table 7.3 summarises the experience of four major seed projects in Nepal, demonstrating the degree to which the projects covered the transaction costs usually associated with organising a seed enterprise. The table illustrates, unfortunately, the general lack of impact of this approach.

The major exception in the Nepal example is the performance of the Seed Sector Support project (SSSP) that is the successor to the Koshi Hills Seed and Vegetable Development Project. The SSSP promotes commercial vegetable seed production among hill farmers.[10] The project helps organise and train groups of farmers (typically about 12 farmers per village) to produce vegetable seed. It also arranges an annual 'workshop' attended by representatives of these producer groups and by seed merchants – wholesalers or retailers – who are members of the Seed Entrepreneurs Association of Nepal (SEAN). During the workshop the farmers make offers of the types and quantities of seed they can produce the following year, and the merchants detail their requirements. The two groups bargain, quantities and prices are agreed, and contracts are drawn up. The project then seeks to acquire sufficient source seed (mostly from government

[10]Much of the information on this project is derived from the author's participation in a project review in Nepal in January 2000.

Table 7.3 Local-level seed projects in Nepal

Project	ActionAid rural developmental programmes for seed production 1984–95	Agriculture Research and Production Project 1980–88	Mechi Hills Development Programme 1987–92 (first phase) 1992–98 (second phase)	Koshi Hills Seed and Vegetable Development Project 1992–7 (successor project initiated)
Donor country	UK	US	The Netherlands	UK
Strategy	Farmer groups are formed to produce and sell seed of food grains.	Farmers are trained to meet local seed demands for food grains.	Groups (mostly females) formed to produce seeds of cereals and vegetables.	Groups formed for the production and sale of seed grains, vegetables and potatoes.
Source seed	Provided by the project. After the project was completed, farmers tried to get some seed from research stations or extension, but were not successful.	Project obtained seed from research stations. After the project, farmers continued trying to get seed from research stations	Project selected varieties for farmers and obtained source seed from research stations.	Project obtained seed from research station for participating farmers.
Seed multiplication	Done by groups, with assistance from project. Farmers with more resources were more likely to participate.	Growers received training, subsidised inputs, storage bins; concentrated on 'progressive' farmers.	Project attempted to target resource-poor farmers as seed producers, but this was not successful.	Seed multiplication done by groups. Training and some subsidised inputs provided.
Seed quality	Project arranged and paid for seed certification.	Project arranged and paid for seed certification.	Technical supervision and seed testing by experiment station staff.	Technical supervision by project staff and seed testing by experiment station staff.
Seed marketing	Originally project bought the seed; later encouraged farmers to sell seed on their own.	Farmers were expected to sell to other farmers, but project bought unsold seed.	Project tried to arrange seed sale to institutional buyers but with little success.	Seed of grains was sold through co-operative associated with project. Vegetable seed sold to merchants.
Current status	Little evidence of any continuing seed sale. In one area a new NGO has been formed for agricultural development including seed production. NGO attempting to make links with an established co-operative for access to source seed and for seed sale.	Most seed production abandoned. A few former participants produce and sell seed, but on a limited scale.	Groups have been disbanded.	Most groups for grain and potato seed have ceased production. Vegetable seed production continues and is supported by a new project (SSSP). Seed is sold to merchants who make contracts in advance, or through a co-operative.

Sources: Joshi, 1995 and 1999

research stations and farms) and sells it to the producer groups for multiplication. In the 1998/9 season, 81 groups delivered a total of 36 tonnes of vegetable seed (of about 10 different species) to the traders.

The project has had considerable success for several reasons. First, it deals with a product that is in high demand. Fresh vegetable production has increased significantly in the past decade, largely in response to growing urban demand. Merchants can earn a significant amount from the sale of vegetable seed; one survey indicates that about one-quarter of the income of small agricultural input shops in Western Nepal is derived from the sale of domestically-produced vegetable seed (Chitrikar, 1999). There is also a small, but growing, market for vegetable seed export, principally to India and Bangladesh. Although most of these vegetables have been grown by hill farmers for many years, farm-level seed production requires extra labour and time. (Seed production for radish, the most widely demanded vegetable, requires keeping the crop in the field an extra few months.) In addition, the hills offer a much better environment for seed production for some of these vegetables than other areas where they may be grown as commercial or subsistence crops. Another reason for success is that the project builds upon commercial traditions. Seed traders in Nepal have several decades of experience contracting individual farmers to grow vegetable seed. (A significant amount of packaged, commercial vegetable seed is also imported, or brought in as loose seed by traders from India.) However, much of this contracting has been done near the capital Kathmandu, while the project has helped extend the activity to more remote regions that have excellent environments for growing vegetable seed. Because most of the seed-growing farmers have exceptionally small landholdings, the establishment of groups facilitates efficient communication with the merchants. In addition, with most of the villages at least several hours' walk from the nearest road, the project has helped form two co-operative organisations that maintain contact with the farmer groups and arrange for delivery of the seed to the merchants, in return for a commission.

The principal challenge to be overcome is the fact that the project still serves as the broker for government source seed. However, a number of seed merchants have recently formed a commercial enterprise ('Seed Service Centre') which plans to produce and sell source seed of a number of vegetables. Merchants can then buy their requirements of source seed and deliver it to the farmer groups (and other farmers) with whom they have established contracts. The example illustrates, once again, the significant bottleneck that can exist when source seed production is controlled by public seed systems.

A number of unexpected developments demonstrate the potential viability of the project's strategy (and indicate possible future directions). In the first place, the project is finding it increasingly difficult to measure the amount of seed produced and delivered because a number of groups and merchants have started to establish contracts independent of the annual workshops and marketing co-operatives. In the area where most villages are far from roads, the marketing co-operative continues to be viable, but in the area where villages are less isolated it is not well utilised. In one case a small seed company (most of whose staff are former employees of a government research station) has contracted for all of the seed production from groups in one district and has stationed someone in the district to help supervise the production. In another case, six merchants in a large town have combined to contract with a number of producer groups in a particular area. On the producers' side, the profitability of the enterprise is indicated by the fact that many of them have taken on outgrowers, other farmers in the community who produce seed and sell it through the group. In one case, a group close to a road has switched to fresh vegetable production (which it finds more profitable) but has developed an associated outgrower group of producers located in a more isolated village. The fact that other farmers have sufficient incentives to grow vegetable seed and market it through the medium of the established groups indicates the strength of this new institutional arrangement and bodes well for the growth of the commercial vegetable seed market.

Another successful local-level seed project is to be found in Ghana (Lyon and Afikorah-Danquah, 1998). The NGO Sasakawa-Global 2000 was instrumental in establishing a system for the production and marketing of OPV maize and cowpea seed after the collapse of the parastatal Ghana Seed Company. The alternative system is based on about 100 seed producers, each with only a few hectares of land. (Many of these were previously contract growers for the state seed company.) The project helped establish three regional growers' associations (SGAs). The growers register with the government seed certification agency (GSID) and obtain foundation seed. They are expected to arrange for the cleaning and storage of their seed (usually at government facilities that belonged to the defunct seed company). They are also expected to arrange for the sale of their seed to input dealers, who in turn sell it to farmers. The input dealers are mostly very small shops operating in cities and larger towns, which sell agricultural chemicals, vegetable seeds and other agricultural equipment, and are now beginning to sell maize and cowpea seed. The system has been in operation since 1990 and has produced as much as 1,000 tonnes of maize seed per year. Its early years saw considerable investment in credit, materials and training from the NGO, but this has declined significantly in recent years. The system continues to operate and, although it is not without problems, it is certainly one of the more viable examples of project-initiated small-scale seed production to be found in Africa.

Table 7.4 summarises some of the differences between expected and actual performance in the Ghanaian case. It illustrates how important the local institutional environment is to the success of seed enterprise development. Line 1 describes the provision of foundation seed, which is handled in a rather mechanical fashion. Although the hope was that the growers, through their associations, would ask for foundation seed based on the perceived demand for different varieties, they are in fact usually able to exert only limited influence over which varieties they grow. In this sense, the system has not promoted an efficient flow of information between the public plant breeding organisation and farmers.

The growers are expected to finance their own production. Although state agricultural development banks are in operation, they are not utilised by the seed growers. Instead, finance is obtained through loans either from seed dealers, who pre-finance the growers in exchange for access to the seed, or from private individuals. The informal loan market

Table 7.4 Expected and actual performance in small-scale seed provision in Ghana

Activity	Expected performance	Actual performance
Gaining access to foundation seed.	Growers should ask for foundation seed based on demand for varieties. Requests should be made through SGA.	Farmers registered for foundation seed with GSID. Little choice of variety.
Financing seed growing.	Growers should use own resources or take loans from agricultural development banks.	Seed dealers pre-finance seed production. Loans also obtained through friends and church members.
Access to conditioning equipment.	Growers should arrange for seed conditioning at government facilities.	Dealers provide loans for conditioning and storage. Some growers develop personal links with equipment operators.
Seed dealers purchase seed from growers.	SGA should co-ordinate contracts between growers and dealers.	MOFA and GSID field staff provide information about seed availability. Growers develop reputations. Growers often provide credit to dealers.
Promotion, advertising.	MOFA extension should promote seed use.	Individual dealers promote seed. Many use agents, including extension personnel, to sell in villages.

GSID = Ghana Seed Inspection Division
MOFA = Ministry of Food and Agriculture
SGA = Seed Growers Association

Source: Lyon and Afikorah-Danquah (1998)

is quite important and tends to be mediated by ties of friendship or often by membership of the same church. So although the formal credit system does not serve the seed producers, there are well-established informal means of obtaining loans.

The growers are also responsible for conditioning and storing their own seed. Most of the cleaning equipment is owned by a government agency that has taken over some of the facilities of the former parastatal. Farmers must pay to have their seed cleaned and, because of the high heat and humidity, must often pay for cold storage until the seed is ready for sale. The costs of these operations are often covered by loans from the seed dealers. There is high demand for the cleaning equipment at harvest time, and growers often develop personal links with the machinery operators to facilitate access.

It should be emphasised that this project does not assume that the growers will sell their seed directly to farmers, but rather relies on established input dealers. In theory the grower associations are supposed to organise the sale of seed to the dealers but in fact most arrangements are made on an individual basis. There is a potential information problem here, with a large number of individual growers seeking to make contact with dealers. The supervisory staff of the certification agency, as well as extension personnel, have emerged in a useful brokering role. They are aware of which growers have seed for sale, and are also able to provide information about the condition of a grower's crop. In addition, as growers and dealers gain more experience, they are able to establish more permanent links that can be exploited in future seasons. Most growers sell their seed to several dealers each season.

Finally, although the seed is popularised through official extension programmes, it is also promoted through the initiative of the dealers, who often arrange their own advertising and demonstrations. Most dealers are small operators who do not have wide coverage. One of the ways they extend their coverage is by the use of agents, who may be small entrepreneurs, farmers, or extension personnel, to sell seed in the villages. Most of these agents receive the seed on credit, and the dealers have to use local contacts and networks to identify trustworthy agents.

The Ghana case demonstrates some strengths and weaknesses as an example of small-scale seed development. Perhaps the greatest strength of this system is the full incorporation of input dealers with the experience, contacts and financial resources for seed marketing. One of its weaknesses is the top-down management of source seed provision and the relative lack of information exchange between the seed system and the public breeding institute. In addition, there are uncertainties and inefficiencies in the management of seed conditioning, but so long as the government manages the old seed company facilities there will be few incentives to look for alternative arrangements.

The case also provides valuable lessons for institutional development. On the one hand, the project's top-down creation of grower associations has failed to lead to viable or effective organisations. On the other hand, the crucial role of established trading contacts and the use of friendships and common church membership to channel credit and to identify trustworthy partners illustrate how entrepreneurial activity is embedded in established social relations. However, this seed system does not rely solely on existing networks for its development. When new opportunities arise for the management of information, unexpected actors may play a role, as with the brokering of information on seed availability by certification personnel. And when opportunities arise for selling seed in distant villages, new commercial relations are formed between dealers and agents. If local-level seed projects are to succeed, they must take advantage of existing networks and encourage their expansion, as illustrated by the Ghana case.

Emergency seed programmes

When a natural disaster such as a drought or flood strikes a farming community, standing crops may be lost and farmers' major source of seed for the next season may be jeopardised. When civil war affects rural areas, farmers may be prevented from planting, have their crops destroyed, or be forced to move to safer areas, which may also affect seed supply. These instances of natural disaster and political strife are increasingly met by relief programmes organised by multilateral agencies, bilateral donors and a range of NGOs. The relief programmes naturally focus on providing food, shelter, and medical assistance, but a significant number of them also include seed provision as part of an effort to re-establish farming after the emergency.

The organisation of any relief programme is fraught with difficulties, and seed provision in post-disaster conditions presents a number of challenges. Aid agencies have not always performed well in these situations. For instance, many emergency seed efforts have paid insufficient attention to identifying appropriate varieties, with the result that farmers have been disappointed by the performance of the seed donated. In addition, emergency seed is sometimes of low quality, and it may be delivered well after the optimum time for planting. However, this is not the place for a detailed examination of the performance of seed provision following acute emergencies.[11] Of more relevance to our interests here are the relationships between emergency seed projects and local seed provision, and the incentives for such projects to become permanent features of donor or government seed strategies.

One of the principal weaknesses of emergency seed provision is its lack of sensitivity to local seed systems. The assumption is often made that local farmers have no access to seed following a disaster. This assumption is often unfounded. A study carried out following the civil war in Rwanda showed that over half the farmers had been able to harvest, even during the height of the crisis. Because food aid had been provided, they were able to save some of their harvest for seed. In addition, small rural markets continued to function, and farmers could obtain fresh seed of a wide range of varieties through these markets, or by bartering with neighbours (Sperling, 1996). The principal problem was probably lack of resources to acquire seed, rather than any absolute shortage.[12]

A particularly useful example of the performance of local seed systems during emergencies is provided by the story of a seed relief project in Ethiopia (Pratten, 1997). An assessment undertaken by an NGO in early 1995 in a highland area of northern Wollo, Ethiopia indicated that poor rainfall the previous season had left many farmers without seed to plant their next barley crop. Seed distribution projects were common in Ethiopia at this time, usually based on loans of seed in order to reduce dependency. Most of these projects were managed through government-supported peasant associations. The NGO was concerned about the lack of accountability of these associations and the low loan repayment rates for most projects. It sought to base its seed loans on a local institution, and chose the *kire*, or burial association, that exists in most villages. These associations have broad membership and an elected leadership. They were asked to identify households that required seed, to manage the dispersal of seed loans, and to monitor the repayment (in kind).

The NGO arranged for the purchase of 100 tonnes of barley from a nearby province. Farmers recognised that the seed provided was a lowland variety but accepted it. The vast majority (89 %) of the recipients of the seed loans took the donated barley to small local markets where they bartered it for grain of more appropriate varieties. Those who

[11]For a review of the subject and a set of guidelines for organising emergency seed provision, see ODI Seeds and Biodiversity Programme (1996).
[12]In Sierra Leone, an NGO working with farmers affected by civil unrest provided funds to a local trader who was able to obtain seed of farmers' preferred rice varieties from other parts of the country (Richards and Ruivenkamp, 1996).

planted the local varieties had generally acceptable crop performance, while the few who experimented with the loaned seed had disappointing results. The loan repayment rate was very high, and much superior to that of government-run projects. The experience of this project illustrates the value of channelling seed loans through local institutions and, more important, provides evidence of the strength and capacity of local markets even in times of crisis. If farmers had had the resources, they could have acquired appropriate seed in the local markets.

A particularly serious problem with emergency seed distribution is that it easily becomes an established part of government or donor programmes. Seed distribution is a highly visible activity that is relatively easy for projects to monitor and report on. Superficially, it has the innocent appearance of providing a valuable input that allows farmers to improve their production, but it can lead to dependence and may threaten the development of sustainable seed provision.[13] In the mid-nineteenth century, the US Department of Agriculture began distributing small packets of free seed to farmers (Kloppenburg, 1988), the original purpose being to provide farmers with access to new varieties (many of which were acquired in other countries or were the results of plant exploration abroad). The seed packs were sent out under the auspices of senators and congressmen, who quickly appreciated the political value of the exercise. The seed (mostly of vegetables and flowers) was very popular with farmers, who experimented with the new varieties and selected those that were useful. The character of the programme gradually shifted, however, and by the turn of the century the distributed seed tended to be of standard, rather than novel, varieties. The programme was attacked as an exercise in political patronage (Fowler, 1994), but the decisive pressure to terminate it came from the commercial seed industry, which complained of unfair competition (Kloppenburg, 1988).

Similar problems are characteristic of seed distribution efforts in developing countries. Following a severe drought in 1991/92, the Government of Zimbabwe initiated a significant seed and fertiliser distribution programme that included more than 500 tonnes of sorghum and pearl millet seed. The efforts were expanded the following year, when the quantity of seed distributed was sufficient to plant the country's entire area under these crops (Rohrbach and Mutiro, 1996). The government continued with seed and fertiliser distribution until 1997. Although many farmers continued to rely at least in part on their own seed stocks (Rohrbach, 1997), farmers become accustomed to the government handing out free seed and complained when there were threats to reduce the programme (Van der Mheen-Sluijer, 1996).[14]

Table 7.5 summarises the recent experience in Malawi with seed distribution projects. The activities began in response to the 1991/92 drought which affected much of southern

---

[13]The sorghum variety that was the most important part of a church-supported seed scheme in Uganda for more than 10 years was found to have low acceptability by farmers. A project report describes its 'relative susceptibility to damage by storage pests and poor taste. Apparently the variety is grown widely only when seeds are made available free of charge' (Anglican Church of Uganda, 1994).

[14]Even immediately after the drought, Zimbabwean farmers used retained seed, or seed obtained in the community, to plant 40% of their white sorghum, 87% of red sorghum, 45% of pearl millet and 100% of finger millet (Friis-Hansen and Rohrbach, 1993).

Table 7.5 Seed distribution in Malawi: some major examples

Programme	Activities
Drought Relief Seeds Distribution Project, 1992/3	In response to drought of 1991/92, 1.3 million farmers each received 10 kg of maize 'seed', purchased on local grain market.
Drought Recovery Inputs Programme, 1994/5	In response to uneven rains the previous year, and collapse of the agricultural credit system, 4139 t of hybrid maize seed was distributed to farmers.
Supplementary Inputs Programme, 1995/6	3451 t of hybrid maize seed and 21 t of sorghum seed distributed. Fertiliser distributed in higher-potential areas.
Starter Pack Scheme 1998/9	Hybrid maize seed, fertiliser and legume seed sufficient for planting 0.1 ha distributed to every farm household in Malawi (2.6 m packs). Total seed distribution 5200 t hybrid maize, 500 t OPV maize, 4000 t groundnut, 1600 t soybean.
Starter Pack Scheme 1999/2000	Starter Pack Scheme repeated for second year.

Source: Longley, Coulter and Thompson (1999)

Africa. But even in the subsequent years of normal rainfall, significant input distribution efforts were organised. In 1998/9 donors and the Malawi Government initiated a 'Starter Pack Scheme' which distributed 2.6 million packs of maize seed, legume seed and fertiliser (enough to plant a tenth of a hectare for every farm household in Malawi). It is probably no coincidence that the scheme was launched shortly before the national elections (Longley et al., 1999). The scheme was continued in 1999/2000. Both the Government of Malawi and the donors who supported the scheme had a range of justifications for its implementation including increasing food production, promoting new technology, promoting crop diversification, improving soil fertility, and providing a safety net to the poor (ibid.). With such a range of objectives, many of which fit neatly into donor priorities, the scheme may find support for several more years.

These projects in Zimbabwe and Malawi are only a small part of the seed distribution activities carried out in sub-Saharan Africa by governments, donors, and NGOs. Such projects are major purchasers of seed, and the few private (and public) seed enterprises in the region naturally turn their attention to addressing these opportunities. Seed companies either produce seed to meet these markets, or purchase grain that can be cleaned and sold as seed. Seed companies in Kenya and Zimbabwe aggressively market to donors and NGOs outside their borders, but find themselves with neither the economic incentive nor the regulatory permission to sell seed to local farmers. In Zimbabwe, for instance, much of the sorghum 'seed' in the distribution schemes was actually grain purchased in local or international markets; at the same time, new public sorghum varieties demanded by Zimbabwean farmers could not be produced as seed because of certification restrictions (Rohrbach and Mutiro, 1996). Meanwhile, no sensible seed company would attempt to establish a market that would compete with these schemes.[15]

In conclusion, seed distribution projects are sometimes justified in order to respond to acute emergencies, but they can easily become expanded and entrenched, in part because they give the appearance that the government, the donor, or the NGO is helping the farmers. However, we have seen that many of these projects establish seed distribution mechanisms that are parallel to, or in conflict with, established institutions of local seed provision. In addition, they become significant disincentives to the growth of local seed enterprises.

Summary

The past decade has seen the emergence of several different types of donor seed projects. They offer novel approaches to improving farmers' access to new varieties and seed, and they attempt to address the new mandates of structural adjustment in the economy and decentralisation in the political system. However, they must also be assessed on the basis of their contributions to institutional development.

In order to strengthen plant breeding efforts that serve farmers in marginal environments, a number of decentralised variety selection and breeding strategies have been instituted. Many of these offer the possibility of increasing contacts between the formal plant breeding system and farmers. Whether information flow is permanently enhanced will depend on the nature of the links that are formed; farmers need to gain direct access to research institutions rather than have their contacts mediated by project staff. One method of improving farmers' voice in the research process is through groups or associations that can exert pressure on research, but farmers require adequate incentives to invest time in such activities. In those cases where projects attempt to strengthen farmers' own research capacities, farmers must see evidence of a useful return before they will invest their time and effort.

In order to address seed needs that have not been met by public or private seed enterprises, a large number of local-level production projects have been funded. Most of these envisage the emergence of viable small-scale enterprises, but very few have achieved this goal. One of the principal problems is the projects' failure to realise that the seed provision process goes beyond seed multiplication. The projects tend to manage the contacts (and cover the transaction costs) involved in obtaining source seed, establishing quality control procedures, arranging for seed conditioning, and marketing the product. Failures to address marketing issues are particularly significant, and in many cases the small-scale enterprise does not address sufficient local demand to make it a viable operation. Little attention is given to the necessity of ensuring that information about seed

[15]In 1933, the Red Cross and other agencies began to distribute free seed to US farm families suffering in the Depression. This was quickly challenged by the American Seed Trade Association, and the result was that farmers were issued with 'seed stamps' that could be exchanged at shops selling commercial seed (Kloppenburg, 1988). Both Malawi and Zimbabwe are currently experimenting with similar seed voucher strategies.

availability or quality is provided to potential clients. These failures are often hidden by the fact that the projects themselves buy much of the seed, or provide it to other NGOs or projects.

In order to meet seed loss during emergencies, a growing number of seed delivery projects have been established. These are often inadequately managed and may deliver seed of inappropriate varieties or poor quality. Although they are organised to supply relief immediately after an acute emergency, many of the projects tend to become institutionalised. Seed delivery is an attractive activity for many donors and NGOs, and it can be an important source of political patronage for governments. Instead of strengthening seed institutions, many of these projects erode farmer demand for new public varieties, discourage seed entrepreneurial activity, bypass local seed markets, and direct seed company attention away from farmer demand towards meeting the needs of donors and governments.

Although all of these types of seed project try to meet local seed needs in an innovative fashion, most do not support institutional growth. Many do not strengthen farmers' links with markets or with public organisations, nor do they take advantage of institutions that are already in place and help farmers gain access to seed. A discussion of what must be done to strengthen the institutions of seed provision is presented in the next chapter.

8 Seed System Development

Previous chapters have discussed how farmers manage and develop their seed supplies, the conditions that led to the emergence of commercial seed trade, the role of the state in supporting the development of seed systems, and the experiences of various seed projects. It is now time to summarise this information and to draw implications for the management of agricultural development.

This concluding chapter begins with a brief review of the institutional approach that has been used throughout the book to interpret seed system development. It then turns the lens around to offer an institutional interpretation of development assistance, including an examination of the project mode, which has been the principal strategy for directing development assistance to the seed sector. This is followed by an attempt to identify the possibilities and limitations of institution-building through development interventions. The discussion then returns to summarise some of the policy requirements for promoting the growth of seed systems and concludes with implications for the direction of agricultural development.

Institutions and agricultural development

This book has used the example of seed provision to demonstrate how institutions that mediate the flow of information help determine the course of agricultural development. There are, of course, many other factors that govern the direction of agricultural change. The growth of the wider economy plays a crucial role in stimulating agricultural development. The availability of physical and financial resources also determines the options that can be pursued. But the flow of information is exceptionally important for the agricultural sector, which is characterised by a large number of independent decision-makers faced with a wide variety of conditions and options. Seed provision is particularly dependent on the availability of information. Adequate information is required to guide the choice of varieties, to seek reliable sources of seed, and to organise plant breeding and seed production.

Three types of information are important for agricultural development. Technical information acquaints farmers with the advantages and disadvantages of various production options, and informs plant breeders, public agencies and merchants about farmers' requirements. Economic information determines what inputs farmers are willing to use and what products are brought to market. Information about the expected performance of partners (their reputations and trustworthiness) determines the willingness of farmers, merchants and consumers to enter into transactions. Efficient institutions must be available to facilitate the transmission of all three types of information.

The discussion of the nature of development in Chapter 1 introduced the distinction between intentional and immanent development, the former being the product of government programmes and policies, while the latter represents change that emerges directly from the actions and motivations of the people involved. We pointed out that this distinction was imperfect, because most immanent development takes place within the context of policies, laws and organisations established by governments. Nevertheless, it is possible to identify many instances of seed sector development that owe their principal impetus to farmers and traders. Chapter 2 summarised the institutional approach that would be followed in the rest of the book and Chapter 3 introduced the basic aspects of variety development and seed management. Chapter 4 described the organisation of farm-level seed provision, illustrating how farmers select varieties and establish access to sources of seed. Chapter 5 described how the increasing formalisation and extension of seed supply channels led to the emergence of the commercial seed sector. As farm-level and commercial seed systems expand, the state often takes on roles that are difficult to organise independently, such as agricultural research and regulation, and Chapter 6 described how these tasks have evolved and how they affect the conduct of seed activities. It also described the outcomes of more concerted programmes such as extension campaigns and the organisation of public seed production. Chapter 7 presented examples of donor and government seed project interventions.

In examining examples of seed system development, we have utilised an institutional perspective based on recent economics and sociological literature to help explain the role of information and its management. Two principal means of information transmission – rules and networks – were emphasised. Institutional economics views institutions as 'the rules of the game'; the institutional environment includes not only the formal laws and regulations but also the informal, but no less important, conventions of market behaviour and social interchange. Rules of this type are necessary for the emergence of the seed trade, which often begins at the local level, with its capacity to expand dependent on the growth of reputations and the efficacy of the formal rules that govern its transactions. As the seed that is traded begins to embody significant investment in research and production there is increasing motivation for the establishment of well defined property rights. In those cases where seed provision strategy envisages community responsibilities, the information requirements of collective action, including monitoring individual contributions and apportioning benefits, determine the possibilities of success. The state makes its major contribution when the difficulties of organising information exchange among large numbers of farmers and the problems of controlling access to that information justify the provision of public goods such as agricultural research and regulatory frameworks.

An institutional approach also highlights the importance of transaction costs for agricultural development. Mechanisms that lower the costs of acquiring information open up new possibilities for technology utilisation and enterprise development. Seed provision entails a sequence of activities, from plant breeding to seed marketing; their integration requires contracting between different types of organisations or, alternatively, the co-ordination provided by a single firm. The choices that are made depend to a large extent on the institutions that are available to manage the flow of information among specialist organisations or to guide the emergence of integrated enterprises.

Sociological perspectives emphasise the importance of networks for transmitting information. Social networks serve a range of purposes and may be adapted to meet new opportunities. They provide individuals with additional scope for acquiring information. At the village level, information about and access to crop varieties are embedded in relations involving kin and friends as well as patrons and clients. In the development of seed enterprises, transaction costs may be lowered through the provision of information from kin, business partners, or officials who have established relationships with farmers or merchants. The stability and efficiency of these interchanges are conditioned by the trust that develops from long-term relationships within networks.

Of particular importance in determining the impact of rules and networks on agricultural development is their breadth of coverage. Those that cover many people and wide areas are more likely to provide the diversity of information that can contribute to productive change. The uniform and effective exercise of legal authority, the scope and reliability of markets, and the opportunities for individuals to expand their networks beyond the local arena all increase the likelihood of agricultural development.

Information flow is not sufficient on its own, of course. No matter how effective the mechanisms for providing information, appropriate incentives are needed for individuals to acquire and utilise that information. In some cases the incentives are obvious. The imperatives of household survival, for instance, are sufficient to motivate farmers to seek productive crop varieties and to ensure a reliable seed supply. Commercial gain is also an obvious stimulus, but the extent to which individuals are likely to make the investments and take the risks required for rural entrepreneurship varies widely within and between cultures and groups. Public service provision, such as agricultural research, also depends on appropriate incentives, which are likely to include a mix of civic duty, professional advancement, and scientific curiosity.

Our examination of the institutional dimensions of seed provision challenges the oversimplifications that characterise much of the contemporary debate about agricultural development and the future of seed systems. We have seen that farmers' own seed management is sophisticated but subject to institutional constraints. Considerable creativity is applied to the development of local varieties, but information about these innovations is not evenly distributed. Contrast this with the view put forward by those who advocate a return to 'traditional agriculture' and who declare that 'saving seed, re-using seed, exchanging and sharing seed are not merely fundamental freedoms of farmers; they are also a fundamental duty' (Shiva, 1999: 4). These are stirring words, but this egalitarian vision of sharing seed and knowledge is a romantic gloss on a much more complex reality.

Those who are concerned about the expansion of commercial agriculture often espouse a contradictory vision of farmer rationality. On the one hand, they see experienced farmers interacting with their environment to create a well-adapted farming system but, on the other hand, those same farmers are presented as being at the mercy of state extension campaigns and easily manipulated by the beguiling publicity of commercial companies. Once again, the reality is much more complex. Incompetent extension strategies and unscrupulous merchants may indeed present problems, but farmers have shown themselves quite capable of utilising information about the alternatives offered by the state and the commercial seed sector.

On the other side of the development debate, a misinformed paternalism may blindly promote 'modern agriculture' without an appreciation of farmers' conditions and constraints. The dominant image here is of benighted farmers requiring guidance to help them emerge from their primitive ways. How many extension and donor reports call for 'improved seeds' without any indication that the authors have any understanding of what precisely might require improvement in farmers' seed provision? Such reports rarely specify the extent to which farmers' seed management is deficient, or precisely what types of new crop varieties would contribute to farming productivity. It is seldom acknowledged that it is usually farmers' access to information that requires most attention.

A similarly incomplete conception of agricultural development is that which holds that the private sector will be able to address all the problems that the public sector has failed to resolve. Liberalisation of the seed sector can certainly open up new possibilities for farmers, but the idea that merely ceasing state activities will automatically lead to the blossoming of private seed provision is an illusion. Commercial seed enterprises do not emerge overnight but are rather the product of a gradual evolution of skills and of increasingly complex mechanisms for combining those skills. Effective rules and networks must be available to allow information about commercial opportunities to be transmitted. Once appropriate incentives are in place, farmers are perfectly capable of incorporating commercial seed markets into their farm management strategies.[1]

The performance of development assistance

This book has presented examples of intentional development, particularly the public research and seed production activities described in Chapter 6 and the seed projects that were the subject of Chapter 7. Development aid is a major source of funding for seed activities in many countries, and there is hope that development activities can support the growth of seed systems. However, we have seen that their projects and programmes have

[1] A particularly distorted and self-serving view from the commercial sector is the defence of 'terminator technology' offered by the technology's owner, Delta and Pine Land. 'The centuries-old practice of farmer saved seed is really a gross disadvantage to Third World farmers who inadvertently become locked into obsolete varieties because of their taking the "easy road" and not planting newer, more productive varieties' (Collins, cited in The Corner House, 1998: 10).

138

had a mixed impact on seed provision. The performance of development aid merits at least a brief discussion.

External aid is a complicated endeavour, subject to a number of motives. In extreme cases, it may simply be an arm of foreign policy, utilised to achieve donor advantages and support under the guise of charity. But even if it is an expression of untainted altruism, the relationships are still complex. This book has emphasised the importance of understanding the incentives that foster agricultural development. The examples have been drawn from the growth of seed systems, and include the motivations of farmers, entrepreneurs, plant breeders, and officials. It is also worthwhile examining the incentives of the aid agencies themselves. Twenty-six years ago, Judith Tendler described the factors that helped set a course of action for USAID:

> the pressure to commit resources; the use of project analysis to rationalise decisions already taken rather than to arrive at decisions; the drumming up of business (i.e., the creation of projects) by departments anxious to keep themselves in existence; and a risk-averse behaviour caused partly by the conspicuousness of mistakes and the less visible, less well-defined standards of success (Tendler, 1975: 40).

There is little reason to believe that this description is not equally valid for the contemporary position of most aid agencies. One of their principal incentives is simply the preservation of the aid bureaucracy. This is accomplished by moving funds as efficiently as possible through projects that conform to an elaborately conceived development grammar and vocabulary, carefully chosen to reflect current government philosophy, to encompass as many interests as possible, and to gloss over potential contradiction or conflict. As hard data for measuring progress are difficult to obtain (and in any case not diligently sought), and as the endeavour requires support from as wide a range of political allies as possible, it attracts an increasing number of special interests, each of which can claim its right to scrutinise projected activities. The particular interests may be valid in their own right, but they detract from the agency's capacity to develop coherent long-term strategies.[2]

The aid agencies, are of course, driven by incentives beyond concern for their own preservation. There is a genuine motivation to assist in alleviating poverty, but the capacity (and often the willingness) to assess the results and use them to inform future plans is deficient. This may seem an odd conclusion in the face of the endless evaluations commissioned by aid agencies. But much of this evaluation activity must be seen as 'a system producing and system maintaining ritual' (Tvedt, 1998: 90). The functions of evaluation are often an area of dispute within aid agencies (Mosley, 1987). Various units will be interested in different outcomes: financial targets, output statistics, or consistency with current agency interests. The weakness of agency evaluation is widely

---

[2]Mellor (1998: 40) describes the special interests that dominate USAID: 'child survival, vitamin A, microcredit, poverty, microenterprise (but excluding agriculture!), empowerment of women, environment, wildlife preservation, and on and on. Extrapolation of the history of special interests in foreign aid suggests that tomorrow the list will be different and longer. Priorities and strategy cannot coexist with such a panoply of special interests, each with its own objectives.'

acknowledged, but this does not lead to significant reform (Carlsson et al., 1994).[3]

Ideally the evaluation of an aid project should be carried out by the recipients, but despite a growing amount of rhetoric about participation, there is little evidence of any serious evaluation managed by recipient governments or organisations. Aid beneficiaries find it difficult to make demands on donors; any serious criticism or initiative might jeopardise the relationship. 'What can a local community do if the donors of foreign aid fail to deliver a good service? They cannot easily turn to a competitor aid donor for a better service' (Putzel, 1998: 88). In addition, there are often strong incentives for officials in recipient countries to respond to foreign aid inducements rather than to try to represent local requirements. It is difficult to know how a more responsive strategy for donor assistance can be encouraged. The current structure already makes a mockery of agencies' incessant preaching about establishing rational, client-oriented incentive systems.

Projects

The predominant strategy for providing aid assistance to agriculture is the project mode, as illustrated in Chapter 7. Projects are an understandably attractive strategy for donors: they operate over a defined timeframe and are consistent with donor budgetary management; they are usually 'owned' by a single donor and can thus be used as a vehicle for promoting its views and priorities; and they lend themselves to standard reporting and evaluation procedures. Unfortunately, these same factors contribute to the failure of many projects to make any lasting contribution: they are often isolated, short-term, myopically conceived efforts that do little to strengthen the institutions that support agricultural development.

The basic criticisms of project aid are well-known. Cassen and Associates (1994: 175) describe '"project proliferation": aid projects are planted here and there in an almost haphazard way and in excessive numbers'. The projects are not only unco-ordinated, but many are actually the outcome of competition among donors (ibid.). In the early 1980s Malawi was the recipient of 188 projects managed by 50 different donors; 44 of these projects were managed by the Ministry of Agriculture. The equivalent figures for Zambia were 614 projects, financed by 69 different donors, including 120 projects in agriculture (Morss, 1984). There is little evidence that the situation has changed since then. In 1998 a single donor was funding three projects in Malawi that focused on seed provision: one supporting the development of the commercial sale of new crop varieties by public research, a second organising community groups to grow and sell their own seed, and a third giving seed packs to all farming households. It is difficult to identify any consistent strategy towards institutional development from this range of activities.

---

[3]The introduction to one of the most influential reviews of aid effectiveness recognises the problem but dismisses its importance. 'If the evaluation of aid is imperfect, how can it be justifiable to conclude that most aid works? The answer is that that conclusion, though not a demonstrable fact, is at least a well-educated assessment' (Cassen and Associates, 1994: 7).

The lack of overall impact is further hidden from view by the excessive attention given to a few show projects that become, in Chambers' (1993: 115) words, 'shining islands of salvation'. Many questions about project efficacy are diverted by pointing to these wholly unrepresentative cases. Some of the local-level seed projects described in Chapter 7 are unfortunately examples of this. Community-produced seed may be purchased and distributed with project funds under the guise of commercial transactions, and farmers are motivated to participate not because of immediate economic returns but rather to take advantage of the potential benefits to be derived from the extra resources and inducements that are invested to keep the project afloat.

What are the implications of the project strategy for our interest in the institutions of agricultural development? We have emphasised the importance of rules and networks for providing the information required for development. Most projects are location-specific and time-bound and offer few opportunities for expanding or strengthening these rules and networks. When several different donor projects compete, they tend to provide conflicting signals to national partners about institutional development.

We have also emphasised the importance of identifying and strengthening the appropriate roles of states and markets. However, there is much about the project strategy, especially as currently practised in agricultural development, that weakens both. Much of the recent history of aid provision has been characterised by a significant shift away from dependence on the state as an agency for development. The trend began in the 1980s when aid agencies became less willing to continue pouring money into inefficient and ineffective government departments. The emphasis shifted to 'getting prices right', eliminating the subsidies and regulations that stood in the way of market development, and achieving fiscal responsibility. At the same time, an increasing proportion of aid funds began to be channelled through NGOs, seen as being more in touch with local needs and more responsible at managing project funding. The result was a significant decentralisation of government services and a move towards supporting 'civil society'.

This is not the place to debate the pros and cons of these major shifts in development strategy. However, it is important to recognise the implications for state roles in seed provision. The state is a source of public goods such as agricultural research. It also has significant responsibility for regulation and consumer protection. One of the major constraints to effective and equitable state provision of services has been farmers' lack of voice for making demands on these services. Rather than developing citizens' capacity to interact effectively with the state, many NGO projects see themselves as establishing alternatives to state service. The power of development vocabulary makes it difficult to understand what is happening. 'By being so enmeshed in rhetoric (for example, the language of popular participation), actual interventions may be described with the right words, while unequal relations are maintained' (Tvedt, 1998: 84). The NGO seed projects described in Chapter 7 demonstrated how NGOs tend to cover the major transaction costs arising from interactions with state agencies, acting both as brokers for the state and as competitors to a declining state service. Farmers are kept at a distance from the public agencies whose efficiency and relevance depend on effective contact with their clients; instead, they are rewarded for being 'participants' in a series of short-lived projects orchestrated by external agencies.

It has become increasingly fashionable for projects to promote a decentralised approach, which allows the donor agency to carve out a manageable portion of the public organisation and to avoid difficult issues of co-ordination. Tendler, examining a number of examples from Brazil, argues that the successful cases represent a mix of local government initiative, civil society involvement, and an active and supportive central government. Indeed, she emphasises the 'paradox of decentralisation' (1997: 143) that links the possibilities of effective local government to the existence of a strong central government. A well organised civil society is a complement to, not a substitute for, a responsible and responsive state. For public responsibilities such as agricultural research, a decentralised approach will only be effective if it can draw upon an adequately funded central research capacity.

Many development projects not only try to act as if the state was unnecessary, but also attempt to substitute for markets, or at least to limit their potential contribution. Some of this is a result of the extreme difficulty NGOs and other development agencies have in coming to terms with markets and commerce (Havers, 1991). Many projects give (appropriate) emphasis to building on local farmers' knowledge, so it is hardly 'convincing to argue that the rural people have these strengths but that the middle and upper classes that have sprung from these rural people do not' (Morton, 1996: 44). Local merchants are regularly portrayed as taking advantage of innocent farmers. In those instances where this is so, the appropriate strategy is to build farmers' capacities to demand an equitable market, rather than to attempt to insulate them from commerce.

Another dimension of the aversion to markets is the attraction of describing farmers' situations in terms that emphasise romantic singularity. A prominent example is the term CDR (complex, diverse and risk-prone) (Chambers, 1997) used to describe the circumstances of the many farmers who have missed out on most agricultural technology development. Without denying the accuracy of the description, it can be argued that it is more useful to reverse the emphasis and to describe these farmers' situation as RDC: remote (from markets and sources of information), diffuse (and unable to specialise or to master particular income-generating activities) and constrained (by inadequate resources), the advantage being to focus attention on the practical requirements for ameliorating the farmers' plight. Rather than emphasise their current isolation we need to improve their access to, and equitable participation in, markets and state services.

Most agricultural development projects fail to address the institutional factors that are so important to determining the course of agricultural change. Far from helping individuals, enterprises, or governments build the rules and networks that foster information exchange, they are directed by the inappropriate incentives of aid agencies and bound by organisational constraints that divert attention from strengthening those rules and networks. In addition, and despite an explicit debate about the relative merits of states and markets, they do little to support sustainable improvements in either public or commercial institutions.

Institutions and organisations

Much has been written about the importance of institution-building in development, and at first glance this would seem to be the strategy that aid agencies need to emphasise. A major problem, however, is agreeing on an appropriate definition. A prominent World Bank examination of the subject defines institution-building as 'the process of improving an institution's ability to make effective use of the human and financial resources available. This process can be internally generated by the managers of an institution or induced and promoted by the government or by development agencies' (Israel, 1987: 11). It is obvious that what is meant here (and in most treatments of the subject) by 'institution' is in fact what we have been calling organisations, entities such as government departments and institutes, educational establishments or commercial associations. These are to be distinguished from the 'rules' interpretation that we have assigned to institutions (Moore, 1995). So long as we are clear about definitions there is no problem, and indeed it is often more feasible and sensible to focus attention on building the capacities of specific organisations rather than trying to address their underlying customs and governance.

The problem is that this type of institution-building (i.e., strengthening specific organisations) is rarely carried out in a consistent or dedicated manner. Institution-building requires 'patience and a long time horizon; experimentation and willingness to admit and learn from mistakes; human skills and sensitivity rather than expensive hardware; and sensitivity to the particular cultural and political environment into which the institution is to fit' (ibid: 90). None of these characteristics is easily accommodated by the structures of conventional donor projects. The usual focus is to provide training and technical support to the organisations involved in implementing a specific project rather than to look at a longer-term strategy.

> There is a striking weakness in the intellectual underpinnings of institution building...compared with the theoretical and quantitative tools used to plan physical investment...[T]here is little guidance for planning institutional requirements of whole sectors, for matching institutional needs with evolving economic structures, or for systematically defining inter-sectoral linkages. (Cassen and Associates, 1994: 171)

When donor support is available for state programmes or market development it rarely pays attention to the types of incentives that allow organisations to be viable or to lower the cost of information management. 'Both the centralisers and the privatisers frequently advocate oversimplified, idealised institutions – paradoxically, almost "institution-free" institutions' (Ostrom, 1990: 22). On the state side, donors support public agencies to manage special projects rather than helping them establish durable interactions with their clientele. Public sector personnel are seconded to special units (or leave the agency entirely to join NGOs that are more likely to receive donor attention). The public agency is taken apart, brick by brick, to build small temporary shelters for the donor's projects. Even the emerging trend towards donor co-ordination across a sector still assigns the primary responsibility for policy formation to the donors.[4] On the market side, liberalisation programmes have concentrated on deregulation and the privatisation of public enterprises rather than on the conditions required to establish competitive markets. The result often has been the acquisition of government assets by the politically well-connected who may simply recreate unresponsive monopolies. At the same time, a continuing lack of adequate mechanisms to support information flow and the establishment of trust means that new commercial relations are slow to emerge.

Institutional development will only take place as an outgrowth of activities that enlist the long-term commitment of their participants. 'Organisations and their entrepreneurs engage in purposive activity and in that role are the agents of, and shape the direction of, institutional change' (North, 1990: 73). People create their own rules and networks in the context of productive organisational activity. The challenge for development assistance is to support the activities that contribute to such institutional evolution.

Rules must emerge from democratic political processes and from the experience of participating in accessible markets. Networks exist for various purposes and can be created or modified to take advantage of new opportunities. The current infatuation with the concept of social capital often ignores that it is a by-product of specific activities mediated by these networks (Coleman, 1988). It is possible to 'create' social capital by encouraging new and expanded networks, but those networks must engage in activities that their participants find useful and worth pursuing.[5] Such social capital can be created by forming links between sectors (civil society, public organisations and private enterprise), and project or NGO staff can contribute by providing the necessary 'bridges' (Brown and Ashman, 1996). But these bridges must have solid foundations that can be maintained by the participants rather than being hastily erected temporary structures that only serve project management.[6]

The process of development can be described in terms of the complementary evolution of organisations and institutions. Helping to build productive organisations contributes to the emergence of effective institutions. An example is the challenge of establishing sufficient trust within a developing market for potential participants to be encouraged to invest their resources and expand their activities. Development programmes need to identify cases where the process has begun and to build upon such

---

[4]Saasa and Carlsson (1996: 135) describe aid co-ordination in Zambia. 'Under such conceptualisation of co-ordination, the government acts more as a servicing organ that tries to understand and reconcile the various donors' activities and priorities at the planning, implementation and monitoring levels. In this scenario, the priorities and procedures of the donors guide and dictate government policy.'

[5]One danger with an over-emphasis on social capital in the conception of development projects is the notion that virtually any activity that involves groups is bound to contribute to the formation of social capital, regardless of its content. For instance, Ostrom, Schroeder and Wynne (1993: 220) suggest that 'grassroots local projects become part of the social capital for the future'.

[6]It is a common (and not always positive) experience that networks established during the management of public enterprises are carried over when these are privatised. Chalfin (1996) describes the privatisation of shea nut marketing in Ghana, where the personnel of the former state Produce Buying Company made use of their contacts with farmers and traders when joining newly formed private marketing firms. The survival and utilisation of communist-era networks in the formation of Russian private enterprise is another important example (Humphrey and Schmitz, 1996).

'islands of trust' (Humphry and Schmitz, 1996: 39) that can serve as examples for the wider economy. In agricultural development, seed provision activities can serve as examples of this kind and their advancement can contribute to institutional growth in the wider agricultural sector. In order for this to happen, however, intentional development activities must adopt a long-term perspective.

Promoting the growth of seed systems

If intentional development activities are to make a contribution to national seed systems, there needs to be much better co-ordination between donor programmes and projects, on the one hand, and national seed policies and priorities, on the other. The blame for the current confusion and inefficiency lies on both sides. There are few incentives for one donor to see how its seed-related projects are related to those of other donors, or to contemplate the implications for consistent national policies. At the same time, weak governments have little capacity to articulate their own policies and few incentives to demand coherent contributions from donors.

Seed system development must address both public and private sector responsibilities. The most effective mix of public and private participation will depend on a number of factors specific to each country. However, both states and markets have essential contributions to make to any national seed system.

On the public side, one of the principal priorities is to reinvigorate and redirect public agricultural research. Although private research will play an increasingly important role in agriculture, there will be many crops and problems that will not attract private research investment, including crops for which there is insufficient commercial demand and areas of research where it is difficult to obtain appropriate returns. We have seen that the incentives for public research are complex, and it will be necessary to ensure that adequate attention is given both to basic research that contributes to the growth of commercial agriculture and to the crops that are important to the livelihoods of resource-poor farming households. Public research must establish a *modus vivendi* with the private sector. In many instances, the course of agricultural development will prompt the public sector to cede responsibilities to the private seed industry, as more commercial opportunities appear. In addition, as we have seen, the public sector is often an important source of training and experience for those who initiate entrepreneurial seed activity. In many cases it has been former public researchers or academics who have had the contacts and experience to initiate commercial seed activities.

A second important public sector role is in regulation. Effective regulation should be the outcome of equitable interactions between the state, producers, and consumers. Seed regulation cannot be imposed top-down, but the state can play a crucial role in helping to provide the environment in which regulatory frameworks are established and modified. Regulation must address the information deficiencies that occur in the seed market and stimulate growth in commercial seed activity. But such regulation cannot emerge unless seed markets are given a chance to innovate and grow. In addition, seed regulatory regimes are now challenged to provide sufficient intellectual property protection to encourage private plant breeding, but to guard against assigning excessive privileges that would curtail public plant breeding and germplasm interchange.

The public sector role in seed production and delivery should diminish considerably, since these are activities that are increasingly being performed by the private sector. During the transition, governments and donors need to pay attention to the physical assets required for production. The major asset, of course, is land for seed multiplication, and this is almost always contracted from individual farmers. Farmers should have access to enough information and training so that seed multiplication is a profitable alternative for those who are located in appropriate environments. In addition, processing equipment and storage capacity are usually required as well. There are often difficulties in making the best use of former parastatal seed processing facilities. Many donor projects add to the confusion by providing equipment of inappropriate capacity for emerging seed enterprises, or by failing to establish clear ownership for donated equipment that provides appropriate incentives for its maintenance and efficient utilisation. The transition from public to private seed production is also hampered by government and donor projects that insist on subsidising or giving away seed.

A major part of seed system development will depend on private commercial activity. Seed production requires relatively modest financial investments and presents relatively few economies of scale. As such, it can provide opportunities for developing small enterprises. Those who might contribute to such an enterprise include agriculturalists, seed growers, grain merchants and input dealers. Seed policy and development aid should be sensitive to the various possibilities and encourage the emergence of commercial ventures that respond to growing seed demand.

In addition, countries must be able to take advantage of the opportunities offered by established seed companies, including foreign enterprises. International seed trade can make a significant contribution to a country's agricultural development. Policy-makers often express concern about the dangers of allowing foreign companies to control national seed supply. The best way to address this is to ensure the development of a robust local commercial seed industry that can effectively compete and collaborate with outside companies. Because agriculture requires location-specific technologies, and because the seed trade depends so heavily on local commercial networks, a strong domestic seed industry will have many bargaining cards to play in its interactions with foreign companies.

Finally, no commercial seed trade can flourish without an effective and competitive system of input marketing. Priority must be given to encouraging the emergence of a strong and responsible network of input dealers. Of equal importance, farmers must be provided with sufficient information, training, and consumer protection so that they demand, and receive, the best service from input dealers.

The direction of agricultural development

Government policies and donor projects that are sensitive to the importance of institutional growth can contribute to agricultural development. But the rules and networks that constitute these institutions must be nurtured and developed by their owners. There is no possibility that (intentional) development aid can substitute for indigenously directed (immanent) growth. The discussion of the nature of development in Chapter 1 suggested that it is useful to view development as the growth of human capacities. What needs to be done to strengthen people's capacities for building institutions to support agricultural development?

The first requirement is good government. Equitable agricultural development is difficult for any country to achieve in the absence of a government that is both competent and representative. Much development aid is wasted when the state is not able to establish and enforce basic rules and to ensure equitable access to resources and opportunities. 'Participatory' projects are no substitute for representative and responsive government. Liberalisation and deregulation can help remove government interference in arenas that are best left to private initiative, but unless there is 'a strong state, with a limited agenda' (Streeten, 1995: 20), there is little hope of establishing the rules and networks that provide the framework on which such initiatives must rest.

It must be emphasised that a focus on the necessarily slow process of institutional growth should not be mistaken for acceptance of a 'trickle-down' approach to poverty alleviation. As development takes place, material wealth, opportunities, and information may indeed spill over. But the channels that deliver these benefits are well worn, and they are more likely to expand their passages than to give rise to alternative courses. It is the task of governments and donors to promote the mechanisms that diversify these channels and allow more widespread participation and access to opportunities. Governments must work towards reducing inequality. Agricultural technology development is more likely to benefit the poor in situations where the initial distribution of assets is more equal. Governments that dedicate resources to reducing inequality can contribute to a significant shift in the direction of agricultural change.[7]

There are other things that governments need to do to promote institutional growth. Farmers' ability to take advantage of new technology and to participate in markets will increasingly depend on their access to adequate education.[8] The performance of agricultural markets also depends heavily on the roads and other infrastructure that government must help provide. The establishment and enforcement of commercial law, consumer education, and technical backstopping for merchants and producers must replace heavy-handed regulation of the seed sector.

The actions of NGOs and community groups can also make a significant contribution. But local-level agricultural development projects should not pretend that they can

---

[7]See the discussion in Lipton and Longhurst (1989: 295–301) about the relationship between assets and technology adoption in the Green Revolution. See Harriss (1992) for an example of the positive effects of government actions to reduce rural inequality.

[8]This is one of the big differences between examples of successful 'grass-roots' seed enterprise development in both industrialised and developing countries, on the one hand, and the current spate of local-level seed projects, on the other. In the successful cases, farmers have enough education to take direct advantage of technical and commercial advice. In contrast, many projects must direct their information to intermediaries (such as NGOs or extension agents) who are expected to guide farmers (e.g., Almekinders and Louwaars, 1999).

substitute for states or markets. Instead, the emphasis should be on ensuring that farmers are able to claim their fair share of state services and negotiate access to as wide a range of market opportunities as possible.

We must not pretend that the development that results from the growth of agricultural institutions is without costs or difficulties. Farmers' participation in markets will contribute to increasing productivity, but this will often imply increasing specialisation and a decrease in the self-sufficiency and independence of individual farms. The image of the self-provisioning farm is appealing but deceptive. While it highlights the multiple capacities of the farm family for managing its resources, it ignores the limited ability of isolated units to respond to external change or to take advantage of the benefits of the larger economy and society.

In addition, agricultural development implies that a decreasing proportion of the population will be involved in farming. There is no way to maintain the myth that tiny farms will somehow provide adequate livelihoods. The transition is difficult and there are no easy answers. Much depends on the development of the wider economy, so that people leaving farming are not turned into landless labourers but rather are able to take advantage of new skills and opportunities to enter other productive endeavours.

If development is related to the expansion of capacities to control and choose, how do we interpret the evolution of seed systems? Development is not judged by whether farmers grow traditional varieties or ones that are the products of formal plant breeding, but rather by the range of productive choices that are at their disposal. Development is not assessed by whether or not farmers save seed, but rather by their security of access to seed, from their own farms or through the market. Development is not dependent on the existence of the latest agricultural innovations, but rather on farmers' access to information about technology, their familiarity with the providers of the technology (public or private), and their ability to press for change or redress if they are not satisfied with its performance. Development is not related to the specific type of property rights accorded new technology, but rather to farmers' equitable access to the technology, the freedom for public and private research to explore new directions, and the ability of new agricultural enterprises to emerge, innovate and grow.

These capacities are the harvest of institutional growth, which requires a long season and careful management to ensure its development. Markets do not emerge full-blown, but grow and evolve as their benefits and opportunities reach an increasing number of participants. Public agencies, such as agricultural research organisations, may benefit from external aid, but they must have internal support and be guided by effective public pressure. Regulations and the definition of commercial property rights cannot be imposed on an economy but must be the products of public debate. New technologies may allow farmers to take advantage of innovations developed elsewhere, but there are no short cuts to establishing the networks of communication and the creation of trust that allow technological change to serve broad-based development.

Seed is both a vehicle for institutional growth in agriculture and a beneficiary of this development. Seed carries information about farmer experience, formal research and market demands. Seed transactions require an environment of trust, and each successful exchange enhances the reputations of the participants. The expansion of seed transactions and the enhanced diversity and quality of the seed require more complex institutions to mediate the exchanges. The utilisation of this seed contributes to agricultural productivity, which in turn supports the institutional growth that spurs further rural innovation.

References

Abeygunawardena, P., Reusche, G. and Suraweera, E. (1990) 'Relative Efficiency of Government Farm Seed Production versus Private Sector Seed Production in Sri Lanka', *Sri Lankan Journal of Agricultural Sciences* 27: 138–47.

Ahmed, Z. (1989) 'Effective Costs of Rural Loans in Bangladesh', *World Development* 17: 357–63.

Akerlof, G. (1970) 'The Market for 'Lemons': Quality Uncertainty and the Market Mechanism', *Quarterly Journal of Economics* 84: 488–500.

Alam, Z., and Saleemi, A. R. (1996) 'Seed Regulatory Frameworks in Pakistan', unpublished paper prepared for Overseas Development Institute/CAZS Seed Regulatory Project.

Alchian, A. and Demsetz, H. (1972) 'Production, Information and Economic Organization', *American Economic Review* 62: 777–95.

Almekinders, C. J. M. and Louwaars, N. P. (1999) *Farmers' Seed Production: New Approaches and Practices.* London: Intermediate Technology Publications.

Almekinders, C. J. M., Louwaars, N. P. and De Bruijn, G. H. (1994) 'Local Seed Systems and Their Importance for An Improved Seed Supply in Developing Countries', *Euphytica* 78: 207–11.

Alston, J. M., Pardey, P. G., and Roseboom, J. (1998) 'Financing Agricultural Research: International Investment Patterns and Policy Perspectives', *World Development* 26: 1057–71.

Ammerman, A. J. and Cavalli-Sforza, L. L. (1971) 'Measuring the Rate of Spread of Early Farming in Europe', *Man*: 674–88.

Anderson, R., Levy, E. and Morrison, B. (1991) *Rice Science and Development Politics.* Oxford: Clarendon Press.

Andren, U., Nkomesha, A., Singogo, L. P. and Sutherland, A. (1991) *National Seed Availability Study: Seed Problems, Practices and Requirements Among Small-Scale Farmers in Zambia.* Lusaka: Ministry of Agriculture, Adaptive Research Planning Team.

Anglican Church of Uganda (1994) 'Karamoja Seeds Scheme Annual Report 1994'. Karamoja Diocesan Development Office.

Arnstein, S. R. (1969) 'A Ladder of Citizen Participation', *Journal of the American Institute of Planners* 35: 216–24.

Ashby, J. (1982) 'Technology and Ecology: Implications for Innovation Research in Peasant Agriculture', *Rural Sociology* 47: 234–50.

Ashby, J. A., Garcia, T., del Pilar Guerrero, M., Quiros, C. A., Roa, J. O. and Beltran, J. A. (1995) *Institutionalizing Farmer Participation in Adaptive Technology Testing with the CIAL.* Agricultural Administration (Research and Extension) Paper No. 57. London: Overseas Development Institute.

Ashby, J., Quiros, C.A. and Rivera, Y. (1987) *Farmer Participation in On-Farm Varietal Trials.* Agricultural Administration (Research and Extension) Network Discussion Paper 22. London: Overseas Development Institute.

Audi, P., Jones, R. and Tripp, R. *Diffusion and Adoption of Nairobi Pigeonpea Variety 670 (NPP 670) in Mwea Division of Mbeere District, Eastern Province, Kenya*. Working Paper No. 1. Nairobi: ICRISAT.

Bardhan, P. (ed.) (1989) *The Economic Theory of Agrarian Institutions*. Oxford: Oxford University Press.

Bardhan, P. and Rudra, A. (1981) 'Terms and Conditions of Labour Contracts in Agriculture: Results of a Survey in West Bengal, 1979', *Oxford Bulletin of Economics and Statistics* 43: 89–111.

Barkley, A. and Porter, L. (1996) 'The Determinants of Wheat Variety Selection in Kansas, 1974 to 1993', *American Journal of Agricultural Economics* 78: 202–11.

Barnett, M. L. (1969) 'Subsistence and Transition in Agricultural Development Among the Ibaloi in the Philippines', in C. R. Wharton (ed.) *Subsistence Agriculture and Economic Development*. Chicago: Aldine.

Barth, F. (1967) 'On the Study of Social Change', *American Anthropologist* 69: 661–9.

Bates, R. H. (1981) *Markets and States in Tropical Africa: The Political Basis of Agricultural Policies*. Berkeley, CA: University of California Press.

Bates, R. H. (1989) *Beyond the Miracle of the Market*. Cambridge: Cambridge University Press.

Bates, R. H. (1995) 'Social Dilemmas and Rational Individuals' in Harriss et al.

Bauer, P.T. (1984) *Reality and Rhetoric. Studies in the Economics of Development*. Cambridge MA: Harvard University Press.

Baumann, P. C. and Turton, C. N. (1998) 'Seed for Regenerating Wastelands in India: Institutional Supply and Demand', *Seed Science and Technology* 26: 53–65.

Baumann, P. C. and Singh, B. (2000) *The Lahaul Potato Society*. ODI Working Paper 136. London: Overseas Development Institute.

Bellon, M. R. and Brush, S. B. (1994) 'Keepers of Maize in Chiapas, Mexico', *Economic Botany* 48(2): 196–209.

Bentley, J. and Vasques, D. (1998) *The Seed Potato System in Bolivia: Organisational Growth and Missing Links*. Agricultural Research and Extension Network Paper No. 85. London: Overseas Development Institute.

Bentley, J., Tripp, R. and de la Flor, R. (2000) 'Liberalization of Peru's Formal Seed Sector'. Unpublished paper.

Benziger, V. (1996) 'Small Fields, Big Money: Two Successful Programs in Helping Small Farmers Make the Transition to High Value-Added Crops', *World Development* 24: 1681–93.

Berg, T., Bjoernstad, A., Fowler, C. and Kroeppa,T. (1991) *Technology Options and the Gene Struggle*. NORAGRIC Occasional Papers Series C; Development and Environment No.8. As: Agricultural University of Norway.

Bernstein, M. (1955) *Regulating Business by Independent Commission*. Princeton, NJ: Princeton University Press.

Biggs, S. (1989) *Resource-Poor Farmer Participation in Research: A Synthesis of Experiences from Nine National Agricultural Research Systems*. OFCOR Comparative Study Paper No.3. The Hague: ISNAR.

Biggs, S. and Clay, E. (1981) 'Sources of Innovation in Agricultural Technology'. *World Development* 9: 321–36.

Biggs, S. and Matsaert, H. (1999) 'An Actor-Oriented Approach for Strengthening Research and Development Capabilities in Natural Resource Systems'. *Public Administration and Development* 19: 231–62.

Bliss, C. J. and Stern, N. H. (1982) *Palanpur: The Economy of an Indian Village*. Oxford: Clarendon Press.

152

Bohn, A. and Byerlee, D. (1993) *The Wheat Breeding Industry in Developing Countries: An Analysis of Investments and Inputs.* Part I of 1992/93 CIMMYT World Wheat Facts and Trends. Singapore: CIMMYT.

Boserup, E. (1965) *The Conditions of Agricultural Growth.* Chicago: Aldine.

Boster, J. (1986) 'Exchange of Varieties and Information among Aguaruna Manioc Cultivators', *American Anthropologist* 88: 428–36.

Boulding, K. (1966) *The Image.* Ann Arbor, MI: University of Michigan Press.

Boyle, J. (1996) *Shamans, Software, and Spleens: Law and the Construction of the Information Society.* Cambridge, MA: Harvard University Press.

Braverman, A., Guasch, J. L., Huppi, M. and Pohlmeier, L. (1991) *Promoting Rural Cooperatives in Developing Countries. The Case of Sub-Saharan Africa.* World Bank Discussion Paper No. 121. Washington, DC: World Bank.

Bray, F. (1986) *The Rice Economies: Technology and Development in Asian Societies.* Oxford: Basil Blackwell.

Brockway, L. H. (1988) 'Plant Science and Colonial Expansion: The Botanical Chess Game' in J. R. Kloppenburg (ed.) *Seeds and Sovereignty.* Durham, NC: Duke University Press.

Brown, L. D. and Ashman, D. (1996) 'Participation, Social Capital, and Intersectoral Problem Solving: African and Asian Cases', *World Development* 24: 1467–79.

Browne, W., Skees, J., Swanson, L., Thompson, P. and Unnevehr, L. (1992) *Sacred Cows and Hot Potatoes. Agrarian Myths in Agricultural Policy.* Boulder, CO: Westview Press.

Brush, S. (1992a) 'Farmers' Rights and Genetic Conservation in Traditional Farming Systems' *World Development* 20: 1617–1630.

Brush, S. (1992b) 'Reconsidering the Green Revolution: Diversity and Stability in Cradle Areas of Crop Domestication', *Human Ecology* 20: 145–67.

Brush, S. B., Carney, H. J. and Huaman, Z. (1981) 'Dynamics of Andean Potato Agriculture', *Economic Botany* 35: 70–88.

Bunting, H. and Pickersgill, B. (1996) 'What is a Plant Genetic Resource?', *Biologist* 43: 227–30.

Busch, L. and Lacy, W. B. (1983) *Science, Agriculture, and the Politics of Research.* Boulder, CO: Westview Press.

Busch, L., Lacy, W. B., Burkhardt, J. and Lacy, L. R. (1991) *Plants, Power and Profit.* Cambridge, MA: Blackwell.

Butler, L.J. and Marion, B.W. (1985) *Impacts of Patent Protection in the US Seed Industry and Public Plant Breeding.* North Central Regional Research Bulletin No.304. Madison, WI: University of Wisconsin.

Byerlee, D. (1994) *Modern Varieties, Productivity, and Sustainability: Recent Experience and Emerging Challenges.* Mexico, D.F.: CIMMYT.

Byerlee, D. and Lopez-Pereira, M. (1994) *Technical Change in Maize Production: A Global Perspective.* CIMMYT Economics Working Paper 94–02. Mexico, D.F.: CIMMYT.

Byerlee, D., Iqbal, M. and Fischer, K. S. (1989) 'Quantifying and Valuing the Joint Production of Grain and Fodder from Maize Fields: Evidence from Northern Pakistan', *Experimental Agriculture* 25: 435–45.

Byres, T. J. (1981) 'The New Technology, Class Formation and Class Action in the Indian Countryside', *Journal of Peasant Studies* 8: 405–59.

Campilan, D., Prain, G. and Bagalanon, C. L. (1999) 'Evaluation from the Inside: Participatory Evaluation of Agricultural Research in the Philippines'. *Knowledge, Technology, and Policy* 11 (4): 114–31.

Carlsson, J., Köhlin, G. and Ekbom, A. (1994) *The Political Economy of Evaluation. International Aid Agencies and the Effectiveness of Aid.* New York: St. Martin's Press.

Cassen, R. & Associates (1994) *Does Aid Work?* Oxford: Clarendon Press.

Ceccarelli, S. (1989) 'Wide Adaptation. How Wide?', *Euphytica* 40: 197–205.

Chalfin, B. (1996) 'Market Reforms and the State: The Case of Shea in Ghana', *Journal of Modern African Studies* 34: 421–40.

Chambers, R. (1993) *Challenging the Professions.* London: Intermediate Technology Publications.

Chambers, R. (1997) *Whose Reality Counts?* London: Intermediate Technology Publications.

Chhetri, P. (1992) 'A Study on the Potato Seed Flow for the Selected Districts of Nepal', *The Economic Journal of Nepal* 15: 1–19.

Chitrikar, D. (1999) *Report on Survey of the Seed Retailers of the West Command Area of SSP.* Kathmandu: Seed Sector Support Project.

Choto, C., Sain, G. and Montenegro, T. (1996) *Oferta y Demanda de Semilla Mejorada de Maíz en El Salvador.* San José, Costa Rica: CIMMYT Programa Regional de Maíz.

Clague, C. (ed.) (1997) *Institutions and Economic Development.* Baltimore: Johns Hopkins University Press.

Clawson, D. (1985) 'Harvest Security and Intraspecific Diversity in Traditional Tropical Agriculture', *Economic Botany* 39: 56–67.

Clunies-Ross, T. (1996) 'Creeping Enclosure. Seed Legislation, Plant Breeders' Rights and Scottish Potatoes', *The Ecologist* 26(3): 110–14.

Coase, R. (1937) 'The Nature of the Firm', *Economica* 4: 386–405.

Cohen, J. I. (1999) *Managing Agricultural Biotechnology: Addressing Research Program Needs and Policy Implications.* Wallingford, UK: CAB International.

Coleman, J. S. (1988) 'Social Capital in the Creation of Human Capital', *American Journal of Sociology* 94 (supp.): S95–S120.

Collins, G. N. (1914) 'Pueblo Indian Maize Breeding', *Journal of Heredity* 5: 255–68.

Collinson, M. (ed.) (2000) *A History of Farming Systems Research.* Wallingford, UK: CAB International.

Commons, J.R. (1934) *Institutional Economics.* New York: Macmillan.

Conklin, H. C. (1957) *Hanunoo Agriculture in the Philippines.* Forestry Development Paper No. 12. Rome: FAO.

Cotterrell, R. (1989) *The Politics of Jurisprudence.* London: Butterworth.

Coughenour, C. M. and Nazhat, S. M. (1985) *Recent Change in Villages and Rainfed Agriculture in North Central Kordofan: Communication Process and Constraints.* Report No. 4 of International Sorghum/Millet Collaborative Research Support Program. Lincoln, NE: Institute of Agriculture and Natural Resources, University of Nebraska.

Cowen, M.P. and Shenton, R.W. (1996) *Doctrines of Development.* London: Routledge.

Crissman, C. C. (1989) *Seed Potato Systems in the Philippines: A Case Study.* Lima: International Potato Center.

Crissman, C. C. and Uquillas, J. E. (1989) *Seed Potato Systems in Ecuador: A Case Study.* Lima: International Potato Center.

Cromwell, E., Friis-Hansen, E. and Turner, M. (1992) *The Seed Sector in Developing Countries: A Framework for Performance Analysis.* Working Paper No. 65. London: Overseas Development Institute.

Crowder, L. V. (1988) 'Agents, Vendors, and Farmers: Agricultural Technology Transfer in Ecuador', *Agricultural Administration and Extension* 30: 215–20.

Dahlman, C. (1979) 'The Problem of Externality', *Journal of Law and Economics* 2: 141–62.

Dasgupta, P. (1988) 'Trust as a Commodity' in D. Gambetta (ed.) *Trust. Making and Breaking Cooperative Relations.* Oxford: Basil Blackwell.

Davis, L. and North, D. (1971) *Institutional Change and American Economic Growth.* Cambridge: Cambridge University Press.

Demsetz, H. (1967) 'Toward a Theory of Property Rights', *American Economic Review* 57: 347–59.

Diaz, C., Hossain, M., Luis, J. and Paris, T. (1994) 'Knowledge, Attitude and Practice of Seed Management Technologies in Rice Farming in Central Luzon', *Philippine Journal of Crop Science* 19: 87–99.

Dorn, J. A., Hanke, S. H. and Walters, A. A. (1998) *The Revolution in Development Economics.* Washington, DC: Cato Institute.

Dorward, A., Kydd, J. and Poulton, C. (1998) *Smallholder Cash Crop Production Under Market Liberalisation.* Wallingford, UK: CAB International.

Dove, M. R. (1985) *Swidden Agriculture in Indonesia. The Subsistence Strategies of the Kalimantu Kantu.* Berlin: Mouton Publishers.

Duvick, D. N. (1988) 'The United States' in M. L. Morris (ed.) *Maize Seed Industries in Developing Countries.* Boulder, CO: Lynne Rienner.

Ellis, F. (1988) *Peasant Economics.* Cambridge: Cambridge University Press.

Ellis, F. (1998) 'Household Strategies and Rural Livelihood Diversification', *Journal of Development Studies* 35: 1–38.

Ensminger, J. (1992) *Making a Market.* Cambridge: Cambridge University Press.

Evans, L. T. (1993) *Crop Evolution, Adaptation and Yield.* Cambridge: Cambridge University Press.

Farrington, J. and Bebbington, A. with Wellard, K. and Lewis, D. (1993) *Reluctant Partners? Non-Governmental Organizations, the State and Sustainable Agricultural Development.* London: Routledge.

Field, A. J. (1984) 'Microeconomics, Norms, and Rationality', *Economic Development and Cultural Change* 32: 683–711.

Firth, R. (1967) *Themes in Economic Anthropology.* London: Tavistock Publications.

Fitzgerald, D. (1990) *The Business of Breeding. Hybrid Corn in Illinois, 1890–1940.* Ithaca, NY: Cornell University Press.

Flannery, K. V. (1965) 'The Ecology of Early Food Production in Mesopotamia', *Science* 147: 1247–56.

Foster, G. M. (1962) *Traditional Cultures: and the Impact of Technological Change.* New York: Harper and Row.

Fowler, C. (1994) *Unnatural Selection. Technology, Politics, and Plant Evolution.* Yverdon, Switzerland: Gordon and Breach.

Fox, H. S. A. (1979) 'Local Farmers' Associations and the Circulation of Agricultural Information in Nineteenth-Century England' in H. Fox and R. Butlin (eds), *Change in the Countryside: Essays on Rural England 1500–1900.* Institute of British Geographers Special Publication No. 10. London.

Francks, P. (1984) *Technology and Agricultural Development in Pre-War Japan.* New Haven, CT: Yale University Press.

Freeman, J. D. (1955) *Iban Agriculture: A Report on the Shifting Cultivation of Hill Rice by the Iban of Sarawak.* Colonial Research Station Paper No. 18. London: HMSO.

Friis-Hansen, E. and Rohrbach, D. (1993) *SADC/ICRISAT 1992 Drought Relief Emergency Production of Sorghum and Pearl Millet. Impact Assessment.* ICRISAT Southern and Eastern Africa Region Working Paper 93/01. Bulawayo: ICRISAT.

Frisvold, G. B. and Condon, P. T. (1998) 'The Convention on Biological Diversity and Agriculture: Implications and Unresolved Debates', *World Development* 26: 551–70.

Fukuyama, F. (1995) *Trust*. New York: Free Press.

Furubotn, E. G. and Pejovich, S. (1972) 'Property Rights and Economic Theory: A Survey of Recent Literature', *Journal of Economic Literature* 10: 1137–62.

Gebrekidan, B. and Kebede, Y. (1979) 'The Traditional Culture and Yield Potentials of the Ethiopian High Lysine Sorghums', *Ethiopian Journal of Agricultural Science* 1: 29–40.

Ghijsen, H. (1996) 'The Development of Variety Testing and Breeders' Rights in the Netherlands' in H. Van Amstel, J. Bottema, M. Sidik and C. Van Santen (eds) *Integrating Seed Systems for Annual Food Crops*. Bogor, Indonesia: CGPRT Centre.

Granovetter, M. (1985) 'Economic Action and Social Structure: The Problem of Embeddedness', *American Journal of Sociology* 91: 481–510.

Green, T. (1987) *Farmer-to-Farmer Seed Exchange in the Eastern Hills of Nepal: The Case of Pokhreli Masino Rice*. Working Paper 05/87. Dhankuta, Nepal: Pakhribas Agricultural Centre.

Greif, A. (1993) 'Contract Enforceability and Economic Institutions in Early Trade: The Maghribi Traders' Coalition', *American Economic Review* 83: 525–48.

Grigg, D. (1982) *The Dynamics of Agricultural Change*. London: Hutchinson.

Gubbels, P. (1997) 'Strengthening Community Capacity for Sustainable Agriculture' in L. van Veldhizen, A. Waters-Bayer, R. Ramirez, D. Johnson and J. Thompson (eds) *Farmers' Research in Practice: Lessons from the Field*. London: Intermediate Technology Publications.

Habib, I. (1999) *The Agrarian System of Mughal India 1556–1707*. (2nd Edition). New Delhi: Oxford University Press.

Haggblade, S. and Hazell, P. (1989) 'Agricultural Technology and Farm – Nonfarm Growth Linkages', *Agricultural Economics* 3: 345–64.

Harlan, J. R. (1988) 'Seeds and Sovereignty: An Epilogue' in J. R. Kloppenburg (ed.) *Seeds and Sovereignty*. Durham, NC: Duke University Press.

Harlan, J. R. (1995) *The Living Fields*. Cambridge: Cambridge University Press.

Harriss, B. (1987) 'Regional Growth Linkages From Agriculture', *Journal of Development Studies* 23: 257–89.

Harriss, J. (1992) 'Does the 'Depressor' Still Work? Agrarian Structure and Development in India: A Review of Evidence and Argument', *Journal of Peasant Studies* 19: 189–227.

Harriss, J., Hunter, J. and Lewis, C.M. (1995) *The New Institutional Economics and Third World Development*. London: Routledge.

Harriss, J. and de Renzio, P. (1997) '"Missing Link" or Analytically Missing?: The Concept of Social Capital', *Journal of International Development* 9: 919–37.

Harriss-White, B. (1996) *A Political Economy of Agricultural Markets in South India*. New Delhi: Sage Publications.

Hassan, R., Njoroge, K., Njore, M., Otsyula, R. and Laboso, A. (1998) 'Adoption Patterns and Performance of Improved Maize in Kenya' in R. Hassan (ed.) *Maize Technology Development and Transfer. A GIS Application for Research Planning in Kenya*. Wallingford, UK: CAB International.

Haugerud, A and Collinson, M. (1990) 'Plants, Genes and People: Improving the Relevance of Plant Breeding in Africa', *Experimental Agriculture* 26: 341–62.

Havers, M. (1991) 'NGOs as Agencies for Small Enterprise Development', *Small Enterprise Development* 2 (3): 14–24.

Hawkins, R. (1984) 'Intercropping Maize with Sorghum in Central America: A Cropping System Case Study', *Agricultural Systems* 15: 79–99.

Hayami, Y. and Ruttan, V. W. (1985) *Agricultural Development: An International Perspective* (2nd Edition). Baltimore: Johns Hopkins University Press.

Hazell, P. and Ramasamy, C. (1991) *The Green Revolution Reconsidered*. Baltimore: Johns Hopkins University Press.

Heisey, P. (ed). (1990) *Accelerating the Transfer of Wheat Breeding Gains to Farmers: A Study of the Dynamics of Varietal Replacement in Pakistan*. Mexico, D. F.: CIMMYT.

Heisey, P. and Brennan, J. (1991) 'An Analytical Model of Farmers' Demand for Replacement Seed', *American Journal of Agricultural Economics* 73: 1044–52.

Heisey, P., Smale, M., Byerlee, D. and Souza, E. (1997) 'Wheat Rusts and the Costs of Genetic Diversity in the Punjab of Pakistan', *American Journal of Agricultural Economics* 79: 726–37.

Heller, M. A. and Eisenberg, R. S. (1998) 'Can Patents Deter Innovation? The Anticommons in Biomedical Research', *Science* 280: 698–701.

Henderson, P. A. and Singh, R. (1990) *NGO-Government Links in Seed Production: Case Studies from the Gambia and Ethiopia*, Agricultural Administration Research and Extension Network Paper No. 14. London: Overseas Development Institute.

Hewitt de Alcantára, C. (1976) *Modernizing Mexican Agriculture: Socio-Economic Implications of Technological Change 1940–1970*. Geneva: UNRISD.

Hill, P. (1972) *Rural Hausa: A Village and a Setting*. Cambridge: Cambridge University Press.

Hodgson, G. M. (1994) 'The Return of Institutional Economics' in Smelser and Swedberg.

Houston, J. E., Centner, T. J. and Morgan, W. (1988) 'Uncertainty and Structural Issues Facing the Seed Handling Industry', *Agribusiness* 4 (4): 347–57.

Humphries, S., Gonzales, J., Jimenez, J. and Sierra, F. (1999) *Searching for Sustainable Land Use Practices in Honduras: Lessons from a Program of Participatory Research with Hillside Farmers*. Agricultural Research and Extension Network Paper No. 104. London: Overseas Development Institute.

Humphry, J. and Schmitz, H. (1996) *Trust and Economic Development*. Discussion Paper No. 355. Brighton: Institute of Development Studies, Sussex University.

Israel, A. (1987) *Institutional Development*. Baltimore: Johns Hopkins University Press.

Jaffee, W. and van Wijk, J. (eds) (1995) *The Impact of Plant Breeders' Rights in Developing Countries: Debate and Experience in Argentina, Chile, Colombia, Mexico and Uruguay*. The Hague: Directorate General International Cooperation (DGIS), Ministry of Foreign Affairs.

Jaffee, S. and Srivastava, J. (1994) 'The Roles of the Private and Public Sectors in Enhancing the Performance of Seed Systems', *The World Bank Research Observer* 9: 97–117.

James, C. (1999) *Global Status of Commercialised Transgenic Crops*. ISAAA Briefs No. 12, Ithaca, NY: International Service for the Acquisition of Agri-Biotech Applications.

Janssen, W., Luna, C. A. and Duque, M. C. (1992) 'Small-Farmer Behaviour Towards Bean Seed: Evidence From Colombia', *Journal of Applied Seed Production* 10: 43–51.

Jennings, P. R. and Cock, J. H. (1977) 'Centres of Origin of Crops and Their Productivity', *Economic Botany* 31: 51–4.

Johannessen, C. L. (1982) 'Domestication Process of Maize Continues in Guatemala', *Economic Botany* 36: 84–99.

Johnston, B. F. and Kilby, P. (1975) *Agriculture and Structural Transformation*. New York: Oxford University Press.

Kaimowitz, D. (1989) *Placing Agricultural Research and Technology Transfer in One Organization: Two Experiences from Colombia*. Linkages Discussion Paper No. 3. The Hague: ISNAR.

Kelley, T. G., Rao, P.P. and Walker, T. S. (1991) *The Relative Value of Cereal Straw Fodder in the Semi-Arid Tropics of India: Implications for Cereal Breeding Programs at ICRISAT*. Resource Management Program Economics Group Progress Report 105. Patancheru, India: ICRISAT.

Kelly, A. F. and Bowring, J. D. C. (1990) ' The Development of Seed Certification in England and Wales', *Plant Varieties and Seeds* 3(3): 139–50.

Kerblay, B. (1971) 'Chayanov and the Theory of Peasantry as a Specific Type of Economy' in T. Shanin (ed.) *Peasants and Peasant Societies.* Harmondsworth, UK: Penguin.

Kimenye, L. and Nyangito, H. (1996) 'Seed Regulatory Frameworks: Kenya', unpublished paper prepared for Overseas Development Institute/CAZS Seed Regulatory Project.

Klein, B. and Leffler, K. B. (1981) 'The Role of Market Forces in Assuring Contractual Performance', *Journal of Political Economy* 89(4): 615–41.

Klitgaard, R. (1997) 'Information and Incentives in Institutional Reform' in Clague.

Kloppenburg, J. R. (1988) *First the Seed.* Cambridge: Cambridge University Press.

Kloppenburg, J. R. and Kleinman, D. L. (1988) 'Plant Genetic Resources: The Common Bowl'. in J. R. Kloppenburg (ed.) *Seeds and Sovereignty.* Durham, NC: Duke University Press.

Knudson, M. (1990) 'The Role of the Public Sector in Applied Breeding R & D', *Food Policy* 15: 209–17.

Koppel, B.M. (ed.) (1995) *Induced Innovation Theory and International Agricultural Development.* Baltimore: Johns Hopkins University Press.

Kshirsagar, K. and Pandey, S. (1996) 'Diversity of Rice Cultivars in a Rainfed Village in the Orissa State of India', in L. Sperling and M. Loevinsohn (eds) *Using Diversity: Enhancing and Maintaining Genetic Resources On-Farm.* New Delhi: IDRC/SARO.

Lamont, J. T. J. (1993) 'Export Success Determinants in the New Product Development Process for Exported Agricultural Products: Evidence from the Dutch Seed Potato Industry'. *Agricultural Systems* 41: 455–74.

Landes, D. (1998) *The Wealth and Poverty of Nations.* London: Little Brown.

Lane, R. E. (1991) *The Market Experience.* Cambridge: Cambridge University Press.

Lazear, E. P. (1987) 'Incentive Contracts' in J. Eatwell, M. Milgate and P. Newman (eds) *The New Palgrave. A Dictionary of Economics.* London: Macmillan.

Le Buanec, B. (1996) 'Globalisation of the Seed Industry: Current Situation and Evolution'. *Seed Science and Technology* 24: 409–17.

Leonard, D. K. (1977) *Reaching the Peasant Farmer: Organization Theory and Practice in Kenya.* Chicago: University of Chicago Press.

Leonard, D. K. (1993) 'Structural Reform of the Veterinary Profession in Africa and the New Institutional Economics', *Development and Change* 24: 227–67.

Lesser, W. (1997) 'Assessing the Implications of Intellectual Property Rights on Plant and Animal Agriculture', *American Journal of Agricultural Economics* 79: 1584–91.

Levins, R. and Lewontin, R. (1985) *The Dialectical Biologist,* Cambridge MA: Harvard University Press.

Lewis, W. A. (1955) *The Theory of Economic Growth.* London: George Allen and Unwin.

Lionberger, H. F. and Chang, H. C. (1970) *Farm Information for Modernizing Agriculture: The Taiwan System.* New York: Praeger.

Lipton, M. and Longhurst, R. (1989) *New Seeds and Poor People.* London: Unwin Hyman.

Little, P. D. and Watts, M. J. (eds) (1994) *Living Under Contract. Contract Farming and Agrarian Transformation in sub-Saharan Africa.* Madison,WI: University of Wisconsin Press.

Long, N. (1968) *Social Change and the Individual.* Manchester: Manchester University Press.

Longley, C., Coulter, J. and Thompson, R. (1999) 'Malawi Rural Livelihoods Starter Pack Scheme, 1998–9: Evaluation Report'. Unpublished paper. London: Overseas Development Institute.

Louette, D. and Smale, M. (1998) *Farmers' Seed Selection Practices and Maize Variety Characteristics in a Traditionally-Based Mexican Community.* CIMMYT Economics Working Paper 98–04. Mexico, D. F.: CIMMYT.

Louwaars, N. P. (1994) 'Integrated Seed Supply: A Flexible Approach', paper presented at the ILCA/ICARDA Research Planning Workshop on Smallholder Seed Production, 13–15 June, Addis Ababa.

Louwaars, N. P. with Marrewijk, G. A. M. (n.d.) *Seed Supply Systems in Developing Countries.* Wageningen: Technical Centre for Agricultural and Rural Cooperation.

Low, A. (1986) *Agricultural Development in Southern Africa.* London: James Currey.

Lupton, F. G. H. (1988) 'History of Wheat Breeding' in F. G. H. Lupton (ed.) *Wheat Breeding: Its Scientific Basis.* London: Chapman and Hall.

Lyoba, B and Tripp, R. 'Linking Adaptive Research to Farmer Seed Systems: The Diffusion of New Varieties in Senanga West, Zambia'. Unpublished paper.

Lyon, F. (1997) 'Vegetable Varieties, Seed Selection and Seed Supply Systems in Brong- Ahafo, Ghana'. Unpublished paper. Chatham, UK: Natural Resources Institute.

Lyon, F. and Afikorah-Danquah, S. (1998) *Small-Scale Seed Provision in Ghana: Social Relations, Contracts and Institutions for Micro-Enterprise Development.* Agricultural Research and Extension Network Paper No. 84. London: Overseas Development Institute.

Makus, L. D., Guenthner, J. F. and Lin, B-H. (1992) 'Factors Influencing Producer Support for a State Mandatory Seed Law: An Empirical Analysis', *Journal of Agriculture and Resource Economics* 17(2): 286–93.

Maredia, M., Howard, J. and Boughton, D. (1999) *Increasing Seed System Efficiency in Africa: Concepts, Strategies and Issues.* MSU International Development Working Paper No.77. East Lansing, MI: Michigan State University.

Martin, G. and Adams, M. W. (1987) 'Landraces of *Phaseolus vulgaris* (Fabaceae) in Northern Malawi. I. Regional Variation'. *Economic Botany* 41: 190–203.

Maurya, D. M. (1989) 'The Innovative Approach of Indian Farmers', in R. Chambers, A. Pacey and L. A. Thrupp (eds) *Farmer First. Farmer Innovation and Agricultural Research.* London: Intermediate Technology Publications.

McGuire, S,, Manicad, G. and Sperling, L. (1999) *Technical and Institutional Issues in Participatory Plant Breeding – Done from a Perspective of Farmer Plant Breeding.* Working Document No.2. Cali: CGIAR Systemwide Program on Participatory Research and Gender Analysis for Technology Development and Institutional Innovation.

McMullen, N. (1987) *Seeds and World Agricultural Progress.* Washington, DC: National Planning Association.

Mellor, J. W. (1998) 'Closing the Last Chapter on U.S. Foreign Aid. What to do About Africa'. *Choices* Fourth Quarter: 38–42.

Merrill-Sands, D. and McAllister, J. (1988) *Strengthening the Integration of On-Farm Client-Oriented Research and Experiment Station Research in National Agricultural Research Systems (NARS): Management Lessons from Nine Country Case Studies.* OFCOR Comparative Study Paper No. 1. The Hague: ISNAR.

Meyer, C. (1992) 'A Step Back as Donors Shift Institution Building from the Public to the 'Private' Sector'. *World Development* 20: 1115–26.

Miclat-Teves, A. and Lewis, D. (1993) 'NGO-Government Interaction in the Philippines: Overview', in J. Farrington and D. Lewis with S. Satish and A. Miclat-Teves (eds) *Non-Governmental Organizations and the State in Asia.* London: Routledge.

Milgrom, P., North, D. and Weingast, B. (1990) 'The Role of Institutions in the Revival of Trade: The Law Merchant, Private Judges, and the Champagne Fairs', *Economics and Politics* 2: 1–23.

Mitnick, B. M. (1980) *The Political Economy of Regulation: Creating, Designing and Removing Regulatory Forms.* New York: Columbia University Press.

Mooney, P. R. (1979) *Seeds of the Earth.* Ottawa: Mutual Press.

Mooney, P. R. (1992) 'Towards a Folk Revolution' in D. Cooper, R. Vellve, and H. Hobbelink (eds) *Growing Diversity: Genetic Resources and Local Food Security*. London: Intermediate Technology Publications.

Moore, M. (1995) 'Promoting Good Government by Supporting Institutional Development?', *IDS Bulletin* 26 (2): 89–96.

Moore, M. (1997) 'Societies, Polities and Capitalists in Developing Countries: A Literature Survey', *Journal of Development Studies* 33: 287–363.

Morin, S. R., Pham, J. L., Calibo, M., Belen, M. G., Jackson, M. T., Erasga, D., and Bellon, M. (1999) 'Rice Variety Classification Among Farmers in the Cagayan Valley Philippines. Its Utility for On-Farm Conservation'. Draft paper. Manila: IRRI.

Morris, M. L. (1998) 'Thailand' in M. L. Morris (ed) *Maize Seed Industries in Developing Countries*. Boulder, CO: Lynne Rienner.

Morris, M. L., Dubin, H. J. and Pokhrel, T. (1992) *Returns to Wheat Research in Nepal*. Economics Working Paper 92–04. Mexico, D.F.: CIMMYT.

Morris, M. L. and López-Pereira, M. (1999) *Impacts of Maize Breeding Research in Latin America, 1966–1997*. Mexico, D.F.: CIMMYT.

Morris, M. L., Risopoulis, J. and Beck, D. (1999) *Genetic Change in Farmer-Recycled Maize Seed: A Review of the Evidence*. CIMMYT Economics Working Paper 99–07. Mexico, D.F.: CIMMYT.

Morris, M. L., Tripp, R. and Dankyi, A. A. (1999) *Adoption and Impacts of Improved Maize Production Technology: A Case Study of the Ghana Grains Development Project*. Economics Program Paper No. 99–01. Mexico, D. F.: CIMMYT.

Morss, E. R. (1984) 'Institutional Destruction Resulting from Donor and Project Proliferation in Sub-Saharan African Countries'. *World Development* 12: 465–70.

Morton, J. (1996) *The Poverty of Nations: The Aid Dilemma at the Heart of Africa*. London: I.B. Tauris.

Mosley, P. (1987) *Overseas Aid. Its Defence and Reform*. Brighton: Wheatsheaf Books.

Msimuko, A. (1997) 'ActionAid's Experience with Small-Scale Seed Production and Distribution in Malawi', in D. Rohrbach, Z. Bishaw and A. J. G. van Gastel (eds) *Alternative Strategies for Smallholder Seed Supply*. Patancheru, India: ICRISAT.

Mulberg, J. (1995) *Social Limits to Economic Theory*. London: Routledge.

Murdock, G. P. (1959) *Africa: Its Peoples and Their Culture History*. New York: McGraw-Hill.

Nabli, M. and Nugent, J. (1989) 'The New Institutional Economics and Its Applicability to Development', *World Development* 17: 1333–47.

Narayan, D. and Pritchett, L. (1997) *Cents and Sociability: Household Income and Social Capital in Rural Tanzania*, Policy Research Working Paper 1796. Social Development and Development Research Group. Washington, DC: World Bank.

Needham, D. (1983) *The Economics and Politics of Regulation: A Behavioural Approach*. Boston, MA: Little, Brown and Company.

Netting, R. McC. (1968) *Hill Farmers of Nigeria*. Seattle: University of Washington Press.

Norskog, C. (1995) *Hybrid Seed Corn Enterprises. A Brief History*. Willmar, MN: Maracom Corp.

North, D.C. (1990) *Institutions, Institutional Change and Economic Performance*. Cambridge: Cambridge University Press.

Nuffield Council on Bioethics (1999) *Genetically Modified Crops: The Ethical and Social Issues*. London: Nuffield Council on Bioethics.

O'Donoghue, M. (1995) 'The Whole Family Training Program on Post-Harvest Technologies. A Program Review'. A Report for the Bangladesh-Australia Wheat Improvement Project. Dhaka.

Olson, M. (1965) *The Logic of Collective Action*. Cambridge: Cambridge University Press.

Ortiz, R., Ruano, S., Juárez, H., Olivet, F. and Meneses, A. (1991) *A New Model for Technology Transfer in Guatemala*. OFCOR Discussion Paper No.2. The Hague: ISNAR.

Ostrom, E. (1990) *Governing the Commons*. Cambridge: Cambridge University Press.

Ostrom, E. (1996) 'Crossing the Great Divide: Co-production, Synergy, and Development'. *World Development* 24: 1073–87.

Ostrom, E. (1997) 'Investing in Capital, Institutions and Incentives' in Clague.

Ostrom, E., Schroeder, L. and Wynne, S. (1993) *Institutional Incentives and Sustainable Development*. Boulder, CO: Westview Press.

Otsuka, K. and Hayami, Y. (1988) 'Theories of Share Tenancy: A Critical Survey', *Economic Development and Cultural Change* 37: 31–68.

Otto, H. J. (1985) 'The Current Status of Seed Certification in the Seed Industry' in M. B. McDonald and W. D. Purdee (eds) *The Role of Seed Certification in the Seed Industry*. Madison, WI: Crop Science Society of America.

Overseas Development Institute Seeds and Biodiversity Programme (1996*) Seed Provision During and After Emergencies*. Relief and Rehabilitation Network Good Practice Review No. 4. London: Overseas Development Institute.

Pal, S., Tripp, R. and Janaiah, A. (forthcoming) *The Public-Private Interface and Information Flow in the Rice Seed System of Andhra Pradesh*. NCAP Working Paper. New Delhi: NCAP.

Pardey, P. G., Roseboom, J. and Beintema, N. M. (1997) 'Investments in African Agricultural Research', *World Development* 25: 409–23.

Parsons, F. G. (1985) 'The Early History of Seed Certification, 1900–1970' in M. B. McDonald and W. D. Purdee (eds) *The Role of Seed Certification in the Seed Industry*. Madison, WI: Crop Science Society of America.

Pattie, P. and Madawanaarchchi, W. (1993) 'Factors Affecting Seed Marketing in Sri Lanka', Peradeniya, Sri Lanka: Diversified Agriculture Research Project.

Peletz, M.G. (1983) 'Moral and Political Economies in Rural Southeast Asia', *Comparative Study of Society and History* 25: 731–9.

Perrin, R. and Winkelmann, D. (1976) 'Impediments to Technical Progress on Small Versus Large Farms', *American Journal of Agricultural Economics* 58: 888–94.

Phiri, M. A. R., Kambewa, P. and Tripp, R. (1999) 'The Diffusion of Seed and Information in the Malawi Smallholder Seed Development Project'. Unpublished paper.

Pingali, P. (1994) 'Technological Prospects for Reversing the Declining Trend in Asia's Rice Productivity' in J. Anderson (ed.) *Agricultural Technology: Policy Issues for the International Community*. Wallingford, UK: CAB International.

Polanyi, K., Arensberg, C. and Pearson, H. (1957) *Trade and Market in the Early Empires*. Glencoe, IL: Free Press.

Popkin, S. L. (1979) *The Rational Peasant: The Political Economy of Rural Society in Vietnam*. Berkeley, CA: University of California Press.

Porter, G. and Phillips-Howard, K. (1997) 'Comparing Contracts: An Evaluation of Contract Farming Schemes in Africa', *World Development* 25: 227–38.

Powell,W. and Smith-Doerr, L. (1994) 'Networks and Economic Life' in Smelser and Swedberg.

Pratt, J. W. and Zeckhauser, R. J. (1985) *Principals and Agents: The Structure of Business*. Cambridge, MA: Harvard Business School Press.

Pratten, D. T. (1997) 'Local Institutional Development and Relief in Ethiopia: A *Kire*-Based Seed Distribution Programme in North Wollo', *Disasters* 21: 138–59.

Pray, C. E. and Umali-Deininger, D. (1998) 'The Private Sector in Agricultural Research Systems: Will It Fill the Gap?', *World Development* 26: 1127–48.

Pray, C. E. and Ramaswami, B. (1991) *A Framework for Seed Policy Analysis in Developing Countries*. Washington, DC: IFPRI.

Pray, C. E., Ribeiro, S., Mueller, R. and Rao, P. (1991) 'Private Research and Public Benefit: The Private Seed Industry for Sorghum and Pearl Millet in India', *Research Policy* 20: 315–24.

Pretty, J. (1995) *Regenerating Agriculture*. London: Earthscan.

Prendergast, C. (1999) 'The Provision of Incentives in Firms', *Journal of Economic Literature* 37: 7–63.

Putnam, R. D. (1993) *Making Democracy Work*. Princeton, NJ: Princeton University Press.

Putzel, J. (1998) 'The Business of Aid: Transparency and Accountability in European Union Development Assistance', *Journal of Development Studies* 34 (3): 71–96.

RAFI (Rural Advancement Foundation International) (1999) 'The Gene Giants: Masters of the Universe?', *RAFI Communique*, March-April.

Rice, E., Smale, M. and Blanco, J-L. (1998) 'Farmers' Use of Improved Seed Selection Practices in Mexican Maize: Evidence and Issues from the Sierra de Santa Marta', *World Development* 26: 1625–40.

Richards, P. (1986) *Coping with Hunger: Hazard and Experiment in an African Rice Farming System*. London: Allen and Unwin.

Richards, P. and Ruivenkamp, G. (1997) *Seeds and Survival: Crop Genetic Resources in War and Reconstruction in Africa*. Rome: IPGRI.

Rivera, W. M. (1996) 'Agricultural Extension in Transition Worldwide: Structural, Financial and Managerial Reform Strategies for Improving Agricultural Extension', *Public Administration and Development* 16: 151–62.

Robertson, A. F. (1987) *The Dynamics of Productive Relationships. African Share Contracts in Comparitive Perspective*. Cambridge: Cambridge University Press.

Rogers, E.M. (1962) *Diffusion of Innovations*. New York: Free Press.

Rohrbach, D. (1997) 'Farmer-to-Farmer Seed Movement in Zimbabwe: Issues Arising' in D. Rohrbach, Z. Bishaw and A. J. G. van Gastel (eds) *Alternative Strategies for Smallholder Seed Supply*. Patancheru, India: ICRISAT.

Rohrbach, D. and Mutiro, K. (1996) 'Formal and Informal Channels of Sorghum and Pearl Millet Seed Supply in Zimbabwe'. Paper presented at the National Workshop on Seed Policies in Zimbabwe, 30–31 July, Harare.

Ronald, P. C. (1997) 'Making Rice Disease-Resistant', *Scientific American* November: 100–5.

Roper, E. M. C. (1989) *Seed Time: The History of Essex Seeds*. Chichester, UK: Phillimore & Co.

Rosales, J. (1995) 'Informe Sobre Enfoques Participativos y Alternativos para la Producción y Distribución de Semillas en Santa Cruz', unpublished paper prepared for Overseas Development Institute/CAZS Seed Regulatory Project.

Rusike, J. (1995) 'An Institutional Analysis of the Maize Seed Industry in Southern Africa'. Unpublished PhD Thesis. Dept. of Agricultural Economics, Michigan State University.

Ruthenberg, H. (1976) *Farming Systems in the Tropics* (2nd Edition). Oxford: Oxford University Press.

Ruttan, V. W. (1988) 'Cultural Endowments and Economic Development: What Can We Learn from Anthropology?', *Economic Development and Cultural Change* 36 (Supplement): S247–71.

Rutz, H. W. (1990) 'Seed Certification in the Federal Republic of Germany', *Plant Varieties and Seeds* 3(3): 157–63.

Saasa, O. and Carlsson, J. (1996) *The Aid Relationship in Zambia. A Conflict Scenario*. Lusaka and Uppsala: The Institute for African Studies and The Nordic Africa Institute.

Salazar, R. (1992) 'Community Plant Genetic Resources Management: Experiences in Southeast Asia', in D. Cooper, R. Vellvé and H. Hobbelink (eds) *Growing Diversity: Genetic Resources and Local Food Security*. London: Intermediate Technology Publications.

Sattar, M. and Hossain, S. M. (1986) 'An Evaluation of Farmers' Technology for Seed Production and Post-Harvest Operations in Aus Rice', *Bangladesh Journal of Extension Education* 1(2): 1–12.

Satyanarayana, A. (1990) *Andhra Peasants Under British Rule*. New Delhi: Manohar.

Scheidegger, U., Prain, G. Ezeta, F. and Vittorelli, C. (1989) *Linking Formal R & D to Indigenous Systems: A User-Oriented Potato Seed Programme for Peru*. Agricultural Administration (Research and Extension) Network Paper No. 10. London: Overseas Development Institute.

Schiff, M. and Valdés, A. (1998) 'The Plundering of Agriculture in Developing Countries' in C. K. Eicher and J. M. Staatz (eds) *International Agricultural Development* (3rd Edition). Baltimore: Johns Hopkins University Press.

Schmitz, H. and Nadvi, K. (1999) 'Clustering and Industrialization: Introduction', *World Development* 27: 1503–14.

Schultz, T. (1964) *Transforming Traditional Agriculture*. New Haven, CT: Yale University Press.

Scott, J.C. (1976) *The Moral Economy of the Peasant: Subsistence and Rebellion in Southeast Asia*. New Haven, CT: Yale University Press.

Scott, J.C. (1985) *Weapons of the Weak*. New Haven, CT: Yale University Press.

Selvarajan, S., Joshi, D. C. and O'Toole, J. C. (1999) *The Indian Private Sector Seed Industry*. Manila: Rockefeller Foundation.

Sen, A. (1988) 'The Concept of Development' in H. Chenery and T. N. Srinivasan (eds) *Handbook of Development Economics, Volume 1*. Amsterdam: North Holland.

Sen, A. (1999) *Development as Freedom*. Oxford: Oxford University Press.

Sheridan, M. (1981) *Peasant Innovation and Diffusion of Agricultural Technology in China*. Special Series on Agricultural Research and Extension No.4. Ithaca, NY: Cornell University Rural Development Committee.

Shimoda, S. (1996) 'The Seeds of Change', *Seed World* June: 6, 8–9.

Shiva, V. (1999) 'Seeds of Hope', *The Guardian*, London, 17 February: G2 4–5.

Simmonds, N. W. (1979) *Principles of Crop Improvement*. Harlow, UK: Longman.

Simmonds, N. W. (1991) 'Selection for Local Adaptation in a Plant Breeding Programme', *Theoretical and Applied Genetics* 82: 363–7.

Simon, H. A. (1959) 'Theories of Decision-Making in Economic and Behavioural Sciences', *American Economic Review* 49: 253–83.

Sims, H. and Leonard, D. (1990) *The Political Economy of the Development and Transfer of Agricultural Technologies*. Linkages Theme Paper No.4. The Hague: ISNAR.

Singh, R.P., Pal, S. and Morris, M. (1995) *Maize Research, Development, and Seed Production in India: Contributions of the Public and Private Sectors*. CIMMYT Economics Working Paper 95–03, Mexico, D.F.: CIMMYT.

Skjønsberg, E. (1989) *Change in an African Village*. West Hartford, CT: Kumarian Press.

Smale, M. (1997) 'The Green Revolution and Wheat Genetic Diversity: Some Unfounded Assumptions'. *World Development* 25: 1257–69.

Smale, M. with Kaunda, Z., Makina, H., Mkandawire, M., Msowoya, M, Mwale, D. and Heisey, P. (1991) *Chimanga Cha Makolo, Hybrids, and Composites: An Analysis of Farmers' Adoption of Maize Technology in Malawi, 1988–91*. CIMMYT Economics Working Paper 91–04. Mexico, D. F.: CIMMYT.

Smale, M., Bellon, M. and Aguirre, J. A. (1999) *The Private and Public Characteristics of Maize Landraces and the Area Allocation Decisions of Farmers in a Center of Crop Diversity*. CIMMYT Economics Working Paper 99–08. Mexico. D. F.: CIMMYT.

Smale, M. and Ruttan, V. W. (1997) 'Social Capital and Technical Change: The *Groupements Naam* of Burkina Faso', in Clague.

Smelser, N. J. and Swedberg, R. (1994) *The Handbook of Economic Sociology*. Princeton, NJ: Princeton University Press.

Smith, T. C. (1959) *The Agrarian Origins of Modern Japan*. Stanford, CA: Stanford University Press.

Song, Y. (1998) ' 'New' Seed in 'Old' China: Impact of CIMMYT Collaborative Programme on Maize Breeding in South-western China'. Unpublished PhD thesis, Wageningen Agricultural University, The Netherlands.

Sperling, L. (1997) *The Effects of the Rwandan War on Crop Production and Varietal Diversity: A Comparison of Two Crops*. Agricultural Research and Extension Network Paper No. 75. London: Overseas Development Institute.

Sperling, L. and Loevinsohn, M. (1992) 'The Dynamics of Adoption: Distribution and Mortality of Bean Varieties among Small Farmers in Rwanda'. *Agricultural Systems* 41: 441–53.

Sperling, L., Loevinsohn, M. and Ntabomvura, B. (1993) 'Rethinking the Farmer's Role in Plant Breeding: Local Bean Experts and On-Station Selection in Rwanda', *Agricultural Systems* 29: 509–19.

Sperling, L., Scheidegger, U. and Buruchara, R. (1996) *Designing Seed Systems with Small Farmers: Principles Derived from Bean Research in the Great Lakes Region of Africa*. Agricultural Research and Extension Network Paper No. 60. London: Overseas Development Institute.

Staatz, J. and Eicher, C. (1998) 'Agricultural Development Ideas in Historical Perspective' in J. Staatz and C. Eicher (eds.) *International Agricultural Development* (3rd Edition). Baltimore: Johns Hopkins University Press.

Staniland, M. (1985) *What is Political Economy?* New Haven, CT: Yale University Press.

Sthapit, B. R., Joshi, K. D., and Witcombe, J. R. (1996) 'Farmer Participatory Crop Improvement. III. Participatory Plant Breeding, A Case Study for Rice in Nepal'. *Experimental Agriculture* 32: 479–96.

Stigler, G. (1971) 'The Theory of Economic Regulation', *The Bell Journal of Economics and Management Science* 2: 3–21.

Stoskopf, N. C. (1981) *Understanding Crop Production*. Reston, VA: Reston Publishing Company.

Streeten, P. (1995) 'Markets and States: Against Minimalism and Dichotomy', in A. de Janvry, S. Radwan, E. Sadoulet and E. Thorbecke (eds) *State, Market and Civil Organizations*. Geneva: ILO.

Streeten, P. and Burki, S. J.(1978) 'Basic Needs: Some Issues', *World Development* 6: 411–21.

Sumberg, J. and Okali, C. (1997) *Farmers' Experiments: Creating Local Knowledge*. Boulder, CO: Lynne Rienner.

Tapia, M. E. and Rosa, A. (1993) 'Seed Fairs in the Andes: A Strategy for Local Conservation of Plant Genetic Resources' in W. de Boef, K. Amanor and K. Wellard, with A. Bebbington (eds) *Cultivating Knowledge*. London: Intermediate Technology Publications.

Tendler, J. (1975) *Inside Foreign Aid*. Baltimore: Johns Hopkins University Press.

Tendler, J. (1997) *Good Government in the Tropics*. Baltimore: Johns Hopkins University Press.

Tetlay, K., Heisey, P., Ahmed, Z. and Ahmad, M. (1990) 'Farmer's Seed Sources and Seed Management' in Heisey.

The Corner House (1998) *Food? Health? Hope? Genetic Engineering and World Hunger.* Sturminster Newton, UK: The Corner House.

Thick, M. (1990a) 'Garden Seeds in England Before the Late Eighteenth Century: I. Seed Growing', *Agricultural History Review* 38: 58–71.

Thick, M. (1990b) 'Garden Seeds in England Before the Late Eighteenth Century: II. The Trade in Seeds to 1760', *Agricultural History Review* 38: 105–16.

Thiele, G. (1999) 'Informal Potato Seed Systems in the Andes: Why Are They Important and What Should We Do With Them?', *World Development* 27: 83–99.

Thiele, G., Gardner, G., Torrez, R. and Gabriel, J. (1997) 'Farmer Involvement in Selecting New Varieties: Potatoes in Bolivia', *Experimental Agriculture* 33: 275–90.

Thirsk. J. (1997) *Alternative Agriculture: A History.* Oxford: Oxford University Press.

Tiffen, M., Mortimore, M. and Gichuki, F. (1994) *More People, Less Erosion.* Chichester: Wiley.

Timmer, P. (1988) 'The Agricultural Transformation' in H. Chenery and T. N. Srinivasan (eds) *Handbook of Development Economics, Volume 1.* Amsterdam: North Holland.

Toye, J. (1995) 'The New Institutional Economics and Its Implications for Development Theory' in Harriss et al.

Traxler, G., Falck-Zepeda, J. and Sain, G. (1999) 'Genes, Germplasm and Developing Country Access to Genetically Modified Crop Varieties'. Paper presented at the conference "The Shape of the Coming Agricultural Biotechonolgy Transformation", Rome, 17–19 June.

Tripp, R. (1989) *Farmer Participation in Agricultural Research: New Directions or Old Problems?'.* Discussion Paper No. 256. Brighton: IDS Sussex University.

Tripp, R. (ed.) (1991) *Planned Change in Farming Systems: Progress in On-Farm Research.* Chichester: Wiley.

Tripp, R. (1996) 'Biodiversity and Modern Crop Varieties: Sharpening the Debate', *Agriculture and Human Values* 13(4): 48–63.

Tripp R. (ed.) (1997) *New Seed and Old Laws: Regulatory Reform and the Diversification of National Seed Systems.* London: Intermediate Technology Publications.

Tripp, R. (2000) 'Strategies for Seed System Development in Sub-Saharan Africa. A Study of Kenya, Malawi, Zambia and Zimbabwe'. Working Paper series no. 2. Bulawayo: ICRISAT.

Tripp R. (forthcoming) 'Can Biotechnology Reach the Poor? The Adequacy of Information and Seed Delivery', *Food Policy.*

Tripp, R. and Pal, S. (2001). 'The Private Delivery of Public Crop Varieties. Rice in Andhra Pradesh'. *World Development* 29: 103–17.

Tripp, R. and Pal, S. (2000) 'Information and Agricultural Input Markets: Pearl Millet Seed in Rajasthan', *Journal of International Development* 12: 133–44.

Tripp, R. and Pal, S. (1998) *Information Exchange in Commercial Seed Markets in Rajasthan.* Agricultural Research and Extension Network Paper No. 83. London: Overseas Development Institute.

Tripp, R. and van der Burg, W. J. (1997) 'The Conduct and Reform of Seed Quality Control, in Tripp (ed.).

Tripp, R., Walker, D., Miti, F., Mukumbuta, S. and Zulu, M. S. (1998a) *Seed Management by Small-Scale Farmers in Zambia.* Wallingford, UK: Natural Resources Institute.

Tripp, R., Walker, D. Opoku-Apau, A., Dankyi, A. A. and Delimini, L. L. (1998b) *Seed Management by Small-Scale Farmers in Ghana.* Wallingford, UK: Natural Resources Institute.

Trutmann, P. and Kayitare, E. (1991) 'Disease Control and Small Multiplication Plots Improve Seed Quality and Small Farm Dry Bean Yields in Central Africa', *Journal of Applied Seed Production* 9: 36–40.

Tudge, C. (1988) *Food Crops for the Future.* Oxford: Basil Blackwell.

Turner, M. R. (1994) 'Trends in India's Seed Sector', paper presented at Asian Seed 94 Chiang Mai, Thailand, 27–29 September.

Tvedt, T. (1998) *Angels of Mercy or Development Diplomats? NGOs and Foreign Aid.* Oxford: James Currey.

UNDP (1999) *Human Development Report 1999.* New York: Oxford University Press.

Uphoff, N. (1994) 'Revisiting Institution Building: How Organizations Become Institutions' in N. Uphoff (ed.) *Puzzles of Productivity in Public Organizations.* San Francisco, CA: Institute for Contemporary Studies.

Vakil, A. C. (1997) 'Confronting the Classification Problem: Toward a Taxonomy of NGOs', *World Development* 25: 2057–70.

Van der Mheen-Sluijer, J. (1996) *Towards Household Food Security.* Harare: SADC/GTZ.

Van Santen, C. and Heriyanto (1996) 'The Source of Farmers' Soybean Seed in Indonesia', in H. van Amstel, J. Bottema, M. Sidik and C. van Santen (eds) *Integrating Seed Systems for Annual Food Crops.* Bogor, Indonesia: CGPRT Centre.

Van Wijk, J. (1997) 'The Impact of Intellectual Property Protection on Seed Supply' in Tripp (ed.).

Veblen, T. (1899) *The Theory of the Leisure Class.* New York: Macmillan.

de Waal, A. (1997) *Famine Crimes: Politics and the Disaster Relief Industry in Africa.* Oxford: James Currey.

Wade, R. (1988) *Village Republics.* Cambridge: Cambridge University Press.

Walker. T. S. (1994) *Patterns and Implications of Varietal Change in Potatoes.* Social Science Department Working Paper Series No. 1994–3. Lima: International Potato Center.

Wallace, H. A. and Brown, W. L. (1988) *Corn and Its Early Fathers.* Ames, IA: Iowa State University Press.

Walton, J. R. (1999) 'Varietal Innovation and the Competitiveness of the British Cereals Sector, 1760–1930', *Agricultural History Review* 47: 29–57.

Whitten, M. J., Jefferson, R. A. and Dall, D. (1996) 'Needs and Opportunities' in G. J. Persley (ed.) *Biotechnology and Integrated Pest Management.* Wallingford, UK: CAB International.

Wiggins, S. and Cromwell, E. (1995) 'NGOs and Seed Provision to Smallholders in Developing Countries', *World Development* 23: 413–22.

Williamson, O. (1979) 'Transaction-Cost Economics: The Governance of Contractual Relations', *Journal of Law and Economics* 22: 233–61.

Williamson, O. (1985) *The Economic Institutions of Capitalism.* New York: Free Press.

Williamson, O. (1993) 'Calculativeness, Trust and Economic Organisation', *American Journal of Law and Economics* 22: 233–61.

Witcombe, J. R., Joshi, A., Joshi, K. D. and Sthapit, B. R. (1996) 'Farmer Participatory Crop Improvement. I. Varietal Selection and Breeding Methods and Their Impact on Biodiversity'. *Experimental Agriculture* 32: 445–60.

Witcombe, J., Virk, D. and Farrington, J. (eds) (1998) *Seeds of Choice.* New Delhi: Oxford and IBH Publishing.

Witcombe, J. R., Petre, R., Jones, S. and Joshi, A. (1999) 'Farmer Participatory Crop Improvement. IV The Spread and Impact of a Rice Variety Identified by Participatory Varietal Selection', *Experimental Agriculture* 35: 471–87.

Wolf, E. (1955) 'Types of Latin American Peasantry: A Preliminary Discussion', *American Anthropologist* 57: 452–71.

Wood, D. and Lenné, J.M. (1997) 'The Conservation of Agrobiodiversity On-Farm: Questioning the Emerging Paradigm', *Biodiversity and Conservation* 6: 109–29.

Woodhouse, P. (1997) 'Virtue or Necessity? Pluralist Agricultural Technology Development in Mozambique', *Journal of International Development* 9: 331–46.

World Bank (1999) *World Development Indicators.* Washington, D.C.: The World Bank.

World Bank (1998) *World Development Report. Knowledge for Development*. Washington, DC: World Bank.

Wright, M., Donaldson, T., Cromwell, E. and New, J. (1994) *The Retention and Care of Seeds by Small-scale Farmers*. Chatham, UK: Natural Resources Institute.

Young, N. (1990) *Seed Potato Systems in Developed Countries: Canada, The Netherlands and Great Britain*. Lima: International Potato Center.

Zimmerer, K. S. (1996) *Changing Fortunes: Biodiversity and Peasant Livelihood in the Peruvian Andes*. Berkeley, CA: University of California Press.

Zimmerer, K. S. and Douches, D. S. (1991) 'Geographical Approaches to Crop Conservation: The Partitioning of Genetic Diversity in Andean Potatoes', *Economic Botany* 45: 176–89.

Zulauf, C. R. and King, K. F. (1985) 'Farm Operators Who Sell Crop Production Inputs: The Case of Ohio Farmers Who Sell Seed', *Agribusiness* 1(2): 193–9.

Zulu, E. and Miti, F. (1999) 'Inventory of the Informal Seed Sector in Zambia'. Unpublished paper.

Index

Lightning Source UK Ltd.
Milton Keynes UK
UKHW021452071118
331938UK00003B/234/P